CARE POVERTY AND UNMET NEEDS

Transforming Care

Series Editors: **Costanzo Ranci**, Polytechnic University of Milan, and **Tine Rostgaard**, Stockholm University and Roskilde University

---

As care and care work have been thrust into the international spotlight, the increased need for empirical, theoretical and methodological investigation into social care and care policy and practice has been revealed. Addressing social care and care policy and practice at an international level, this series provides a crucial platform for scholars researching early childhood care, care for adults with disabilities and long-term care for frail older people.

Also available in the series:

Unpaid Work in Nursing Homes
edited by **Pat Armstrong**

Reablement in Long-Term Care for Older People
edited by **Tine Rostgaard**, **John Parsons**
and **Hanne Tuntland**

A Care Crisis in the Nordic Welfare States?
edited by **Lise Lotte Hansen**, **Hanne Marlene Dahl**
and **Laura Horn**

Find out more at:
policy.bristoluniversitypress.co.uk/transforming-care

CARE POVERTY AND UNMET NEEDS

Inequalities in Theory and Practice

Edited by
Teppo Kröger, Nicola Brimblecombe,
Ricardo Rodrigues and Kirstein Rummery

First published in Great Britain in 2025 by

Policy Press, an imprint of
Bristol University Press
University of Bristol
1–9 Old Park Hill
Bristol
BS2 8BB
UK
t: +44 (0)117 374 6645
e: bup-info@bristol.ac.uk

Details of international sales and distribution partners are available at policy.bristoluniversitypress.co.uk

British Library Cataloguing in Publication Data
A catalogue record for this book is available from the British Library

ISBN 978-1-4473-7009-3 paperback
ISBN 978-1-4473-7011-6 ePub
ISBN 978-1-4473-7010-9 ePdf

Cover design: Robin Hawes
Front cover image: iStock/shuoshu
Bristol University Press uses environmentally responsible print partners.
Printed and bound in Great Britain by CPI Group (UK) Ltd, Croydon, CR0 4YY

Bristol University Press' authorised representative in the European Union is:
Easy Access System Europe, Mustamäe tee 50, 10621 Tallinn, Estonia,
Email: gpsr.requests@easproject.com

Contents

List of figures and tables

Notes on contributors

Mari Aaltonen is Chief Researcher at the Finnish Institute for Health and Welfare. She has a title of Docent in Social Policy. Her research interests include ageing, health and social care policies, long-term care, home care, dementia, and needs and unmet needs of older people. Recently, she has conducted quantitative research using extensive register-based data in Finland (*Scandinavian Journal of Public Health*, 2024) and Canada (*Journal of American Medical Directors Association,* 2021). In addition, she has conducted interviews with people with dementia and published qualitative research on their daily life and care (*Dementia*, 2021).

Nicola Brimblecombe is Assistant Professorial Research Fellow in the Care Policy and Evaluation Centre, London School of Economics and Political Science, UK. Her research focuses on support for unpaid carers, carers and employment, unmet need for care, inequalities in care, and the wider determinants of care need and use, including housing and care. Recent relevant publications include 'Inequalities in unpaid carer's health, employment status and social isolation' (in *Health & Social Care in the Community*, 2022), and 'Inequalities in receipt of long-term care services by disabled or older people and co-resident carer dyads in England' (in *Journal of Poverty and Social Justice*, 2022).

Daniela Brüker is Doctoral Researcher at the Institute for Social Work and Social Policy at the University of Duisburg-Essen, Germany. She is a social gerontologist by training and her research interests are: ageing societies, dementia care, informal care, social inequality, reconciliation of caring and paid employment. Her publications include *Sorgende Angehörige. Eine intersektionale Analyse* [Family Caregivers: An Intersectional Analysis] (Westfälisches Dampfboot, 2020, co-authored with Diana Auth et al).

Natasha Cortis is Associate Professor at the Social Policy Research Centre, University of New South Wales, Sydney, Australia. Her research examines the ways social services are organised, delivered and evaluated, and focuses on themes relating to quality and market regulation, funding, workforce and sustainability, and women's employment and economic security. Her publications feature in Australian and international journals, and in policy and evaluation reports that have shaped government, non-governmental organisation and trade union practice and advocacy. Natasha is co-chief editor of the *Australian Journal of Social Issues*.

Päivi Eskola is University Teacher of Gerontology at the Open University of the University of Jyväskylä, Finland. Her research focuses on dementia and couplehood, and the agency of older people living at home with dementia. She defended her PhD thesis within gerontology and public health, titled *From a Reciprocal Relationship to a Care Relationship? Dementia and Couplehood*, at the University of Jyväskylä in December 2023.

Maria Evandrou is Professor of Gerontology and Director of the Centre for Research on Ageing at the University of Southampton, UK. She is also Co-Director of the Economic and Social Research Council (ESRC) Centre for Population Change and the Connecting Generations research partnership. Her research interests include inequalities in later life, the health and social in later life, informal care and paid employment in mid-life, and intergenerational flows of support. She has published over 200 journal articles, book chapters, books, reports and papers, and supervised 20 PhD students to completion. She has acted as an advisor to government departments in the UK and internationally, and also to non-governmental organisations.

Jane Falkingham is Professor of Demography and International Social Policy at the University of Southampton, UK, Director of the ESRC Centre for Population Change and Principal Investigator of the ESRC Connecting Generations research collaboration. She pursues a multidisciplinary research agenda, located at the interface between population studies and social policy. She has published over 200 journal articles, books and book chapters. She was President of the European Association for Population Studies (2018–20) and a Member of the ESRC Council (2017–22) and chaired the COVID-19 Rapid Response panel. In January 2023 she was honoured as a Commander of the British Empire.

Maša Filipovič Hrast is Associate Professor of Sociology at the University of Ljubljana and Head of the Centre for Welfare Studies in Slovenia. Her research focuses on vulnerability, social exclusion, social policy, welfare state development and quality of life, with particular focus on quality of life in old age. Her (co-authored) recent publications include a chapter on Eastern European welfare states (in *De Gruyter Handbook of Contemporary Welfare States*, 2022) and articles 'Moving house and housing preferences in older age in Slovenia' (*Housing Theory and Society*, 2019) and 'Life course pathways into intergenerational caregiving' (*The Journals of Gerontology: Series B*, 2022).

Myra Hamilton is Associate Professor at the University of Sydney and Principal Research Fellow at the Australian Research Council's Centre of Excellence in Population Ageing Research. She is a sociologist and policy researcher whose focus is on gender, ageing and care. She combines traditional academic research with applied policy research. She makes regular contributions to scholarly and public debate on issues such as balancing work and care, aged care services and navigation, young carers, grandparenting, and policies for parents and carers. She is Reviews Editor of the *International Journal of Care and Caring* and sits on the New South Wales Carers Advisory Council.

Trish Hill is Honorary Senior Lecturer at the Social Policy Research Centre and Associate Investigator at the Ageing Futures Institute at the University of New South Wales, Sydney, Australia. She has a research focus on informal caring across the life course, ageing and aged care, poverty and inequality, and gender and social policy. Her research is published in academic journals and research and evaluation reports for government and non-government organisations.

Valentina Hlebec is Professor at the University of Ljubljana, Faculty of Social Sciences, Slovenia. She has an extensive knowledge of social methodology, and lately she has focused on social welfare and informal/formal social care. Her research experience covers projects on reducing old-age social exclusion, active and healthy ageing, and addressing the needs of informal carers. Her recent (co-authored) publications include the articles 'Ethical considerations when conducting pan-European research with and for adolescent young carers' (*Ethics and Social Welfare*, 2023) and 'The first cross-national study of adolescent young carers aged 15–17 in six European countries' (*International Journal of Care and Caring*, 2023).

Miriam Hurtado Monarres is Research Assistant at the Faculty of Social Sciences, University of Ljubljana, Slovenia, and a PhD student in sociology. In her research she focuses on the welfare state and social policy, quality of life in old age, informal carers, and social exclusion. Her (co-authored) publications include the book chapter 'Homelessness services during the COVID-19 pandemic in Slovenia' (in *Quality of Life in COVID-19 Pandemic*, University of Ljubljana, 2022) and the article 'Scaling-up an integrated care for patients with non-communicable diseases' (*Slovenian Journal of Public Health*, 2021).

Christine Kelly is Associate Professor in Community Health Sciences and a research affiliate with the Centre on Aging at the University of Manitoba, Canada. She is a health policy researcher with expertise in home care services for people with disabilities and older people, especially directly funded home care. She is co-editor of *Dispatches from Disabled Country* (2023), *The Aging–Disability Nexus* (2020), *Mobilizing Metaphor: Art, Culture and Disability Activism in Canada* (2016) and author of *Disability Politics and Care* (2016), all published by UBC Press.

Teppo Kröger is Professor of Social and Public Policy at the University of Jyväskylä, Finland, and Director of the Centre of Excellence in Research on Ageing and Care (CoE AgeCare). His research has focused, for example, on care systems for older people, integration of formal and informal care, conditions of care work and reconciliation of caring and paid employment. His publications include *Care Poverty: When Older People's Needs Remain Unmet* (Palgrave Macmillan, 2022) and *Combining Paid Work and Family Care: Policies and Experiences in International Perspective* (Policy Press, 2013, co-edited with Sue Yeandle). He is the recipient of the 2024 Nordic Prize in Gerontology (the Sohlberg Prize).

Simone Leiber is Professor of Social Policy at the Institute for Social Work and Social Policy, University of Duisburg-Essen, Germany. Her research focuses on intersectionality in care, care migration, informal care, reconciliation of caring and paid work. Her publications include 'Contestations in coping with elderly care: an intersectional analysis addressing family caregivers in Germany' (*European Journal of Politics and Gender*, 2023, co-authored with Diana Auth and Sigrid Leitner).

Jiby Mathew Puthenparambil is Postdoctoral Researcher within the Faculty of Humanities and Social Sciences at the University of Jyväskylä, Finland. His research focuses mainly on the ongoing changes in the care service for older people in Finland. His research deals with the marketisation of care, service utilisation, care poverty and care workers. He has contributed articles to international journals, the most recent of which is 'Being able to provide sufficiently good care for older people: care workers and their working conditions in Finland' (*International Journal of Care and Caring*, 2023).

Márton Medgyesi is a sociologist and works as Senior Researcher at TÁRKI Social Research Institute and at the Child Opportunities Research Group of the HUN-REN Centre for Social Sciences in Budapest, Hungary. His main research interests are the analysis of income distributions and of intergenerational transfers in the family and the welfare state. Recent publications include *Reducing Inequalities: A Challenge for the European Union* (Palgrave Macmillan, 2018, co-edited with Renato Carmo and Cédric Rio) and articles in journals such as *Frontiers in Sociology*, *Social Indicators Research*, *PLOS ONE* and *Social Policy & Administration*.

Carmelle Peisah is Conjoint Professor and Ageing Futures Institute Investigator, University of New South Wales; Clinical Professor, University of Sydney; and Special Instructor, Chiang Mai University, Thailand. She is a medical practitioner, specialist Old Age Psychiatrist, Consultation-Liaison psychiatrist and Family-Systems Therapist. She is Founder-President of the human rights charity Capacity Australia, and in 2021 was recognised as a World Expert in Human Rights, rated in the top 0.1 per cent of human rights scholars. She is widely published in the areas of aged care, capacity and human rights and is co-author of the e-Text, *Capacity and the Law*, https://austlii.community/wiki/Books/CapacityAndTheLaw/.

Tjaša Potočnik is Research Assistant at Faculty of Social Sciences, University of Ljubljana, Slovenia. In her research she focuses on social policy and its outcomes, quality of life of older adults and informal caregivers, reconciliation of paid work and informal care, and long-term care in the community. Her co-authored publications include 'Cross-national analysis of legislation, policy and service frameworks for adolescent young carers in Europe' (*Journal of Youth Studies*, 2022) and 'The awareness, visibility and support for young carers across Europe: a Delphi study' (*BMC Health Services Research*, 2020).

Min Qin is Senior Research Fellow at the ESRC Centre for Population Change (Connecting Generations) and the Centre for Research on Ageing, University of Southampton, UK. Her research focuses on population aging, intergenerational exchange and later-life health. She has co-authored publications including 'Dynamics of unmet need for social care in England' (*Ageing & Society*, 2022) and 'The impact of changing social support on older persons' onset of loneliness during the COVID-19 pandemic in the United Kingdom' (*The Gerontologist*, 2022).

Ricardo Rodrigues is Assistant Professor of Sociology of Work at the Lisbon School of Economics and Management, University of Lisbon, Board Member of SOCIUS, the Research Centre in Economic and Organisational Sociology, Portugal, and a consultant for the World Health Organization Kobe Centre. His main research focuses on financing of long-term care, inequalities in health and inequalities in the use and provision of care, mostly from a comparative view across different care systems and care norms. His publications include *Facts and Figures on Healthy Ageing and Long-term Care* (European Centre, 2012, co-edited with Manfred Huber and Giovanni Lamura).

Tine Rostgaard is Professor at the Department of Social Sciences and Business, Roskilde University, Denmark, and at the Department of Social Work, Stockholm University, Sweden. She holds a PhD in comparative welfare analysis and specialises in research on care policies and practices in parental leave, childcare and long-term care. Tine is the co-chair of the international researcher network Transforming Care with more than 700 members, http://www.transforming-care.net/. She has recently co-edited *Reablement in Long-Term Care for Older People*, also in the Transforming Care book series (Policy Press, 2023) and is presently co-editing the *Handbook of Social Care* (Elgar Publishing).

Kirstein Rummery is Professor of Social Policy at the University of Stirling, UK. Her research interests include comparative long-term and health care, personalisation of care services, partnership working between health and social care, disability, gender, ageing and dementia. Her publications include *What Works in Improving Gender Equality: International Best Practice in Childcare and Long-term Care Policy* (Policy Press, 2021, with Craig McAngus and Alcuin Edwards).

Petra Ulmanen is Senior Lecturer at the Department of Social Work, Stockholm University, Sweden. Her main research interests concern social care, social policy and gender, and she has focused on informal care for older persons and its social and economic consequences. Her publications include 'From the state to the family or to the market? Consequences of reduced residential eldercare in Sweden' (*International Journal of Social Welfare*, 2015, co-authored with Marta Szebehely) and 'Reversed socioeconomic pattern in the costs of caring regarding well-being and paid work among women in Sweden' (*Social Policy & Administration*, 2021).

Lina Van Aerschot is Senior Researcher at the University of Jyväskylä and Lecturer at the University of Tampere, Finland. Her research interests include care policies, unpaid care, needs and unmet needs of older people and persons with dementia. Recently, she has published 'Community-dwelling older adults and their informal carers call for more attention to psychosocial needs: interview study on unmet care needs in three European countries' (*Archives of Gerontology and Geriatrics*, 2022) and 'Psychophysical burden and lack of support: reasons for care workers' intentions to leave their work in the Nordic countries' (*International Journal of Social Welfare*, 2021).

Athina Vlachantoni is Professor of Gerontology and Social Policy in the Department of Gerontology and the Centre for Research on Ageing, University of Southampton, UK. Her research interests are at the interface of ageing, gender and social policy. She is currently Principal Investigator of an ESRC-funded project on promoting inclusivity in pension protection and saving for later life among minority ethnic groups in the UK, and Co-Investigator on the Centre for Population Change Connecting Generations project focusing on intergenerational support and exchange.

Eszter Zólyomi is Researcher at the European Centre for Social Welfare Policy and Research in Vienna, Austria. Her research interests include poverty, non-monetary aspects of well-being, social and gender inequalities, and care. Her recent publications include 'Cohort trajectories by age and gender for informal caregiving in Europe adjusted for socio-demographic changes' (*The Journals of Gerontology: Series B*, 2023) and 'Gender differences in access to community-based care: a longitudinal analysis of widowhood and living arrangements' (*European Journal of Ageing*, 2022). She is co-editor of the book *Women's Work and Pensions: What is Good, What is Best? Designing Gender-Sensitive Arrangements* (Routledge, 2010).

PART I

Introduction

Introduction: Unmet care needs and care poverty in international perspective

*Teppo Kröger, Nicola Brimblecombe,
Ricardo Rodrigues and Kirstein Rummery*

Introduction

The ongoing rapid population ageing and the resulting increase in care needs has made securing the provision of care a burning policy question around the world. Populations are ageing practically everywhere, in the Global South as well as in the Global North, in the East as well as in the West. Along with climate change, demographic change is increasingly recognised as a grand societal challenge that, if not adequately addressed, can threaten not only the quality of life and human dignity of older people, but also the labour market participation of their family members, the balance of national economies and even the legitimacy of political decision-making. As a sign of awakening to these threats, the European Union launched in 2022 its European Care Strategy, stressing the need for Member States to provide affordable and adequate access to high-quality long-term care services for all those in need (European Union, 2022). The fact that such a high-level policy announcement was deemed necessary implies that the reality across Europe is far from this goal, that in practice care services are often of low quality, unaffordable and inadequate, and that many people in need do not have access to them – and that informal care can no longer solve the situation. And on a global scale, Europe is certainly not in the weakest position to meet the growing care needs of older people.

This bleak situation is the starting point for this book. We know from previous research that in every country there seem to be at least some older people who do not get the help and support that they need, either from the state or from their families and social networks. Their care needs are not being adequately covered, so they have 'unmet needs'. This term is most commonly used in North American gerontology, where a specific stream of research developed in the 1990s to measure and examine the incidence of such situations and their determinants and consequences (for example,

Allen, 1994; Tennstedt et al, 1994; Allen and Mor, 1997; see also Kröger, 2022). In the early 21st century, this research has also developed in Europe and other parts of the world (for example, Tomás Aznar et al, 2002; Gureje et al, 2006; Vlachantoni et al, 2011; Peng et al, 2015).

Recently, research on the unmet long-term care needs of the older population has grown in several countries. Knowledge of the problem and its occurrence has increased and new methods of analysis have been developed. However, this progress is overshadowed by the fact that this research has mainly focused on the individual level of older people and has mostly been carried out in isolation from social policy research. As a result, its contribution to highlighting the inadequacies of current policies and the way forward in developing more appropriate policy models has remained limited.

In order to establish a closer link between research on unmet needs and social policy, and social science more generally, a new conceptual framework has recently been proposed. The concept of 'care poverty' highlights the structural and policy contexts of the phenomenon of unmet needs and emphasises the need to understand deprivation of adequate care in the same way as deprivation of material resources, that is, as a social inequality rooted in how resources are distributed between different population groups in society (Kröger et al, 2019; Kröger, 2022). According to this approach, only by addressing these structural issues is it possible to find effective strategies to address the unmet needs that older people experience in their daily lives.

This book aims to promote research on unmet care needs, particularly through international collaboration, which has been limited to date. Research on this topic has more than academic value. Without knowing which groups of older and disabled people are particularly at risk of going without the support they need, which of their needs are most often unmet, and what the negative consequences of such a situation are for their health and quality of life, it is difficult, if not impossible, to develop policies that could eradicate the problem. At the same time, by introducing the conceptual approach of care poverty and its potential contributions to research and policy, this volume aims to go beyond previous literature on unmet needs. Solving a social problem requires a comprehensive understanding of its scope, causes and mechanisms, as well as the impact that different policy interventions may have on it. Such an understanding requires a more expansive perspective than that offered by the concept of unmet need, and the new care poverty approach, which brings together gerontology, social policy and poverty research, can contribute to such a broader perspective.

The concepts of unmet needs and care poverty

As already mentioned, the concept most commonly used in research on the lack of adequate care and support for disabled and older people is that of unmet need. There are several different definitions of this concept. For example, Williams et al (1997: 102) state that '[u]nmet need occurs in long-term care when a person has disabilities for which help is needed, but is unavailable or insufficient'. Typically, unmet need is measured using lists of Activities of Daily Living and sometimes Instrumental Activities of Daily Living, looking at whether there is a gap between help needed and help available in one or more of these activities (for example, Allen and Mor, 1997). Most studies of unmet needs are based on questionnaire surveys in which either disabled/older people or their family members or care professionals have reported their needs and whether or not these are being met.

Compared to the concept of unmet need, the concept of care poverty is more recent. It has been developed to build links between studies of unmet needs and social policy research, particularly feminist care policy research (Kröger, 2022). Care poverty has been defined as 'inadequate coverage of care needs resulting from an interplay between individual and societal factors' (Kröger et al, 2019: 485). It highlights the structural background of unmet care needs and shifts attention from the individual level to the societal level, emphasising how the problems of disabled and older people and their carers are embedded in structural contexts. Care poverty is not seen as part of material poverty, but as a parallel concept: poverty is about deprivation of material resources, while care poverty is about deprivation of informal and formal care resources (Kröger, 2022). Both are expressions of social inequality between those who have sufficient resources and those who do not. By making the conceptual link between lack of adequate care and poverty, the aim is to learn from the rich conceptual and methodological toolkit of poverty research and, where possible, apply it to care research.

Aims of the book

This book suggests a change of perspective for international research on care for older and disabled people. Up to now, research has largely focused on inputs – in particular care expenditures – and outputs – that is, the volume of services provided. Knowledge of these is undoubtedly useful, but care policies need to be evaluated primarily in terms of their main objectives. The key objective of long-term care systems is to meet the support and care needs of the older and disabled population, as well as informal carers, and whether or not this is happening deserves to be the main focus of the evaluation. In addition to inputs and outputs, more attention needs to be paid to outcomes. Are some policies more effective than others in reducing unmet needs? Are there differences between countries and their long-term care systems in their ability to meet care needs and eliminate care poverty? What is the role of informal versus formal care in ensuring access to adequate support? How can the perspectives and experiences of people in need of care be taken into account when examining these issues?

The aim of this volume is to advance this discussion at the international level. As noted earlier, there is a gradually growing literature at the national and local level in several countries examining the unmet care needs of older people, but there has been little international discussion or research on this issue and no collective attempt to consolidate empirical evidence, theories and concepts on the issue in a coherent way within a common framework.

Based on a collaboration of social policy researchers from a number of countries and welfare settings, this book reviews and synthesises the state of the art of research on unmet care needs of older and disabled people. It brings together not only the empirical evidence but also the theoretical and methodological approaches of this emerging strand of research literature. This empirical, theoretical and methodological knowledge is then framed and discussed under a new concept, that of care poverty, and its relevance and potential for research on the lack of adequate care in different social and cultural contexts is explored. The book thus develops the theoretical and methodological foundations of this rapidly expanding area of social policy analysis.

The book also presents new empirical evidence on how care poverty is distributed across different groups from a range of welfare states in and outside Europe. These studies strengthen the knowledge base on which the value of different policy approaches and practices can be discussed. In doing so, the book updates and extends the review of previous literature on unmet care needs. This book represents a collective international effort to outline the way forward for research on unmet needs and care poverty.

Background of the book

The book is based on an international research network. In January 2020, the Care Policy Evaluation Centre of the London School of Economics and Political Science and the Centre of Excellence in Research on Ageing and Care from Finland co-organised a workshop in London where around 25 care policy researchers from over ten different countries shared their research on unmet long-term care needs of older and/or disabled people. During the workshop, the participants formed a new international research network called 'Unmet Needs, Inequalities and Care Poverty' (UNICAP). The network aims to promote research on the inadequate provision and receipt of care and support for older and disabled people through international collaborative research, joint publications and research events focusing on the issue.

This book is a product of collaboration within the UNICAP network. Its authors are experienced researchers from 11 different countries (Australia,

Austria, Canada, Denmark, Finland, Germany, Hungary, Portugal, Slovenia, Sweden, United Kingdom). Most of them are from Europe, representing its different welfare models: Nordic, Bismarckian, British, Central and Southern European systems, plus Australia and Canada. The chapters reflect the policy traditions and research approaches in these countries, while all addressing unmet needs and care poverty and contributing to the overall aim of the book to analyse care inequalities from an international perspective. Draft chapters were discussed and developed in two author workshops, one online in March 2023 and the other held in conjunction with the Transforming Care 2023 conference in Sheffield in June 2023.

Structure of the book

In addition to and between this introductory chapter (Part I) and the concluding chapter (Part IV), the book is divided into two main parts, one focusing more on theoretical and methodological issues (Part II) and the other presenting new empirical analyses of care poverty and unmet needs from different national contexts (Part III).

Part II includes chapters that develop new conceptual and measurement approaches to the study of unmet needs and care poverty. It begins with two chapters that assess the theoretical value of the concept of care poverty and link it to other ongoing conceptual debates. First, in Chapter 2, Rummery situates the care poverty approach in the context of other care theories and reviews the conflicts inherent in these theories. She connects care poverty to social citizenship – to the right to access resources to meet needs, in this case care needs. The chapter applies ideas about care poverty to offer a theoretical way of synthesising previous conflicting theories of care, and uses this synthesis as a lens through which to understand gendered citizenship.

In Chapter 3, Kelly also discusses the theoretical value of the care poverty approach. In particular, she links care poverty to the concept of the care economy, which positions care as a mode of production with tangible implications for other sectors of the economy and for those who participate (or not) in the care workforce. Using Canada as a case example, the chapter shows how a care poverty framework moves the concept of unmet needs from documentation and measurement towards solutions and policy change. It concludes that care poverty is a more complete accounting of unmet care needs in context, an indicator of a malfunctioning care economy, and a reminder that transformative change can occur through the way societies organise care.

These two theoretical chapters are followed by two methodological chapters. In Chapter 4, Hill et al review 29 different measures of unmet need drawn from the disciplines of health, gerontology, social sciences and human rights, and propose a holistic approach to measuring unmet care needs of older people. Using Australia as an example, the chapter highlights the role that measurement can play in transforming a system based on rationing substandard care into one that enforces a universal right to quality care based on assessed need.

Furthermore, in Chapter 5, the final chapter of Part II, Medgyesi et al start to develop methods for measuring care poverty. Building on existing approaches to (income) poverty measurement, they discuss the advantages and disadvantages of different ways of assessing unmet needs and care inequalities, and how poverty measurements could be adapted to quantify care poverty. They place a particular emphasis on different approaches to comparative research.

Part III of the book contains chapters that empirically analyse care poverty and unmet needs in a range of different societal and cultural contexts, each bringing a unique perspective and broadening the understanding of care poverty. These chapters open up new ways of analysing unmet needs and related phenomena and move the field forward, taking into account national contexts. An important contribution is to show that care poverty affects not only older and disabled people but also their family members, in particular their informal carers. Unmet needs of older or disabled family members can become transformed to unmet needs of carers if adequate support is not available. Taken together, these chapters show the diversity of people experiencing care poverty and its various manifestations.

In Chapter 6, Vlachantoni et al examine patterns of met and unmet care needs over time. Drawing on evidence from the English Longitudinal Study of Ageing and making comparisons between different types of older people's social networks, the chapter identifies groups at increased risk of persistent unmet need, with implications for social policy design. They show that both informal and formal care need to increase in order to reduce unmet need, and that policies need to target the most vulnerable networks by providing them with additional care resources.

Survey data are also used in Chapter 7 by Mathew Puthenparambil et al, who compare care poverty among three groups of older people: those who use only formal care services; those who receive only informal care; and those who rely on both formal and informal care. Their results show that in Finland the majority of older people with personal care needs receive a combination of formal and informal care, while those with practical care needs tend to receive only informal care. However, even when older people receive care from a combination of formal and informal sources, this user group is the most likely to have unmet care needs.

Also in Chapter 8, Rostgaard analyses survey data and finds that the coverage of home care in Denmark has fallen dramatically. The results show a significant increase in inadequate coverage of care needs due to an interplay between individual and societal factors, where local political priorities clash with cultural understandings of how care needs are best met. This points to a substantial change with implications for the core elements of the Nordic public service model, in terms of generosity and universalism, and for the extent of the phenomenon of care poverty and the inequalities it entails.

With Chapter 9, the attention of the volume turns to family carers. In this chapter, Potočnik et al analyse how people from different socioeconomic backgrounds transition into caring and how they navigate their care responsibilities. By analysing the different care trajectories of Slovenian family carers, the chapter finds that the inadequate provision of formal home care has a significant impact on the organisation and navigation of care responsibilities in everyday life, especially in families with a low socioeconomic status who are unable to supplement the inadequate public home care provision with private care services. Care poverty thus overlaps with (income) poverty, as low-income carers often report feeling trapped and overburdened in their role.

In Chapter 10, Leiber and Brüker highlight that not only people in need of care but also carers are at risk of having unmet needs. In their intersectional analysis of the situations of family carers coming from both Western and Eastern Germany, they identify different type-specific unmet needs along an intersectional typology of coping with caring, as well as overarching unmet needs across the coping types. Coping with caring was also found to be different in Western and Eastern Germany, due to structural deficits, but also due to the high level of employment among carers in the East.

In Chapter 11, Aaltonen et al examine a specific but central and rapidly growing group of older people and carers: people with dementia and their informal carers. The chapter combines the analysis of survey data and in-depth interviews from Finland and finds that, although people with dementia receive more care than people without the condition, they still have more unmet needs. The authors conclude that the current social and health care system in Finland is inadequately prepared for the complex care needs of people with dementia, leading to unmet needs and care poverty, and affecting the well-being and health of their carers.

Part III concludes with Chapter 12 by Ulmanen who examines 'managerial care', that is, how families secure and manage care for their older members. Faced with the risk of care poverty, family members use their economic, cultural and social capital to try to ensure that care services meet the needs of the older person and reduce their own care responsibilities. This includes identifying what services are needed and whether they are available, accessing and mobilising services, and monitoring and orchestrating services. The chapter concludes that while managerial care has alleviated care poverty for many older people in Sweden, the needs of female carers, in particular, remain unmet.

Finally, Chapter 13, which forms Part IV of the book, draws on the previous chapters and critically discusses current research approaches to understanding unmet needs and care poverty. It summarises the theoretical, methodological and policy lessons learned and also outlines future directions for this area of research. Theoretically, the care poverty framework is seen as a significant step forward, particularly in bridging feminist and disability scholarship. Methodologically, the volume opens up new avenues, for example, by discussing ways of defining care poverty thresholds and measuring the intensity of care poverty. Empirically, new evidence presented in the book shows that care poverty exists even in the most developed welfare states and that socioeconomic status is very closely linked to unmet needs of older people and their carers. The links and even trade-offs between the unmet needs of care recipients and their carers become clear, as does the importance of the socio-emotional dimension of care poverty. Policy-wise, there is an apparent need to increase the availability of care, to better tailor support to existing needs, and to recognise and address the needs of carers through adequate support and financial protection. The chapter – and thus the book – concludes with a call for comparative care policy research informed by the care poverty approach.

References

Allen, S.M. (1994) 'Gender differences in spousal caregiving and unmet need for care', *Journal of Gerontology*, 49(4): S187–95.

Allen, S. and Mor, V. (1997) 'The prevalence and consequences of unmet need: contrasts between older and younger adults with disability', *Medical Care*, 35(11): 1132–48.

European Union (2022) 'Proposal for a Council Recommendation on access to affordable high-quality long-term care', *European Union* [COM/2022/441 final], 7 September. Available from: https://eur-lex.europa.eu/ [Accessed 30 March 2024].

Gureje, O., Ogunniyi, A., Kola, L. and Afolabi, E. (2006) 'Functional disability in elderly Nigerians: results from the Ibadan study of aging', *Journal of the American Geriatrics Society*, 54(11): 1784–9.

Kröger, T. (2022) *Care Poverty: When Older People's Needs Remain Unmet*, Cham: Palgrave Macmillan.

Kröger, T., Mathew Puthenparambil, J. and Van Aerschot, L. (2019) 'Care poverty: unmet care needs in a Nordic welfare state', *International Journal of Care and Caring*, 3(4): 485–500.

Peng, R., Wu, B. and Ling, L. (2015) 'Undermet needs for assistance in personal activities of daily living among community-dwelling oldest old in China from 2005 to 2008', *Research on Aging*, 37(2): 148–70.

Tennstedt, S., McKinlay, J. and Kasten, L. (1994) 'Unmet need among disabled elders: a problem in access to community long term care?', *Social Science & Medicine*, 38(7): 915–24.

Tomás Aznar, C., Moreno Aznar, L.A., Germán Bes, C., Alcalá Nalváiz, T. and Andrés Esteban, E. (2002) 'Dependencia y necesidades de cuidados no cubiertas de las personas mayores de una zona de Salud de Zaragoza' [Dependency and unmet need of care in older people in a health area of Saragossa, Spain], *Revista Española de Salud Pública*, 76(3): 215–26.

Vlachantoni, A., Shaw, R., Willis, R., Evandrou, M., Falkingham, J. and Luff, R. (2011) 'Measuring unmet need for social care amongst older people', *Population Trends*, 145: 1–17.

Williams, J., Lyons, B. and Rowland, D. (1997) 'Unmet long-term care needs of elderly people in the community: a review of the literature', *Home Health Care Services Quarterly*, 16(1–2): 93–119.

PART II

Theory and methods

2

Care poverty and conflicts in social citizenship: the right to care?

Kirstein Rummery

Introduction

In this chapter the theory of care poverty is placed in the context of other theories of care, providing an overview of the conflicts inherent in these theories, including the idea of 'social citizenship' – the right to access resources to meet needs, in this case care needs. Ideas about care poverty are used to offer a theoretical way of synthesising previous conflicting theories of care, testing this against kinship versus formal care provision.

Conflicting theoretical models of care

'Care' is a contested site of critical tension in contemporary social theory, policy and practice, and theories of care poverty draw on several histories to reframe and understand this tension. Feminist scholarship has highlighted the importance of understanding the intersection between emotion (Bowden, 1997) and labour (Twigg, 2000) – including the physical, emotional and economic costs of that labour (Himmelweit, 1999). Theorists have sought to distinguish between caring *about* and caring *for* (Knijn and Kremer, 1997) and the ethical dimensions of that tension (Tronto, 1998). Care is also understood as having both ethical and competency dimensions for both family (informal) and professional (formal) carers (McKechnie and Kohn, 1999). Crucially, care, whether it takes place in a formal or informal relationship, needs to be viewed as being a *social* relationship: an often complex and difficult relationship involving power and dependency (Lloyd, 2000). This power and dependency relationship is not simple, and involves the risk of loss of autonomy and independence, and the risk of exploitation, on both sides (Fine, 2005).

Theoretical definitions of 'care' have also had a normative influence on, and been influenced by, scholarship in social policy, which has looked not only at the *gendered* dimensions of care, but also other social divisions pertaining, for example, to ethnicity and class (Williams, 1995). Poverty and inequality in care has been highlighted by research on migrant care workers, who work to address care poverty in developed welfare states (Hochschild, 2000). Understanding the relationships between state, community, family and individual responsibilities for care is now accepted as part of mainstream social policy analysis (Ungerson, 2005). Caring *for* and *about* people is no longer seen as a private relationship between individuals but one of public concern.

The strength of feminist research in this area does mean that the values of justice and care are seen as both gendered and oppositional (Crittenden, 2001) – care having emotional and subjective value. Knijn and Kremer (1997) argued that a justice framework can help us to conceive of the right to *receive* care, as well as the right to *give* care as a matter for citizenship, making it increasingly difficult to sustain the claim that ethical values based on care violate the ideals of justice. Williams (2001) frames it as the *right* to give and receive care being a struggle for social justice.

A 'justice' model of care can be seen to resonate with a concern with social citizenship: it allows a focus on the social rights associated with care: both the right to have the *giving* of care recognised and legitimated, choice over whether and how to provide care supported, and the recognition of the right to *receive* care and support (Knijn and Kremer, 1997; Williams, 2018). Reformulating care as an issue of justice underpins the political approach to care adopted by feminists and social justice campaigners and to research on caregiving (Fine, 2007). It is important, when thinking about care poverty, to note that the political response to the isolation, poverty and social exclusion of primary caregivers draws heavily on the feminist framing of care as a matter for civic justice.

Set against the view of care as site of social justice are the voices of disability rights authors such as Morris (2001; 2004) and Brisenden (1989). Their concern with the view of care as social justice is that this framing relies on the empirical and theoretical perspectives of those who *provide* care, excluding those who *receive* care. To illustrate this, Waerness asserted that 'the receiver of care is subordinate in relation to the caregiver' (Waerness, 1984: 189), and Ungerson (1990) and Daly (2002) assert that care receivers are 'dependent' upon caregivers due to incapacity and inability to care for themselves. Brisenden (1989: 10) has argued that relying for support on unpaid carers is exploitative to both care giver and receiver. Morris (1997) argued that care itself is a form of oppression against disabled people – because care involves removing choice and control from disabled people (who are assumed to be unable to exercise it), it cannot be empowering.

Kröger (2009: 406) asserts that the disability rights and feminist perspectives are portrayed as being 'poles apart and fully incompatible with each other'. Reciprocity appears to be the key to unlock this stalemate: reconciliation of these conflicting positions has been achieved by some authors by arguing that the marketisation and personalisation of care services is a way of achieving social justice in care for both givers and receivers (Watson et al, 2004).

Theoretically, opening up choice to both givers and receivers of care recognises its reciprocal nature and empirically can be supported in the case of informal care, and where those with care needs are also giving care (for example, as parents, spouses and carers) (Williams, 2001). However, in cases of vulnerability of care recipients, the role of ethical care arguably becomes even more important – for example, near the end of life, with dementia or profound impairments that make the exercise of choice difficult (Brannelly, 2011; Rogers, 2016). This means that practically, and therefore also theoretically, relying on choice does not work to achieve social justice for all those who give and receive care.

One argument, particularly supported by Nordic feminists, is that the state should provide care (Parker, 1992). This would free carers from having to provide unpaid care if they do not want to, and reduce the risk of abuse and disempowerment on care receivers. However, disability rights campaigners have fought long and hard to free themselves from the oppression, paternalism and segregation associated with state care (Kröger, 2009). We could look to the market rather than the state (Beckett, 2007) but belief in markets as a way of achieving social justice is not shared by feminist writers. They point out that undervaluing of care work is due to its feminisation, which itself drives down wages. Marketising care also places formal carers at the risk of exploitation and abuse, and it can place additional burdens on informal carers. There is a high risk of leaving vulnerable people needing care unprotected (Pascall and Lewis, 2001).

Improved longevity and well-being, and declining availability of family support, can be seen as social policy successes, but they have led to a rising demand for long-term care and support across developed welfare states (Barber et al, 2020). The form and practice of oppression along the lines of gender, disability, class and age need to inform our understanding of the payment for and provision of care (Lewis, 2002). Most theoretical developments concerning the role these different constituent parts play in the 'welfare mix' which draw on feminist theory have focused on the gendered roles associated with *providing* care. Feminist analysis of care has given us a rich empirical and theoretical basis to draw on. However, the perspectives of those *receiving* care have, with a few notable exceptions (Kröger, 2009), not necessarily drawn on this heritage. In this chapter theoretical frameworks are drawn on and developed that are concerned with both those *providing* and *receiving* care to address this gap.

Increasing demands for services coupled with the politicisation of disability rights organisations have resulted in important changes in the policy direction in the provision of care services. In particular, there has been a rejection of state-provided long-term care services as being increasingly fragmented and unresponsive, and of reliance on informal care as being disempowering and exploitative (Brisenden, 1989; Morris, 2004).

Social citizenship and the right to receive care

Citizenship can be defined as:

> [T]hat set of practices (juridical, political, economic and cultural) which define a person as a competent member of society, and which as a consequence shape the flow of resources to persons and social groups. ... Citizenship is concerned with (a) the content of social rights and obligations; (b) with the form or type of such obligations and rights; (c) with the social forces that produce such practices; and finally (d) with the various social arrangements whereby such benefits are distributed to different sectors of society. (Turner, 1993: 2–3)

For Marshall, 'citizenship is a status bestowed on those who are full members of a community' (Marshall, 1992 [1950]: 18). Social citizenship is affected both by giving and receiving care, partly because work is an important way in which people discharge their citizenship obligations. The valuation and form of that work (whether it is paid or unpaid, whether it is recognised and recompensed, whether it is freely offered, whether it protects from or increases the risk of poverty) directly affects whether those giving care are able to be social citizens (Marshall, 1992 [1950]; Lister, 2003). For care receivers, how care is delivered (whether they can exercise choice and control over it, whether they can combine receiving with giving care, whether care enables them to participate in society, whether care is accessed as a social right) has a direct effect on their social participation, which is their ability to exercise choice and self-determination over their lives, shaped by their access to resources (Sen, 1990; Townsend, 1993). Social citizenship means the ability to participate in social life, which is affected by access to resources. This works also as a way to theorise care: the *giving* of care and having *access* to care are seen as an important part of the resources which are needed for social citizenship (Knijn and Kremer, 1997; Williams, 2001).

There is an inherent tension in conceptualising care as a citizenship right. Rights are 'enforceable choices' (Turner, 1993): they are claims that can and should be enforced by the state on behalf of individual citizens. It takes resources to enforce rights: civil rights are meaningless without a police force and criminal justice system to enforce them, and political rights similarly need a democratic political and judicial system (Barbalet, 1988). Care can be conceived as a 'social right' (Marshall, 1992 [1950]), that is, a right to resources to meet needs. As with other rights, resources are needed to protect access to those rights. However, unlike civic and political rights, which can essentially be seen to have little impact in terms of costs to individuals (it costs very little to not infringe the rights of others or to vote), social rights do have a cost to individuals (Plant, 1992). The production of welfare generally involves people: practitioners in fields such as education, health, welfare, criminal justice and so on. Giving their labour is not a no-cost endeavour – although as professionals they receive remuneration, if working in the 'caring' professions they are giving emotional as well as physical and intellectual labour (Kittay, 2002).

An example of this can be seen in the 'right' to health care in developed welfare states. A citizen has the right – the enforceable choice – to access health care, but this does not translate into an enforceable choice to any particular service or treatment. Marshall (1992 [1950]) illustrated this by articulating that under the newly formed British National Health Service, every citizen had the right to be registered with a General Practitioner and to be seen by a doctor when ill. However, the treatment or service then offered is contingent on the professional judgement of the practitioner and the availability of resources (Rummery and Glendinning, 1999). If we translate that to care – particularly care provided or commissioned by the welfare state, rather than family care – someone in need of care can have an enforceable choice to accessing an assessment of needs, but not any specific service to meet those needs. The power to allocate resources to meet needs resides in the practitioner acting on behalf of the state (Ellis, 2011), which they often do by exercising discretion or acting as street-level bureaucrats (Trappenburg et al, 2020). Crucially, the person requiring care has very little say in the allocation of those resources.

There is another conceptual problem with seeing care as a social right. As was explored earlier, care is not just physical labour for the person providing it, it is also emotional labour that entails costs (Himmelweit, 1999). Moreover, if care is to be provided ethically, we cannot divorce the emotional labour: care means caring about as well as caring for (Sevenhuijsen, 2003). Care that is not provided in an ethical, emotional way will almost inevitably be disempowering, paternalistic and mechanistic for both parties. Even the physical labour of care is not one that can be easily decoupled from the material reality of bodies providing that care: it is often intimate and personal, and needs to take account of the material and emotional reality of the person receiving as well as the person providing the care (Kittay, 2011). How then can we have an enforceable right to receive care when that would involve enforcing emotional labour in a way which feminists would recognise as being difficult at best and abusive at worst?

Here there is a clear difference between care that is provided by families, and that which is provided by formal, paid carers. A care relationship between someone needing care and a practitioner providing it can be negotiated like any other employment contract. An exchange of payment for labour gives both the provider and receiver of care protection through the ability to freely choose whether to enter the contract, and the terms of that contract. There are of course limits to that choice: on the care receiver side, there may be little choice of provider who can provide care in a way that the receiver needs; on the care provider side, there may be little choice on wage negotiation or pressure to accept undesirable conditions of work. Payment also does not remove the need for emotional connection between caregiver and recipient: there needs to be trust for intimate care to take place without fear of abuse. It does, however, offer both parties the opportunity to exit the caring relationship and reduces the risk of exploitation. In this way care can be conceived of as an enforceable choice: the enforcement is through agreeing the terms of a relationship that can be altered or exited by either side if the terms are unsatisfactory, but which can reasonably be expected to be fulfilled if satisfactory. Mladenov (2016) goes so far as to argue that this intimate employer/employee relationship between the givers and receivers of care is part of the fundamental human rights needed by disabled people to achieve equality.

This is not the case if care is provided by family members. When kinship bonds are involved, personal relationships cannot realistically include a 'right', as in an enforceable choice, to receive care. The only way the choice can be enforced is through emotional and familial ties and responsibilities: by definition these are only breakable in extreme circumstances, probably involving the breakdown of the relationship itself. Feminism would point out that you cannot have a right to care any more than you can have a right to sex: both choices, to be enforced, would involve access to emotional and/or physical intimacy, and any enforcement of that intimacy would by definition be exploitation or abuse. Care relationships within families are also difficult to conceive as rights-based because of the 'burden of gratitude' (Galvin, 2004) experienced by the care recipient, which means they cannot rely on or control the care given.

However, this is not to say that paid care is unproblematic from a social rights perspective. Hughes et al point out that: 'As "master" of "his" own destiny and PA [personal assistance] at "his" command, the disabled person is able to acquire control over many of the mundane but vitally important aspects of everyday existence which, hitherto, were delivered, if at all, to a timetable that suited the "carer"' (Hughes et al, 2005: 263). Masculinist language has been deliberately used here to highlight that this is a justice model of care – responding to the 'annihilation of the autonomy of the other' (Bauman, 1993: 11) that Morris (1993) and others have criticised. However, by deliberately separating the ethical, emotional aspects of care and turning it into a simple contractual exchange, Hughes et al (2005) reveal an important theoretical and ethical issue. If the power in the caring relationship has moved from the caregiver to the care receiver, that does not, per se, address a power imbalance in the ability to enforce social rights: it simply switches roles.

It should be noted that countries that have developed personalised care have often done so as a cost containment measure, rather than embracing the ideological emancipation of those who need care. In the UK, for example, direct payments are a way of shifting the rising costs of state-provided care onto service users (Pearson, 2000). In countries such as France and the Netherlands, payments are seen as a way of supporting a mix of family and formal care, and avoiding unsustainable growth in demand for state care from an ageing population. In more familial welfare states such as Austria and Italy, care payments directly to care users are more of a way to 'formalise' family care and support migrant labourers to provide intimate personal care, reducing demand on state services and replacing familial care. The ideological basis that dictates how, and in whose interests, the policy of personalised care operates is about neoliberal individualisation of responsibility, rather than a rights-based approach to the emancipation of care users (Rummery, 2009).

Demands for the personalisation of care came, particularly in neoliberal welfare states, from strong disability/user led political organisations. Personalisation has been much slower to take shape in the Nordic/ Scandinavian/universal welfare states: schemes there tend to be seen as additional to, rather than replacing, state-provided care. A strong ideological commitment to gender equality in these states recognises the problem that unpaid care in families disproportionately falls on women, and thus care services have within the context of welfare state provision been seen as universal and the responsibility of the state rather than individual families. However, that commitment does not necessarily translate into a commitment to user empowerment: the state not only decides who should receive care, but who should give care (and the nature and timing of that care). Hence it is the state, rather than individual carers, who take on the oppressive side of care – that 'annihilation of the other' that concerned Bauman (1993) and Keith (1992). Moreover, if practitioners are employed by the state to provide care, the way that care is provided is dictated by employers and professional practice: not by the care user. While there can be said to be a meaningful 'right' to access social care, it does not necessarily translate into full citizenship.

The right to give care

Social citizenship does not just involve rights to access resources. It also involves duties and obligations which accompany those rights: 'if citizenship is involved in the name of rights, the corresponding duties cannot be ignored' (Marshall, 1992 [1950]: 41). In most developed welfare states, the right to access resources to meet needs is contingent in some ways on contributing to the cost of the welfare state through work – usually either through taxation or insurance or a mixture of both. Therefore, for citizens to have a right to receive care, they must have contributed in some way to the provision of that care. Depending on the ideology and configuration of the welfare state in question, there are various ways in which that can happen. Welfare states which are based on an ideological commitment to state provision of services usually have work-based citizenship duties, as do those of a neoliberal bent. As Sainsbury (2009), Lister (2003) and others have pointed out, discharging your citizenship duties via the direct provision of care to your family has always been seen as bestowing a second-class citizenship on women, compared to those who engage in paid work. This can be seen through relatively low welfare benefits for carers, lack of paid leave or work-based support for carers, and lack of investment in support services for family carers. Nevertheless, the reliance on family carers in neoliberal welfare states is high (ILO, 2022).

Can the option to give care be seen as a social right – an enforceable choice? To some extent, in the case of family care, it can be. Many welfare regimes offer payments to family carers, either directly, or routed through care receivers. However, these payments are almost always set low (in comparison to median wages, and in some cases even in comparison to poverty-alleviation benefits), reflecting the undervaluation of care work (particularly that done by family carers). Family members choosing to provide care under these payments are 'choosing' under constrained conditions: the income they receive will almost certainly put them, and their family, at risk of material poverty. Family care does, usually, fit the ethic of care precept of having an emotional connection component – but this can be dangerous if the intimate nature of relationships is put under strain by material poverty. Nevertheless, although constrained, it is still a choice. Some families prefer the emotional connection of a family carer, others prefer trained strangers to deliver intimate personal care, and these preferences are cultural as well as political, economic and rational.

Care can be an enforceable choice where family carers and/or care recipients prefer family over paid care: apart from very rare cases where abuse, neglect or harm is evident, the state has very few options to impose state care and remove family care. However, at the time of writing it was #internationaldayofdisabilityremembrance – a Twitter-led campaign to honour those disabled and older people 'killed by filicide, or family carers'. People over 60 are routinely not included in general domestic abuse statistics, but one small-scale survey estimated that around 120,000 older people in the UK are suffering from physical, psychological, emotional or monetary abuse – 40 per cent from a spouse and 44 per cent from an adult family member such as a parent, sibling or adult child. Although the extent of the problem is unknown, it is clear that providing and receiving care within family relationships places them under strain, and the intimate private nature of these relationships means it is easy to hide abuse. The right to provide care can too easily become the right to exert power and control in a dangerous way, and the hidden nature of care can lead to abuse of carers as well.

It should not, however, be supposed that the danger of the abuse of caring relationships is confined to those in family caring relationships. Two in three care practitioners working in residential care reported that they have engaged in abusive acts towards older residents (Yon et al, 2017), with some studies estimating that rates of abuse in community-based settings rose by 84 per cent during COVID-19 (Chang and Levy, 2021). Care workers are also at risk of violence and abuse in residential and domestic care settings (Ford et al, 2022).

Care poverty and social citizenship

I have argued that the idea of 'care poverty' as articulated by Kröger et al (2019) moves away from the idea of 'vulnerability' or a 'dependency' on a particular form of support – deemed demeaning by care recipients and those arguing for a social justice model of care – towards a more politically engaged understanding of care (Rummery, 2022): 'Care poverty means a situation where, as a result of both individual and structural issues, people in need of care do not receive sufficient assistance from informal or formal sources, and thus have care needs that remain uncovered' (Kröger et al, 2019: 487). This formulation allows us to engage with the idea of care as a social right with more political and epistemological power. Poverty is a contested concept: scholars and policy makers argue over whether it should be measured in absolute or relative terms (Sen, 1983; Townsend, 1993), and whether it is a cause or consequence of oppression (George, 1988). However, there is universal agreement that poverty – whatever it is or has been caused by – is something negative that merits policy attention and political action (D'Arcy and Goulden, 2014). It leads to social exclusion (Levitas, 1996), which has significant economic and social costs for the state.

Living with 'care needs uncovered' is detrimental in terms of social exclusion and citizenship. If there are no ways to enforce the choice to access resources to meet basic needs, then citizens will be socially excluded from being 'full members of the community' (Marshall, 1992 [1950]). Not only will they have their capacities to self-actualisation limited (Sen, 1983), they will also not be able to fulfil the duties part of their membership of the community. As noted earlier, the duty to be a citizen can be discharged in various ways: through paid and care work, but also through family and community engagement, parenting, grandparenting, volunteering and other myriad ways to enhance family and community life.

In the case of older citizens whose capacity to provide service has been diminished through frailty, most have spent a lifetime working, caring and paying taxes. Disabled parents often struggle to have their parenting recognised as a citizenship contribution: it is often pathologised by a paternalistic state that cannot recognise disabled people generally as engaged citizens, let alone caregivers. Even people who are severely impaired have personal relationships which are meaningful and contribute to families and friendships (Kittay, 2011). Disability rights scholars and campaigners have asserted that every contribution to social well-being is valuable, and addressing poverty means addressing oppression, alienation and lack of connection as well as addressing material needs (Campbell and Oliver, 1996).

Changing our conception of care from one of imbalanced emotional and material relationships to a site of political and ideological struggle opens up new ways to break away from the care receiver/caregiver dichotomy. This dichotomy does not always recognise the care *given* by disabled and older people – the often reciprocal nature of the emotional aspect of caring – requiring both an ethics and justice approach to understanding care demands. Care poverty offers the opportunity to make the area of care a political one, needing scholarly theoretical and empirical attention.

Care poverty and social citizenship from a comparative perspective

How useful is a reframing of our understanding of lack of sufficient care as 'care poverty' in understanding and evaluating contemporary developments in long-term care provision? Most ways of approaching comparative analysis of welfare regimes (or sectors within those regimes) have depended on categorising by systems: organisations, actors, funding and governance. Although these are useful, particularly those that have paid attention to welfare outcomes in terms of gender equality (Orloff, 2009), they do not give us the full story. Kröger et al (2019) argue that the idea of unmet need relied on policy makers defining need, and scholars measuring need in terms of access to long-term care (Brimblecombe et al, 2017). Care poverty, in contrast, is 'lack of sufficient assistance' (Kröger et al, 2019: 487), which allows for the possibility that access to care – whether that be through families or paid carers – in itself does not necessarily provide that assistance in a way that enables 'being a fully competent member of the community'.

Conclusion

We have seen in this chapter how the conflicts underpinning an articulation and definition of care have to a certain extent led to an ideological and policy impasse between the needs of caregivers and care receivers. It has been articulated how using concepts derived from social citizenship theory offers a way forward in articulating care as a site of rights and duties, as well as one of emotional and physical labour and connection. It has also been argued that the concept of care poverty draws on the theory of care as a site of the operation of social citizenship: a site of publicly articulated rights and duties of citizens and states. This lends the idea of care poverty an ontological power: it enables us to talk about the need for care as a social right, to reframe our thinking away from vulnerabilities and needs and towards a more emancipatory approach to care provision. It also gives care a political power: poverty is universally seen not only as a negative state of affairs, but one which needs addressing, and one which states should be addressing as part of their duties towards their citizens.

However, care poverty is relatively new, in epistemological, ontological and empirical terms. While the work of developing care poverty as a nuanced and useful way to understand care will continue, it also needs to be empirically tested. As the lack of assistance that leads to care poverty could be addressed through personal, family, marketised or state means (or any combination of these), there is important work to be done in comparative social policy to examine the ideas, institutions and actors that exacerbate and alleviate care poverty, and this work has implications for policy and practice.

References

Barbalet, J.M. (1988) *Citizenship: Rights, Struggle and Class Inequality*, Milton Keynes: Open University Press.

Barber, S.L., Ong, P. and Han, Z.A. (2020) 'Long-term care in ageing populations', in R. Haring, I. Kickbusch, D. Ganten and M. Moeti (eds) *Handbook of Global Health*, Cham: Springer, pp 1–34. DOI:10.1007/978-3-030-05325-3_65-1.

Bauman, Z. (1993) *Postmodern Ethics*, Oxford: Blackwell.

Beckett, C. (2007) 'Women, disability, care: good neighbours or uneasy bedfellows', *Critical Social Policy*, 27(3): 360–80.

Bowden, P. (1997) *Caring: Gender-sensitive Ethics*, London: Routledge.

Brannelly, T. (2011) 'That others matter: the moral achievement – care ethics and citizenship in practice with people with dementia', *Ethics and Social Welfare*, 5(2): 210–16.

Brimblecombe, N., Pickard, L., King, D. and Knapp, M. (2017) 'Perceptions of unmet needs for community social care services in England: a comparison of working carers and the people they care for', *Health and Social Care in the Community*, 25(2): 435–46.

Brisenden, S. (1989) 'A charter for personal care', *Progress*, 16.

Campbell, J. and Oliver, M. (1996) *Disability Politics: Understanding Our Past, Changing Our Future*, London: Routledge.

Chang, E.S. and Levy, B.R. (2021) 'High prevalence of elder abuse during the COVID-19 pandemic: risk and resilience factors', *The American Journal of Geriatric Psychiatry*, 29(11): 1152–9.

Crittenden, C. (2001) 'The principles of care', *Women and Politics*, 22(2): 81–105.

Daly, M. (2002) 'Care as a good for social policy', *Journal of Social Policy*, 31(2): 251–70.

D'Arcy, C. and Goulden, C. (2014) *A Definition of Poverty*, York: Joseph Rowntree Foundation.

Ellis, K. (2011) '"Street-level bureaucracy" revisited: the changing face of frontline discretion in adult social care in England', *Social Policy & Administration*, 45(3): 221–44.

Fine, M. (2005) 'Dependency work: a critical exploration of Kittay's perspective on care as a relationship of power', *Health Sociology Review*, 14(2): 146–60.

Fine, M. (2007) 'The social division of care', *Australian Journal of Social Issues*, 42(2): 137–49.

Ford, J.L., Zhu, Y. and Barrett, A.K. (2022) 'Structurational divergence, safety climate, and intentions to leave: an examination of health care workers' experiences of abuse', *Communication Monographs*, 89(1): 1–24.

Galvin, R. (2004) 'Challenging the need for gratitude: comparisons between paid and unpaid care for disabled people', *Journal of Sociology*, 40(2): 137–55.

George, V. (1988) *Wealth, Poverty and Starvation*, Hemel Hempstead: Wheatsheaf Books.

Himmelweit, S. (1999) 'Caring labor', *The Annals of the American Academy of Political and Social Science*, 561(1): 27–38.

Hochschild, A.R. (2000) 'The nanny chain', *The American Prospect*, 11(4): 32–6.

Hughes, B., McKie, L., Hopkins, D. and Watson, N. (2005) 'Love's labours lost? Feminism, the Disabled People's Movement and an ethic of care', *Sociology*, 39(2): 259–75.

ILO (International Labour Organization) (2022) 'Care work and care jobs: for the future of decent work', *International Labour Organization*. Available from: https://www.ilo.org [Accessed 1 February 2024].

Keith, L. (1992) 'Who cares wins? Women, caring and disability', *Disability Handicap and Society*, 7(2): 167–75.

Kittay, E. (2002) 'Love's labor revisited', *Hypatia*, 17(3): 237–50.

Kittay, E.F. (2011) 'The ethics of care, dependence and disability', *Ratio Juris*, 24(1): 49–58.

Knijn, T. and Kremer, M. (1997) 'Gender and the caring dimension of welfare states: toward inclusive citizenship', *Social Politics*, 4(3): 328–61.

Kröger, T. (2009) 'Care research and disability studies: nothing in common?', *Critical Social Policy*, 29(3): 398–420.

Kröger, T., Puthenparambil, J.M. and Aerschot, L.V. (2019) 'Care poverty: unmet care needs in a Nordic welfare state', *International Journal of Care and Caring*, 3(4): 485–500.

Levitas, R. (1996) 'The concept of social exclusion and the new Durkheimian hegemony', *Critical Social Policy*, 16(46): 5–20.

Lewis, J. (2002) 'Gender and welfare state change', *European Societies*, 4(4): 331–57.

Lister, R. (2003) *Citizenship: Feminist Perspectives*, Basingstoke: Macmillan.

Lloyd, L. (2000) 'Caring about carers: only half the picture?', *Critical Social Policy*, 20(1): 136–50.

Marshall, T.H. (1992 [1950]) *Citizenship and Social Class*, London: Pluto Press.

McKechnie, R. and Kohn, T. (1999) 'Introduction: why do we care who cares?', in T. Kohn and R. McKechnie (eds) *Extending the Boundaries of Care: Medical Ethics and Caring Practices*, Oxford: Berg, pp 1–14.

Mladenov, T. (2016) 'Disability and social justice', *Disability & Society*, 31(9): 1226–41.

Morris, J. (1993) 'Feminism and disability', *Feminist Review*, 43(1): 57–70.

Morris, J. (1997) 'Care of empowerment? A disability rights perspective', *Social Policy & Administration*, 31(1): 54–60.

Morris, J. (2001) 'Impairment and disability: constructing an ethics of care that promotes human rights', *Hypatia*, 16: 1–16.

Morris, J. (2004) 'Independent living and community care: a disempowering framework', *Disability & Society*, 19(5): 427–42.

Orloff, A.S. (2009) 'Gendering the comparative analysis of welfare states: an unfinished agenda', *Sociological Theory*, 27(3): 317–43.

Parker, G. (1992) *With this Body: Caring, Disability and Marriage*, Buckingham: Open University Press.

Pascall, G. and Lewis, J. (2001) 'Care work beyond Beveridge', *Benefits: The Journal of Poverty and Social Justice*, 32: 1–6.

Pearson, C. (2000) 'Money talks? Competing discourses in the implementation of direct payments', *Critical Social Policy*, 20(4): 459–77.

Plant, R. (1992) 'Citizenship, rights and welfare', in A. Coote (ed) *The Welfare of Citizens: Developing Social Rights*, London: Institute of Public Policy Research, pp 15–29.

Rogers, C. (2016) *Intellectual Disability and Being Human: A Care Ethics Model*, Abingdon: Routledge.

Rummery, K. (2009) 'A comparative discussion of the gendered implications of cash-for-care schemes: markets, independence and social citizenship in crisis?', *Social Policy and Administration*, 43(6): 634–48.

Rummery, K. (2022) 'The right to care? Social citizenship and care poverty in developed welfare states', *International Journal of Sociology and Social Policy*, 43(1/2): 33–47.

Rummery, K. and Glendinning, C. (1999) 'Negotiating needs, access and gatekeeping: developments in health and community care policies in the UK and the rights of disabled and older citizens', *Critical Social Policy*, 19: 335–51.

Sainsbury, D. (2009) *Gender, Equality and Welfare States*, Cambridge: Cambridge University Press.

Sen, A. (1983) 'Poor, relatively speaking', *Oxford Economic Papers*, 35(2): 153–69.

Sen, A. (1990) 'Gender and cooperative conflict', in I. Tinker (ed) *Persistent Inequality*, Oxford: Oxford University Press, pp 123–48.

Sevenhuijsen, S. (2003) 'The place of care: the relevance of the feminist ethic of care for social policy', *Feminist Theory*, 4(2): 179–97.

Townsend, P. (1993) *The International Analysis of Poverty*, London: Harvester Wheatsheaf.

Trappenburg, M., Kampen, T. and Tonkens, E. (2020) 'Social workers in a modernising welfare state: professionals or street-level bureaucrats?', *The British Journal of Social Work*, 50(6): 1669–87.

Tronto, J. (1998) 'An ethic of care', *Generations San Francisco*, 22(3): 15–20.

Turner, B.S. (1993) *Citizenship and Social Theory*, London: SAGE.

Twigg, J. (2000) *Bathing: The Body and Community Care*, London: Routledge.

Ungerson, C. (1990) 'The language of care: crossing the boundaries', in C. Ungerson (ed) *Gender and Caring: Work and Welfare in Britain and Scandinavia*, Hemel Hempstead: Harvester/Wheatsheaf.

Ungerson, C. (2005) 'Care, work and feeling', *The Sociological Review*, 53(2 suppl): 188–203.

Waerness, K. (1984) 'The rationality of caring', *Economic and Industrial Democracy*, 5(2): 185–211.

Watson, N., McKie, L., Hopkins, D. and Gregory, S. (2004) '(Inter) dependence, needs and care: the potential for disability and feminist theories to develop an emancipatory model', *Sociology*, 38(2): 331–50.

Williams, F. (1995) 'Race/ethnicity, gender, and class in welfare states: a framework for comparative analysis', *Social Politics*, 2(2): 127–59.

Williams, F. (2001) 'In and beyond New Labour: towards a new political ethics of care', *Critical Social Policy*, 21(4): 467–93.

Williams, F. (2018) 'Care: intersections of scales, inequalities and crises', *Current Sociology*, 66(4): 547–61.

Yon, Y., Mikton, C.R., Gassoumis, Z.D. and Wilber, K.H. (2017) 'Elder abuse prevalence in community settings: a systematic review and meta-analysis', *The Lancet, Global Health*, 5(2): e147–56.

3

Care poverty: centring older and disabled people in the care economy

Christine Kelly

Introduction

In early 2023, media sources in the mid-sized city of Winnipeg, Manitoba, Canada reported a personal story reflecting a complete failure of public home care services. Katherine Ellis was facing end of life due to pancreatic cancer. Ellis was discharged from the hospital as she opted for at-home palliative care. Ellis and her husband Eric de Schepper were given information detailing the amount and type of palliative home care services they would receive. For five long weeks, the services never materialised, leaving de Schepper and Ellis to struggle until her passing. De Schepper went public with his story and filed a complaint with the provincial Ombudsman. Media reports questioned the government about the incident, which cited staffing issues. Unions representing most of the home care workers in the province commented on the lack of incentives to bring more people to home care. In solidarity, a local group of home care workers risked their job security and composed a public letter highlighting system issues that likely contributed to de Schepper and Ellis' situation, arguing 'scheduling concerns and labour issues raised by health-care aides and home care workers aren't being taken seriously, and it's hurting their patients the most' (Bergen, 2023).

This tragic account in one specific context is, unfortunately, not rare. Examples of home care failures are common in media stories in countries worldwide – a sure sign of a system in distress. Home care breakdowns have implications for three groups, namely paid workers, unpaid caregivers and people who need support. Paid workers express being ignored, disrespected and stressed due to unsustainable work assignments. Worker experiences are shaped by localised working conditions as well as socioeconomic policies that govern this sector (for example, immigration rules, educational policies). The account of Ellis' situation also demonstrates implications for unpaid caregivers (de Schepper in this case), who face physical, emotional and financial strains (Adelman et al, 2014; Arriagada, 2020). Caregiver issues are shaped by health and social system decisions that implicitly (and at times explicitly) rely on unpaid labour for the system to function. Finally, Ellis' and de Schepper's account reveals the implications for the person in need of support, who may experience neglect, stress, pain and lack of dignity.

The potential harms of inadequate care services are layered and interdependent. For many people with disabilities[1] and older people who need care at home whether at the end of life or in an ongoing way, even minor disruptions can have serious social, economic and health implications. Such disruptions then increase the burden on unpaid caregivers, who unlike in the opening story, are disproportionately women and women of colour (Parmar et al, 2021). Gaps in care are linked to numerous inequities affecting the well-being of unpaid caregivers and care recipients alike – that is a situation where a person may be living in what Kröger terms 'care poverty' (Kröger, 2022). Care poverty captures situations of system failure by considering the structural issues that shape the availability of care in conjunction with a detailed description of different needs (Kröger et al, 2019; Kröger, 2022). Care poverty underscores that individuals have unmet needs not because of disability or age, but because formal services are not functioning as they aim to, and informal supports may not be available for structural reasons. Beyond the health and well-being of home care clients and caregivers, there are serious economic risks associated with gaps in home care, which are captured by recent work on the *care economy*. The care economy 'refers to the sector of economic activities, both paid and unpaid, related to the provision of social and material care' and is integral to overall economic functioning (Peng, 2018).

This chapter zooms out from Ellis and de Schepper's story to demonstrate how both population levels and individual experiences of care poverty are indicators of a strained care economy. It describes how 'unmet needs' are documented and understood in Canada as a case example and argues that a care poverty approach offers a more complete framework requiring a different set of methods and assumptions. In addition, care poverty allows for a fuller description of the multiple aspects of the care economy in ways that avoid repeating previous erasures of care scholarship and helps further bridge contemporary disability studies' scholarship on the politics of care. In this way, care poverty is a more complete accounting of unmet home care needs in context, an indicator of a malfunctioning care economy, and a reminder that transformative change can happen through how societies organise care.

What is care poverty?

As mentioned throughout this collection, care poverty is 'where, as a result of both individual and structural issues, people in need of care do not receive sufficient assistance from informal or formal sources' (Kröger et al, 2019). The concept of care poverty describes the situation of *not enough* care. It is a comprehensive approach to documenting unmet needs, but also a conceptual intervention that transforms individualised accounts of 'unmet needs' into indicators of structural issues. This chapter suggests it is particularly useful for signalling strain or malfunction in the care economy and the urgent and dire consequences for those who need care.

In terms of measurement, Kröger (2022) details three domains of need and two measures of care poverty. The '*personal domain*' refers to the need for help with the Activities of Daily Living (ADLs) – a concept that is prevalent in health care sectors. Many ADL assessments are based on Katz et al's (1963) scale of six tasks: bathing, dressing, going to the toilet, continence, transferring and eating (Liu et al, 2012). Earlier international research on unmet home care needs tended to emphasise the personal domain of care poverty (for example, Desai et al, 2001).

The '*practical domain*' reflects the Instrumental Activities of Daily Living (IADLs), often assessed using screening tools based on the Lawton Instrumental Activities of Daily Living Scale that covers eight complex activities such as transportation, shopping and laundry (Lawton and Brody, 1969; Kelbling et al, 2024). The practical domain is inconsistently represented in unmet needs literature, with increased consideration in recent work for the interplay between personal and practical domains (for example, Black et al, 2019; Vlachantoni, 2019).

The third domain is the '*socio-emotional domain*' and pertains to feelings of belonging and connection, drawing on research on social isolation and loneliness. The last domain is the least likely to be included in existing unmet needs research and frontline service assessments yet is crucial to receiving high-quality care. Care poverty centres on the person in need of support, and aims to detail all potential needs and assess available supports; at present, care poverty does not necessarily position one domain as more important than another nor formal services as more important than informal support from unpaid caregivers. Care poverty can be measured as *absolute*, when a person needs assistance but receives no formal or informal support at all, or *relative*, when a person receives insufficient support (referred to as 'partially unmet needs' in Canada) (Vlachantoni, 2019; Kröger, 2022).

Without needing to document the needs of the couple in the opening vignette, it is clear Ellis was in a situation of relative care poverty in all three domains as her spouse was able to provide basic level help during that time. The public letter prepared by the paid care workers does the other work of care poverty by illuminating how the failures were structural and embedded in programme design.

Care poverty is described as bridging unmet care needs literature as well as the body of scholarship on the 'care gap', that is, the decreasing availability of formal and informal care due to social and economic changes such as falling birth rates, ageing populations and the increased paid workforce participation of women (Redfoot et al, 2013; Pickard, 2015). The chapter turns now to developments in this second body of work to consider what care poverty adds.

What is the care economy?

In parallel to, but disconnected from, scholarship on care poverty, there is increasing international and national focus on the care economy (for example, Addati et al, 2018; Peng, 2018; ILO, 2022). The concept of the care economy is linked to the long evolution of care gap research and commentary concerned with the availability of a care workforce. Instead of discussing the care gap where care labour supply is interpreted as *an outcome* of social and demographic trends, scholarship on the care economy flips the discussion to position care as a mode of production with tangible implications for other economic sectors and the populations who participate (or not) in the care workforce.

The concept of the care economy resists dichotomising paid and unpaid care by grouping them as a foundational workforce and economic subsector (Peng, 2018). Recent groundbreaking international work found women's participation in paid and unpaid care work is predictive of the extent, quality and trajectory of their general labour force participation in countries around the world – and, further, care workers, predominantly women, are crucial to the overall functioning of society, governments and economies (Addati et al, 2018). Even seemingly unrelated economic activities, such as distribution and manufacturing, are upheld by paid and unpaid care work supporting children, adults, people with disabilities and older people. Early waves of the COVID-19 pandemic, for example, saw extreme disruptions to the care economy where failures of care in residential care, home care and primary care settings rippled out to affect multiple aspects of the economic infrastructure.

Social reproduction is a long-standing concept used to recognise contributions of women's *unpaid* invisible labour (Bakker, 2007), yet the premise of the care economy goes further to describe an interwoven network of paid and unpaid individuals. In returning to the opening vignette as well as other research, even if the paid and formal services had been delivered for the couple, home care services rarely function properly without supplementary and substantial unpaid care provided by family and friends (Pickard, 2015; Kelly et al, 2023). At the same time, paid care work is characterised by poor working conditions and high turnover – the effects of which are poorly tracked (Addati et al, 2018; ILO, 2022). Volatility in the paid care sector can lead to an over-reliance on the unpaid care sector to compensate for system deficits, leading to inadequate care for older people and people with disabilities and at the same time straining unpaid caregivers.

Canada is also playing a role in advancing and drawing attention to the concept of the care economy. In Canada, a collective of academics, non-profits, economists and health advocates released the *Care Economy Statement* in 2021 and are steadily gathering signatures to advocate for care to be a top political priority (Armstrong et al, 2021). In parallel, Canadian national statistics are also working to document and describe the care workforce. Based on Canadian census data from 2016, it was found that about one in five of the total employed population are people working in paid care occupations, with women accounting for three-quarters of all care workers (Khanam et al, 2022). Understanding paid and unpaid care work as an 'economy' draws attention to the disadvantages and characteristics of those who work in this sector. Further, it underscores how larger systems and individuals benefit (and are even upheld) by invisible care work. This focus on the inequities linked to care work demonstrates how the care economy functions and malfunctions in different contexts and situations.

What does care poverty add?

What does it mean for the care economy to 'malfunction'? In exploring matters of care, it is imperative to resist the 'conflation of care with affection, happiness, attachment, and positive feeling as political goods', which is common even among feminist, global health and other critical scholars (Murphy, 2015). Murphy (2015) calls for the 'unsettling of care' in ways that consider 'multiply fraught histories and structures' including within feminist care scholarship. There is an unfortunate tendency within care theorising and scholarship to erase and at times patronise those in need of care – which is particularly challenging for those who need care in an ongoing way, such as older people and people with disabilities (Thomas, 2007). In advancing the concept of a care economy, it is imperative that we do not repeat these histories and consider other indicators of malfunction beyond the labour market participation of care workers. That is, what are the indicators and effects when the care economy fails the 'consumers' of care? This is the missing piece of care economy work and a key indicator of economic system malfunction – that is, care poverty.

Conceptually, care poverty makes an important advancement to unmet needs scholarship, which has often taken a deductive theoretical approach based on ADL/IADL scales. Once measured, explanations for situations of care poverty consider structural issues, such as political agendas and policy frameworks, and social location, for example, gender and immigration status. As described earlier, care poverty connects unmet needs (typically from gerontology) and care gap research (typically from feminist political economy) – helping position individuals on the social landscape. Care poverty is also linked to economic poverty and inequality research, which 'allows us to move beyond needs to understand the relationship to deprivation and disadvantage in society' (Kröger, 2022). This is the key distinguishing feature of care poverty, that one may live with a variety of unmet needs not because of individual characteristics but because of structural factors that shape meanings and experiences.

But what does care poverty add to the burgeoning attention to the care economy? The concept of care economy grows from care gap literature and is embedded in a theoretical genealogy of feminist political economy. The new face of this work on the care economy, while extremely compelling, risks repeating the same troubling exclusions of the theoretical legacy it builds upon – the tendency to de-centre the experiences and perspectives of those in need of care. As such, care poverty brings to the care economy a renewed focus on the urgent situations it can create where people with care needs who are often and already marginalised in our current social structures are left with basic needs unmet.

In disability studies' evolution around care, recent iterations elaborate on the complex interdependences of those who need support and those who provide it. Nishida (2022: 11) reflects on much of feminist care theory, where care is positioned as 'labour' and even 'dirty work'. Such an approach to care illuminates and problematises the inequality on one side of the care equation – caregiving. What is rarely mentioned in such analysis is the other side of the equation – care receiving and the stories of those who are exclusively situated as objects of burden or dischargers of the 'dirt'. Nishida's work blurs the lines of care worker and care receiver, demonstrating how the conditions of care can debilitate marginalised workers to the point that they acquire disabilities and need support themselves. Nishida (2022: 14) comments: 'I resist the widespread assumption that care workers are nondisabled or immune to pain, fatigue, and other disabling conditions, and disabled people are not agents of caregiving.'

Nishida (2022) positions care as both an object and mechanism of social change – that is, a policy topic and system to galvanise around as well as micro-daily interactions. This can, in the end, be transformative – that is, a form of *just* care. Care is not only a system that can fail and should be changed, but rather includes practices to be reclaimed. Nishida (2022: 7) describes situations of 'care injustice where people – whether they are situated as care workers, care receivers, and others – deteriorate under the name of care when care is used as a mechanism to enhance the political economy and neglect the well-being of those situated as care workers and care recipients'. In this way, the notion of care poverty is a way to document Nishida's concept of care injustice – further bridging this long-standing gulf between disability and feminist care theorists.

Nishida is not the first scholar to attempt this bridge. Coming from the other side of the gulf, Cranford (2020) argues home care programmes represent a negotiation between workers' quest for security and recipients' struggle for flexibility – a struggle that can be resolved through 'intimate community unionism' such as forms of collective social action or shared norms of reciprocity. Both scholars look towards each other, in ways that help us envision care and home care as a space for transformative change rather than only failures and governance.

Home care and unmet needs in Canada

This chapter now presents Canada as a case example to demonstrate what a care poverty framework adds to the existing ways of measuring unmet needs and emerging discussions about the care economy. In Canada, residential long-term care and home care services run through, or adjacent to, the health care system. Canada does not have a clearly delineated social care sector as in other countries. Canada ranks 10th in an overall assessment of health care systems in 11 high-income countries, with particularly poor performance for 'income-related inequities' (Schneider et al, 2021). Canada's health care system is organised both federally and then by the ten provinces and three territories in the north, with operational decisions made at the provincial/ territorial level (for more details on Canada's health care system, see Allin et al, 2020).[2]

Canada's health care systems are strained by issues that are familiar to many countries. Canada is grappling with the politicisation of public health, burnout and health human resource gaps, especially among nurses, lack of access to primary care, long waitlists for certain services, growing awareness of the failures and perhaps inappropriateness of residential long-term care, and inequities in access and outcomes for marginalised populations (PHAC, 2022).

Home care in Canada operates in this complex health landscape. Home care availability, eligibility and coverage vary greatly from province to province (Marier, 2021; Contandriopoulos et al, 2022). Some provinces have means-testing while others aim for more universal coverage. National data find that 27 per cent of the Canadian households receiving home care services pay 'solely out of pocket' (Gilmour, 2018a). Canadian home care is often and long-described as 'piecemeal' and 'siloed' (Donner et al, 2015; Peckham et al, 2018).

The complex health and home care infrastructure does not necessarily mean it is not functioning well, with the more salient issue being whether the services are meeting the needs of Canadians. American researchers conclude that unmet needs are 'common' and most of them are 'non-medical' (Black et al, 2019). International research identifies groups at risk of having unmet needs (Liu et al, 2012; Wilkinson-Meyers et al, 2014), such as recent immigrants (Yung, 2021), adults with disabilities (McColl et al, 2010) and older adults with intellectual disabilities (Shooshtari et al, 2012). There is compelling research on the outcomes of leaving home care needs unmet (LaPlante et al, 2004; Quail et al, 2011; Freedman et al, 2014; Hass et al, 2017). For example, greater unmet needs are predictive of residential care placement for people living with dementia (Gaugler et al, 2005).

As described at the outset, there are relatively frequent stories featured in the media of home care system failures. More systematically, the common source for reporting population estimates of unmet home care needs is data drawn from the Canadian Community Health Survey (CCHS), an annual longitudinal cross-sectional survey that collects information related to 'health status, health care utilization, and health determinants for the Canadian population' (Statistics Canada, 2019). CCHS is housed at Statistics Canada – the national statistical office that operates with a high degree of sampling and analytical rigour. An analysis of the CCHS reports that in 2021, 6 per cent of Canadian households[3] reported using formal home care services for someone over the age of 18 in the past year, and an additional 3 per cent of households reported an instance of needing home care but not receiving it (Statistics Canada, 2022). The previous publication in 2016 focused on individual estimates (rather than households), finding that 3.2 per cent of Canadians over the age of 18 received home care in the past year, with 1.6 per cent reporting perceived unmet needs (Gilmour, 2018b).

Unmet needs in CCHS are established through responses to the standardised question: 'During the past 12 months, was there ever a time when you or anyone in the household felt that home care services were needed but were not received?' (HMC-Q040). CCHS allows for proxy reporting and reports on the health practices of the entire household (anyone who lives in the same dwelling). The approach in Canada is a hybrid between the 'self-reported' approach defended in Kröger (2022) and the approach that gathers information from unpaid caregivers, depending on which member answers the survey questions for the household. The survey includes a follow-up question that would make it possible to discern if the answers are about the respondent specifically or about other household members – perhaps presenting an opportunity to further validate and consider the methodological issue of self-reporting unmet needs.

In the 2021 CCHS report of unmet needs, home care is distinguished as 'home health care' and 'support care' (Statistics Canada, 2022). The former refers to health services such as nursing care, physiotherapy and medical services provided at home. The latter, home support care, is what is more commonly thought of as home care services – assistance with personal needs and other services. It is notable that, unlike a care poverty framework, it is not possible to distinguish personal, practical and socio-emotional domains of needs even globally in CCHS. CCHS also does not assess receipt or extent of unpaid care. For example, the report comments: 'In 2021, among the 6% of Canadian households that reported using formal home care in the previous 12 months, almost half (48%) received only home health care, while nearly one-third (32%) received only support home care and 20% received both types of care' (Statistics Canada, 2022) – arguably information that does not help identify populations facing absolute or relative care poverty.

The final numbers produced and cited are extremely limited, providing only a glimpse of the extent of unmet needs in the Canadian population, with possible analyses based on gender, geography, economic status and other routinely collected demographic information. CCHS does reveal the scope of the issue but loses the granular depth that is needed for policy design and response. For example, casting back to the couple featured in the opening vignette, the current approach would not capture the severity or urgent temporality in their situation, but rather, that story would be folded in with larger populations who may have only one instance of home care services failing to arrive over the past 12 months. Further, the single global question about perceived unmet needs does not enable an analysis of the level, frequency, type or severity of unmet needs, as a respondent could have one instance of home care needs being unmet and be classified in this way (see also Chapter 5). It is thus difficult to consider the needs and descriptors of households facing absolute care poverty – that is, those with a need for home care but not receiving formal or informal care at all.

There are a few other possible data sources in Canada, yet each carries distinct limitations. The Canadian Longitudinal Study on Aging (CLSA), for example, catalogues ADL/IADL needs but does not assess the ability to meet each need. The CLSA assesses social supports and connections, and as such, is a valuable source for evaluating socio-emotional care gaps. Statistics Canada also houses the General Social Survey: Caregiving and Care Receiving, which includes a detailed assessment of care receivers' informal sources of care and needs; however, like in CCHS, unmet needs are measured through a single global question, and there is limited exploration of formal sources of support. Finally, the Home Care Reporting System, more commonly known as InterRAI, collects data on resource utilisation from publicly funded sources via paid workers (CIHI, nd). It is not collected in all provinces, does not assess informal support and cannot provide information about people lacking access to services. At present, the Canadian data landscape presents multiple opportunities that fall short of creating a complete picture of the nature and effects of living in care poverty.

Conclusion

A care poverty approach to understanding unmet needs allows for an in-depth and holistic consideration of what the needs of a person are in three domains, the extent of the 'unmetness' and an assessment of the available resources (informal and formal), and potential confounding factors linked to structural and social forces. Yet, there is a practical challenge to advancing a care poverty framework in Canada and other similar policy contexts. Canadian health policy makers are likely to have reservations about the broad scope of care poverty, perhaps that it encompasses 'too much'.

As home care services are part of the health care system in Canada, using a care poverty framework to assess system failures and population-level needs brings a much broader range of needs under the purview of health. In this context, the care poverty framework could potentially medicalise social needs and is likely to reveal more gaps within the current services. Many home care programmes in Canada are open to those who need help with personal care needs and only then will provide support with practical care needs. A care poverty framework illuminates the importance of supporting a wide array of needs – and documenting the various rates of care poverty would challenge the service approach of many Canadian programmes. This is a difficult criticism to face in resource-strained policy contexts facing significant human resourcing issues.

Turning to the landscape of care theory, care poverty is a practical bridge – a way to concretely measure care injustice faced by those who need care, perhaps to document the needs and gaps of unpaid caregivers. Conceptually, by seeing unmet needs as a form of systematic poverty, and *a malfunction of the care economy*, we can also see how care workers become disabled through their work, that unpaid caregivers are often also older people themselves, and the complex types of care and contributions that people who need care make. Indeed, by adding care poverty to the unmet needs and care economy literature, we head further towards listening and centring the experiences of disabled and older people in need of support.

Returning to the account of Ellis and de Schepper once more, using a care poverty framework reveals a situation of relative care poverty and an instance where the care economy has failed. Yet, care poverty does not focus on the effects on economic productivity and labour market participation of paid and unpaid care workers, but rather opens a conversation about the policy context that enabled such a failure. The workers draw attention in their open letter to the policy and practice norms that contributed to the system failure experienced by the couple. Perhaps if we pause to learn from the lived experiences of care poverty, we can better design our services to support a vibrant care economy that centres the well-being of those who need and work in care.

Notes

[1] In Canada, many community organisations, official government sources and individuals use the person-first terminology of 'people with disabilities'. Others, however, prefer to use the term 'disabled person' to indicate the centrality of disability to identity and life experience. This is a contentious issue in Canada and there is not consensus among key stakeholders. As such, this chapter uses both phrases to acknowledge strongly held and highly personal ways of identifying.

[2] The federal government is responsible for providing supports to specific populations, namely, First Nations and Inuit people who live on reservations, and veterans.

[3] This survey uses the household as the unit of analysis and not individuals. As such, there may be more than one person using home care services in a given household. The CCHS excludes people in residential settings such as long-term care facilities and correctional facilities.

References

Addati, L., Cattaneo, U., Esquivel, V. and Valarino, I. (2018) *Care Work and Care Jobs for the Future of Decent Work*, Geneva: International Labour Organization.

Adelman, R.D., Tmanova, L.L., Delgado, D., Dion, S. and Lachs, M.S. (2014) 'Caregiver burden: a clinical review', *JAMA*, 311(10): 1052–60.

Allin, S., Marchildon, G. and Peckham, A. (2020) 'Canada', *The Commonwealth Fund* [International Health Care System Profiles], 5 June. Available from: https://www.commonwealthfund.org/international-health-policy-center/countries/canada [Accessed 1 February 2024].

Armstrong, P., Cohen, M.G., Ritchie, L., Vosko, L.F. and Yalnizyan, A. (2021) 'The care economy statement'. Available from: https://thecareeconomy.ca/statement/ [Accessed 1 February 2024].

Arriagada, P. (2020) 'The experiences and needs of older caregivers in Canada', *Statistics Canada* [Insights on Canadian Society], 24 November. Available from: https://www150.statcan.gc.ca/n1/pub/75-006-x/2020001/article/00007-eng.htm [Accessed 1 February 2024].

Bakker, I. (2007) 'Social reproduction and the constitution of a gendered political economy', *New Political Economy*, 12(4): 541–56.

Bergen, R. (2023) 'Home-care workers cite a litany of systemic failures in letter to Winnipeg widower denied palliative care', *CBC News*, 23 February. Available from: https://www.cbc.ca/news/canada/manitoba/home-care-palliative-winnipeg-letter-1.6758802 [Accessed 27 February 2023].

Black, B.S., Johnston, D., Leoutsakos, J., Reuland, M., Kelly, J., Amjad, H., et al (2019) 'Unmet needs in community-living persons with dementia are common, often non-medical, and related to patient and caregiver characteristics', *International Psychogeriatrics*, 31(11): 1643–54.

CIHI (Canadian Institute for Health Information) (nd) 'Home care reporting system metadata', *Canadian Institute for Health Information*. Available from: https://www.cihi.ca/en/home-care-reporting-system-metadata [Accessed 18 February 2022].

Contandriopoulos, D., Stajduhar, K., Sanders, T., Carrier, A., Bitschy, A. and Funk, L. (2022) 'A realist review of the home care literature and its blind spots', *Journal of Evaluation in Clinical Practice*, 28(4): 680–9.

Cranford, C. (2020) *Home Care Fault Lines: Understanding Tensions and Creating Alliances*, Ithaca, NY: Cornell University Press.

Desai, M.M., Lentzner, H.R. and Weeks, J.D. (2001) 'Unmet need for personal assistance with activities of daily living among older adults', *The Gerontologist*, 41(1): 82–8.

Donner, D.G., Fooks, C., McReynolds, J., Sinha, S., Smith, K. and Thomson, D. (2015) *Bringing Care Home: Report of the Expert Group on Home and Community Care*, Toronto: Government of Ontario.

Freedman, V.A., Spillman, B.C. and Kasper, J. (2014) *Hours of Care in Rounds 1 and 2 of the National Health and Aging Trends Study (No. 7)*, Baltimore: Johns Hopkins University.

Gaugler, J.E., Kane, R.L., Kane, R.A. and Newcomer, R. (2005) 'Unmet care needs and key outcomes in dementia', *Journal of the American Geriatrics Society*, 53(12): 2098–105.

Gilmour, H. (2018a) 'Formal home care use in Canada', *Health Reports*, 29(9): 3–9.

Gilmour, H. (2018b) 'Unmet home care needs in Canada', *Health Reports*, 29(11): 3–11.

Hass, Z., DePalma, G., Craig, B.A., Xu, H. and Sands, L.P. (2017) 'Unmet need for help with activities of daily living disabilities and emergency department admissions among older Medicare recipients', *The Gerontologist*, 57(2): 206–10.

ILO (International Labour Organization) (2022) 'The care economy', *International Labour Organization*. Available from: https://www.ilo.org/glo bal/topics/care-economy/lang--en/index.htm [Accessed 5 February 2024].

Katz, S., Ford, A.B., Moskowitz, R.W., Jackson, B.A. and Jaffe, M.W. (1963) 'Studies of illness in the aged: the index of ADL: a standardized measure of biological and psychosocial function', *JAMA*, 185(12): 914–19.

Kelbling, E., Ferreira Prescott, D., Shearer, M. and Quinn, T.J. (2024) 'An assessment of the content and properties of extended and instrumental activities of daily living scales: a systematic review', *Disability and Rehabilitation*, 46(10): 1990–9.

Kelly, C., Dansereau, L., FitzGerald, M., Lee, Y. and Williams, A. (2023) 'Inequities in access to directly-funded home care in Canada: a privilege only afforded to some', *BMC Health Services Research*, 23: Article 51.

Khanam, F., Langevin, M., Savage, K. and Uppal, S. (2022) 'Women working in paid care occupations', *Statistics Canada* [Insights on Canadian Society], 25 January. Available from: https://www150.statcan.gc.ca/n1/en/pub/ 75-006-x/2022001/article/00001-eng.pdf?st=aTQUqXsK [Accessed 1 February 2024].

Kröger, T. (2022) *Care Poverty: When Older People's Needs Remain Unmet*, Cham: Palgrave Macmillan.

Kröger, T., Mathew Puthenparambil, J. and Van Aerschot, L. (2019) 'Care poverty: unmet care needs in a Nordic welfare state', *International Journal of Care and Caring*, 3(4): 485–500.

LaPlante, M.P., Kaye, H.S., Kang, T. and Harrington, C. (2004) 'Unmet need for personal assistance services: estimating the shortfall in hours of help and adverse consequences', *The Journals of Gerontology: Series B*, 59(2): S98–S108.

Lawton, M.P. and Brody, E.M. (1969) 'Assessment of older people: self-maintaining and instrumental activities of daily living', *The Gerontologist*, 9(3, Part 1): 179–86.

Liu, Y.H., Chang, H.J. and Huang, C.C. (2012) 'The unmet activities of daily living (ADL) needs of dependent elders and their related factors: an approach from both an individual- and area-level perspective', *International Journal of Gerontology*, 6(3): 163–8.

Marier, P. (2021) *The Four Lenses of Population Aging: Planning for the Future in Canada's Provinces*, Toronto: University of Toronto Press.

McColl, M.A., Jarzynowska, A. and Shortt, S.E.D. (2010) 'Unmet health care needs of people with disabilities: population level evidence', *Disability & Society*, 25(2): 205–18.

Murphy, M. (2015) 'Unsettling care: troubling transnational itineraries of care in feminist health practices', *Social Studies of Science*, 45(5): 717–37.

Nishida, A. (2022) *Just Care: Messy Entanglements of Disability, Dependency, and Desire*, Philadelphia: Temple University Press.

Parmar, J., Anderson, S., Dobbs, B., Tian, P.G.J., Charles, L., Triscott, J., et al (2021) 'Neglected needs of family caregivers during the Covid-19 pandemic and what they need now: a qualitative study', *Diseases*, 9(4): Article 70.

Peckham, A., Morton-Chang, F., Williams, A.P. and Miller, F.A. (2018) 'Rebalancing health systems toward community-based care: the role of subsectoral politics', *Health Policy*, 122(11): 1260–5.

Peng, I. (2018) 'Why Canadians should care about the global care economy', *Canadian International Council* [Open Canada], 16 March. Available from: https://opencanada.org/why-canadians-should-care-about-global-care-economy/ [Accessed 1 February 2024].

PHAC (Public Health Agency of Canada) (2022) *A Vision to Transform Canada's Public Health System: Chief Public Health Officer's Report on the State of Public Health in Canada 2021*, Ottawa: Public Health Agency of Canada.

Pickard, L. (2015) 'A growing care gap? The supply of unpaid care for older people by their adult children in England to 2032', *Ageing & Society*, 35(1): 96–123.

Quail, J.M., Wolfson, C. and Lippman, A. (2011) 'Unmet need for assistance to perform activities of daily living and psychological distress in community-dwelling elderly women', *Canadian Journal of Aging/La Revue Canadienne de Vieillissement*, 30(4): 591–602.

Redfoot, D., Feinberg, L. and Houser, A. (2013) 'The aging of the baby boom and the growing care gap: a look at future declines in the availability of family caregivers', *AARP Public Policy Institute* [Insight on the Issues], August. Available from: https://www.aarp.org/content/dam/aarp/resea rch/public_policy_institute/ltc/2013/baby-boom-and-the-growing-care-gap-insight-AARP-ppi-ltc.pdf [Accessed 1 February 2024].

Schneider, E.C., Shah, A., Doty, M.M., Fields, K. and Williams II, R.D. (2021) 'Mirror, mirror 2021: reflecting poorly: health care in the U.S. compared to other high-income countries', *The Commonwealth Fund* [Fund Reports], 4 August. Available from: https://doi.org/10.26099/01dv-h208 [Accessed 1 February 2024].

Shooshtari, S., Naghipur, S. and Zhang, J. (2012) 'Unmet healthcare and social services needs of older Canadian adults with developmental disabilities', *Journal of Policy and Practice in Intellectual Disabilities*, 9(2): 81–91.

Statistics Canada (2019) 'Canadian Community Health Survey: Annual Component (CCHS)'. Available from: https://www23.statcan.gc.ca/imdb/p2SV.pl?Function=getSurvey&SDDS=3226 [Accessed 26 March 2021].

Statistics Canada (2022) 'Home care use and unmet home care needs in Canada, 2021', *Statistics Canada* [The Daily]. Available from: https://www150.statcan.gc.ca/n1/daily-quotidien/220826/dq220826a-eng.htm [Accessed 27 February 2023].

Thomas, C. (2007) *Sociologies of Disability and Illness: Contested Ideas in Disability Studies and Medical Sociology*, New York: Palgrave Macmillan.

Vlachantoni, A. (2019) 'Unmet need for social care among older people', *Ageing & Society*, 39(4): 657–84.

Wilkinson-Meyers, L., Brown, P., McLean, C. and Kerse, N. (2014) 'Met and unmet need for personal assistance among community-dwelling New Zealanders 75 years and over', *Health and Social Care in the Community*, 22(3): 317–27.

Yung, S. (2021) 'Immigrant status and unmet home care needs: results from the Canadian Community Health Survey', *Journal of Immigrant and Minority Health*, 24(1): 154–61.

4

From rationing to rights: measuring unmet care needs to transform aged care systems

Trish Hill, Natasha Cortis, Myra Hamilton and Carmelle Peisah

Introduction

In many countries, older people's social care needs are left unmet by formal and informal care, affecting their health and well-being, and their families and communities (Harrison et al, 2014; Low et al, 2015; ABS, 2019a; AIHW, 2019; RCACQS, 2019a; Yu and Byles, 2020). In Australia, official reviews have documented inadequacies in the availability, delivery and quality of formal care services, and reiterated concerns about how aged care systems fail to uphold older people's rights (RCACQS, 2019b).[1] The Final Report of Australia's Royal Commission into Aged Care Quality and Safety (the Commission) called for a shift to policies preoccupied with government-provider financial relations and spending restraint, to emphasise older people's rights to the care they need (RCACQS, 2021: 12, 32). Drawing from the International Covenant on Economic, Social and Cultural Rights (ICESCR) (United Nations, 1966), the Commission contended that a human rights approach should inform new legislation prioritising older people's well-being (RCACQS, 2021).

The Commission's inquiry identified concerns about unmet needs among older people resulting from: neglect, abuse, restrictive practices, poor quality care and infection control, poor access to services, long waiting times, and the under-resourcing of paid and unpaid carers (Counsel Assisting, 2020: 10–39). Unmet or poorly met needs were attributed to: ageism, lack of 'dignity and self-determination', insecure funding, little 'shared understanding of high quality' care beyond minimum standards, inadequate responses to diverse groups' needs, poor regulation and complaints mechanisms, and inadequate data, precluding measurement and monitoring (Counsel Assisting, 2020: 30–9).

This chapter focuses on measurement and its role in identifying and addressing unmet need. In care systems, measurement underpins eligibility, resource allocation and service delivery decisions, and is essential for monitoring care standards and distribution. In Australia's case, the Commission's legal counsel found 'reticen[ce] to measure quality' among those responsible for the aged care system restricted knowledge about 'substandard care' (Counsel Assisting, 2020: 21) and thus unmet need. They further argued that 'Australians have a right to know how their aged care system is performing' (Counsel Assisting, 2020: 21).

We contend that new measurement approaches are needed to improve transparency about how older people's needs are met and which needs are not met, and to enact a vision of universal rights to high-quality care. The chapter identifies limitations of dominant approaches to measuring need and unmet need and argues for an interdisciplinary measurement approach to better understand opportunities for equitable access and how to reduce unmet need. First, we consider the disciplinary silos that limit the ways need is conceptualised and measured. Using the Australian case, we review current measures of need and unmet need, then identify alternative international tools, and highlight the role measurement can play in transforming a system based on rationing care to enacting universal rights to quality care, based on assessed need. Such a shift requires that concepts and measures encompass the salient dimensions of quality care and quality of life, and reveal how aged care needs are met and remain unmet, and why.

Disciplinary perspectives on aged care needs and unmet need

Aged care needs arise when older people require support to undertake instrumental and other activities of daily living due to frailty, disability or health conditions.[2] To meet these needs, governments determine eligibility to aged care using prioritisation criteria. Existing measurement tools and assessments inform care providers' and recipients' understandings of the needs services can meet, and frame policy and service priorities (Dickson et al, 2022). Measures and tools are embedded in disciplinary perspectives, which define the phenomena studied, theories about causes and behaviours, concepts and vocabularies, and ways of producing knowledge (Repko and Szostak, 2020). As such, different assumptions underpin social science-based, legal-based and health-based approaches to conceptualising and measuring need.

In the social sciences, social policy concepts may distinguish 'need' from 'want', by identifying whether or not 'harm' will result from a need not being met (Lister, 2010) or through agreement about which needs give rise to rights to access socially provided support (Ignatieff, 1985). While 'need' is a problem requiring a welfare state or service response (Spicker, 2014), 'scarce' resources may mean all 'needs' cannot be met. Bradshaw's (1972) taxonomy of how policy processes recognise needs and allocate resources differentiates between felt, expressed, normative and comparative need, highlighting whether individuals, experts or policy makers define need and how needs are compared to standards and across groups.

In liberal welfare contexts, using markets to meet aged care needs assumes that allocative 'efficiency' will result from consumer 'preference' or 'choice' and that 'empowering' consumers to select and purchase services in a market will result in good quality and outcomes (Davidson, 2011; Brennan et al, 2012; Meagher and Baldwin, 2022). These economic frameworks also assume that markets exist to meet care needs, and that consumers have full information and will act rationally to maximise 'utility' (Blank, 2000; Davidson, 2011). In practice, care needs and eligibility, the distribution of costs, and service availability and quality depend on policy contexts (Gingrich, 2011, in Meagher and Baldwin, 2022).

Sen's (1993) alternative to economic metrics of utility and resources focuses on 'capabilities', or individuals' opportunities to be and do what they value. Rather than emphasising resources to meet needs, the capabilities framework highlights individual, social or institutional 'conversion factors' that transform resources into opportunities for being and doing (Sen, 1993). This conceptual approach underpins quality of life measures for older people, such as the Adult Social Care Outcomes Toolkit (ASCOT: Netten et al, 2012; van Loon et al, 2018) and ICEpop CAPability measure for Older people (ICECAP-O: Grewal et al, 2006), where unmet needs are the lack of such opportunities.

Social science assessments of unmet need also examine Activities of Daily Living (ADLs) and Instrumental Activities of Daily Living (IADLs)[3] and whether support is provided by paid care workers or informal carers (Vlachantoni et al, 2011; Vlachantoni, 2019). Kröger goes further, noting that lack of 'sufficient assistance from informal or formal sources' constitutes a form of 'care poverty' (Kröger et al, 2019: 487; Kröger, 2022).

Social science frameworks discuss need through referring to harms, rights, collective obligations, individual autonomy, empowerment, choice, distribution and poverty. These ideas incorporate different perspectives on processes for defining and allocating resources to meet needs. Correspondingly, unmet needs can be differently defined, with causality variously attributed to administrative, institutional and/or market mechanisms.

Legal concepts of needs focus on ensuring rights are respected, protected and fulfilled, requiring states to provide protection from interference and to enable people to fulfil their rights (AHRC, 2019: 10). Human rights frameworks, such as the ICESCR, provide for 'the enjoyment of the highest attainable standard of physical and mental health' (United Nations, 1966: Article 12(1)), while the Convention on the Rights of Persons with Disabilities articulates principles of dignity, autonomy and self-determination, respect for will and preferences, support for decision-making, and the right to safeguards against neglect (United Nations, 2006: Articles 1, 12, 16). Unmet needs are thus conceptualised as violation of rights or lack of entitlements, protections or quality standards (Spanier and Doron, 2016; AHRC, 2019).

In health, need and unmet need are framed in terms of normative standards of physical and mental health (McIntyre et al, 2009). Needs may also be framed in terms of care recipients' subjective perceptions (see Allin et al, 2010, in Smith and Connolly, 2020) and expert views on 'capacity to benefit from a health care intervention' (Culyer and Wagstaff, 1993; McIntyre et al, 2009).[4]

The diverse social science, legal and health disciplinary perspectives have implications for how needs and unmet needs are conceptualised and measured in aged care systems and inform:

- the purpose and context of needs assessment;
- which domains of needs are assessed or prioritised;
- how need and unmet need are defined, assessed, measured (subjectively, against normative standards and by whom);
- explanations for need or unmet need;
- expectations about how needs should be met, and by which systems/actors (see Hill et al, 2021; Dickson et al, 2022; Hill, 2022).

The next section outlines concepts and measures applied to assess need, using the Australian example. Then, to establish alternatives, we identify measurement instruments from the international literature that can help build more comprehensive, integrated insights to strengthen responses to unmet aged care need.

Measuring unmet aged care need: an Australian example

Concepts and measures of need and unmet need are operationalised in legislation, eligibility rules, resource allocation processes and system performance indicators.

Legislation defines which aged care needs should be respected, protected and fulfilled, and how. Australia's existing Aged Care Act 1997 refers to quality care and quality of life, however, these domains are framed by economic imperatives in the context of targeting government-subsidised services to those most in need to ration care. The Commission recommended a new Act including 'a universal right to high quality, safe and timely support and care to assist older people to live an active, self-determined and meaningful life' (RCACQS, 2021: 121). Such aspirations are informed by legal conceptions of needs underpinned by fundamental human rights (RCACQS, 2021).[5]

Eligibility for government-subsidised aged care assesses older people's medical, physical, psychological, safety, vulnerability and social needs, their goals, and support from informal carers and services (Department of Health,

2018).[6] Assessments consider the availability of informal carers, including carer burden measures (Robinson, 1983; Onega, 2008; Department of Social Security, 2019). While needs assessments for aged care services encompass multidimensional domains, resource allocation through prioritisation criteria ration care and focus on needs relating to risks to older people's health and safety, risks of entering hospital or residential care, and the sustainability of informal care relationships (Department of Health, 2018; Hill, 2022). Specific needs assessment tools are used for residential care, allocating and rationing resources to individuals and providers. The new Australian National Aged Care Classification estimates a 'casemix class cost' based on identifying needs that are 'the most significant cost drivers in residential aged care' (Westera et al, 2019: 6).

Need and unmet need are also measured in outcome and output measures that frame evaluation of system performance (SCRGSP, 2023: 16). Appealing to broad notions of quality of life, health and well-being, government objectives emphasise 'accessible', 'appropriate', 'person-centred', 'high quality' and safe care (SCRGSP, 2023: 5). However, performance indicator framework measures and data are limited (SCRGSP, 2023: 17) and, to date, rights primarily reflect consumer rights (ACQSC, 2024a; 2024b).

While measures of aged care needs in eligibility assessments, resource allocation and performance indicators draw on indicators of need based in health, gerontology and social sciences, to date, these exist within an overarching economic framing prioritising fiscal savings in the context of population ageing and growing care demands. The resulting rationing imperative limits full understanding of the nature and extent of need and unmet need. There is little emphasis on measures of well-being and human flourishing (social sciences approach) or on rights-based measures of dignity and choice for older people as citizens (legal approach), rather than as aged care 'consumers'.

Data and measures to enact rights to care

Current data used to assess need and monitor aged care system performance are often limited with concerns about inadequate conceptualisation, measurement and monitoring of high-quality aged care and human rights (RCACQS, 2021). Proposals to broaden the human rights framework underpinning Australian aged care (Byrnes, 2020) raises challenges of how a new Act should measure and monitor how the aged care system respects, protects and fulfils rights. The next section reviews alternative international measurement tools that could help support the system to shift from a focus on rationing scarce care resources to more fully realise rights to care.

We examined international literature and assessed 29 measurement tools relevant to the needs and unmet needs of older people, encompassing health, functioning, well-being, quality of life and rights. While non-exhaustive, Table 4.1 encompasses common instruments. Clusters of measures focus on quality of life and health-related quality of life. Some have been developed for older people with dementia, including Quality of Life in Late-stage Dementia Scale (QUALIDEM) and Bath Assessment of Subjective Quality of Life in Dementia (BASQID), relying on proxy measures rather than older people's self-reports. Some are intended for assessment or clinical monitoring (Tilburg Frailty Indicator), or for population monitoring via surveys like the Australian Bureau of Statistics' Survey of Disability, Ageing and Carers (SDAC). Studies document instrument design, development, validation, refinement and application (Trigg et al, 2007; Resnick et al, 2018; Sopina et al, 2019), sometimes emphasising underlying conceptual frameworks or measurement, and informants' diverse perspectives (Hill et al, 2021).

Few instruments directly measure which aged care needs are unmet, and how (Table 4.1). Camberwell Assessment of Need for the Elderly indicates whether respondents have 'no needs', 'met needs' or 'unmet needs' across physical, psychological, environmental and health domains. Type of Unmet Need Assessment (TUNA) captures unmet need for people with dementia across social interaction, sensory deprivation, discomfort, meaningful activity, relaxation, control and pain domains (Cohen-Mansfield et al, 2015: 62). ASCOT also distinguishes between those with no, some or high needs in quality-of-life domains affected by social care, while SDAC identifies whether unmet needs are due to lack of formal or informal care.

Most instruments *indirectly* indicate older people's needs and unmet needs based on low scores. This is the case for many indicators of functional status and quality of life (Table 4.1). In addition, International Older Persons' Human Rights Index, which stems from a human rights approach, can show lack of legal protections, and the Missed Care measure (MISSCARE), derived from nursing to indicate which care delivery tasks were omitted, can indicate likely unmet needs of care recipients (as tasks required to meet need were not performed).

Few instruments show *why* needs are left unmet. SDAC identifies a range of reasons for unmet need for formal care such as: 'did not know of service', 'need was not important enough', 'won't ask or pride', 'unable to arrange service', 'costs too much' or 'doesn't provide sufficient hours' (ABS, 2019a; 2019b). SDAC also identifies reasons for unmet need for informal assistance, including: 'has not asked family or friends', 'needs more help than family or friends can provide' or 'family or friends not available or too far away' (ABS, 2019a; 2019b). MISSCARE captures service-related reasons needs may be left unmet, asking whether care was not performed due to communication, material or labour resource reasons, while the Tilburg Frailty Indicator asks if enough support is received from others, and Control, Autonomy,

Table 4.1: Measures reviewed

Emphasis	Instrument	References	Indicates which needs are unmet?	Indicates reasons needs are unmet?
Unmet need	1. Camberwell Assessment of Need for the Elderly 2. SDAC measures of unmet need for ADLs, IADLs 3. Type of Unmet Need Assessment (TUNA)	Reynolds et al (2000) ABS (2019a; 2019b) Cohen-Mansfield et al (2015)	Shows 'no needs', 'met needs', or 'unmet needs' across physical, psychological, environmental and health domains Shows whether needs are fully, partly or not met across ten domains of ADLs and IADLs Shows type of unmet need (for example, social interaction, pain, meaningful activity)	No Yes, with different reasons for unmet need for formal services and unmet need for informal support No, but application in nursing homes implies unmet need due to poor quality care
ADL functioning	4. Katz Index of Independence in Activities of Daily Living 5. Lawton Instrumental Activities of Daily Living (IADL) Scale 6. Barthel/Modified Barthel Index	Katz et al (1963) Lawton and Brody (1969) Shah et al (1989)	Low functional status indicates need	No No No
Quality of life scales and well-being scales	7. ICEpop CAPability measure for Older people (ICECAP-O) 8. World Health Organization Quality of Life Instrument-Older Adults (WHOQOL-Old) 9. Older People's Quality of Life 10. Control, Autonomy, Self-realization and Pleasure (CASP-19)	Grewal et al (2006) Power et al (2005) Bowling (2009) Hyde et al (2003)	Low scores indicate need	No No No Some information to attribute unmet need to health, financial, family and age related factors
Social participation	11. Australian Community Participation Questionnaire	Brett et al (2019)	Low scores indicate need	No

(continued)

Table 4.1: Measures reviewed (continued)

Emphasis	Instrument	References	Indicates which needs are unmet?	Indicates reasons needs are unmet?
Health status	12. Tilburg Frailty Indicator	Gobbens et al (2010)	High frailty could indicate need	No, but one item asks 'Do you receive enough support from other people'
	13. Quality of Well-being Scale (QWB)	Andresen et al (1998)	Asks if person needed help but not if needs were met	No
Dementia-specific quality of life	14. Quality of life in late-stage dementia scale (QUALID) 15. QUALIDEM 16. Alzheimer's Disease-Related Quality of Life 17. Bath Assessment of Subjective Quality of Life in Dementia (BASQID)	Weiner et al (2000) Ettema et al (2007) Rabins et al (1999) Trigg et al (2007)	Low scores indicate need	No No No No
Human rights				
Human rights for older people	18. International Older Persons' Human Rights Index 19. Ageism Survey	Spanier and Doron (2016) Palmore (2004)	Identifies lack of legal protections No	No No
Human rights in health care	20. FREDA/FREIDA/FREDAR	Butchard and Kinderman (2019)	No	No
Outcomes and delivery of care				
Social care related quality of life	21. Adult Social Care Outcomes Toolkit (ASCOT) 22. Australian Community Care Outcomes Measure (ACCOM)	Netten et al (2012) Cardona et al (2017)	Yes, identifies high needs, some needs, no needs	No No, but used as an outcome measure which attribute change to service

Table 4.1: Measures reviewed (continued)

Emphasis	Instrument	References	Indicates which needs are unmet?	Indicates reasons needs are unmet?
Health related quality of life	23. EuroQol – 5 Dimensions (EQ-5D) 24. Dementia Quality of Life Measure	Rabin and de Charro (2001) Smith et al (2007)	Low scores indicate need	No No
Quality of care	25. Home and Community-Based Services Consumer Assessment of Healthcare Providers and Systems (HCBS CAHPS)	Medicaid.gov (2020)	Yes, identifies unmet need in several domains	Captures unmet need due to service-related factors, for example, if hungry they are asked if that is because there were no staff to assist
	26. Thriving of Older People Assessment Scale (TOPAS)	Baxter et al (2019)	Low 'thriving' indicates need	No
	27. PCAT- Person centred care assessment tool	Edvardsson et al (2010)	Not directly, but indicates capacity of the care environment to meet needs	No
	28. MISSCARE	Kalisch and Williams (2009)	Shows which care tasks were not performed	Yes, indicates whether communication, material resources or labour resources are reasons for missed care
Measurement framework for long-term care	29. WE-THRIVE	Corazzini et al (2019)	Yes, within broad measurement framework	Not yet clear

Self-realization and Pleasure (CASP-19) poses questions such as 'shortage of money stops me from doing the things that I want to do', enabling attribution to health, financial, family or age-related factors.

In response to the limitations of narrow, discipline-based concepts of need, a number of multidisciplinary measures of more comprehensive dimensions have been developed. Older People's Quality of Life (Bowling, 2009), for example, recognises how ageing affects several areas of life. Alzheimer's Disease-Related Quality of Life (Kasper et al, 2009) and QUALIDEM also recognise multiple aspects of quality of life, across health, social and other domains (Ettema et al, 2007). Another multidisciplinary approach, WE-THRIVE, aims to develop common data infrastructure and cross-national measures for long-term care. While not integrating items into a single instrument, WE-THRIVE brings together a wide range of measures of care quality, covering organisational contexts, workforce and staffing, person-centred care and care outcomes (including ICECAP-O, the World Health Organization Quality of Life Instrument [WHOQOL], EuroQol – 5 Dimensions [EQ-5D] and Thriving of Older People Assessment Scale [TOPAS]). This approach is a shift from deficit-oriented measures focused on functional decline to emphasise healthy ageing and person-centred models of care (Edvardsson et al, 2019).

Disciplinary perspectives are also used to reframe the concept underpinning the measure using what might be regarded as an *interdisciplinary* approach. For example, while originally a medical concept, 'frailty' has been reconceptualised to include social and psychological domains of human functioning alongside physical domains. Gobbens et al (2010: 344) note that rather than relating narrowly to disease or infirmity, frailty is a 'dynamic state affecting an individual who experiences losses in one or more domains of human functioning (physical, psychological, social)'. This conceptual basis for more comprehensive social, psychosocial and physical frailty measures recognises that narrow concepts limit measures and can fragment care, reducing care quality (Gobbens et al, 2010: 344; Gobbens et al, 2017).

Older people's perspectives are sometimes incorporated in instrument development and through self-reported need. Instrument development is largely expert-led (see the Quality of Life in Dementia Scale [QUALID] and the World Health Organization Quality of Life of Older People Instrument [WHOQOL-OLD] in Weiner et al, 2000; Bowling, 2009). However, the Person-centered Care Assessment Tool, for example, was developed using interviews and focus groups with aged care staff, people with dementia and family members exploring person-centred care (Edvardsson et al, 2010). Some require older people to self-report (including ICECAP-O, Australian Community Participation Questionnaire, ASCOT and CASP-19), while others may use a proxy, including late-stage dementia-specific measures, which can be completed by formal care workers or family (QUALID, QUALIDEM, Dementia Quality of Life Measure, TUNA, TOPAS, EQ-5D).

Strengthening evidence through better measures

This chapter examined how concepts and measures can reinforce and challenge aged care systems focused on targeting and rationing care. New data approaches are needed to monitor and help enact universal rights to high-quality care. Many measures relate to aged care quality and outcomes, yet few directly identify 'unmet need' and instead infer it indirectly. None utilise concepts and thresholds of 'care poverty', despite the concept's promise of highlighting the nature of care inequalities and underpinning factors. Chapter 5 reviews principles of income poverty measures that could help operationalise measures of care poverty to assess unmet need.

Measurement tools offer some ways forward. Some aim to directly identify unmet need and are underpinned by multidisciplinary approaches, providing insight into levels of unmet need across different domains. They do less well at contextualising these unmet needs. Few measures identify reasons for unmet need or the role of providers or systems in meeting/ failing to meet need.

Measures used to determine eligibility, allocate resources and assess performance could be broadened to recognise citizen entitlements and the social determinants of healthy and inclusive ageing. Informal carer support is crucial, yet assessment of carer needs and care relationships that contribute to unmet aged care needs is limited. Measures assessing carers' needs (such as burden, self-efficacy or loneliness) are underutilised, as are measures reflecting care workforce perspectives regarding quality of care, including person-centred care and the institutional environment.

More comprehensive, rigorous measures could drive paradigmatic shifts in aged care: from a rationed, consumer market to a citizen's entitlement based on assessed need. As noted by Dickson et al (2022), assessment tools shape care providers' and care receivers' perceptions of needs to be met through services, priorities and 'policy problems'. Disciplinary perspectives contribute to definitions and perceptions of ageing and care needs. A critical interdisciplinary lens regarding age-related needs and their genesis is required to generate more holistic policy and care responses.

Tools to measure and monitor aspirational outcomes of supporting older people to live active, self-determined, meaningful and safe lives will be most effective if informed by interdisciplinary approaches that identify the multiple domains, components, influences and appropriate responses to meeting care needs. The more comprehensive instruments bring together multiple disciplinary frameworks or measures and include concepts that have been expanded through interdisciplinary understandings (such as the Tilburg Frailty Index). The measurement of aged care needs and unmet needs is interwoven with questions about which are the most important needs, older people's priorities, how to honour their will and preferences, and how to identify and address reasons for unmet needs. The measurement tools reviewed here may contribute to more holistic and robust evidence about unmet aged care needs.

Notes

[1] In Australia, the aged care system includes supports for older people to live at home, such as personal care and support with everyday living, and residential care for older people who cannot live at home.

[2] Other policy and service systems also support older people's well-being, including income support and urban planning, however our focus is on aged care systems.

[3] ADLs refer to basic activities to sustain well-being, such as eating, bathing, dressing and toileting. IADLs are more complex activities such as shopping, cooking and managing finances.

[4] For the latter, needs exist only where a form of care can address it, and unmet need refers to health system failure.

[5] A new Aged Care Act, informed by these ideas, is undergoing a consultation process. For a review of aged care and public health law, see Peisah et al (2023).

[6] Needs assessments for eligibility for aged care services are conducted by Aged Care Assessment Teams in the Aged Care Assessment Program (for older people who may need higher-level support including residential aged care) and Regional Assessment Service assessments (for those who may need support to help them stay at home).

Acknowledgements

This research was supported by a UNSW Sydney Ageing Futures Institute 2020 Seed Funding Grant.

References

ABS (Australian Bureau of Statistics) (2019a) *Disability, Ageing and Carers, Australia: Summary of Findings, 2018*, Canberra: Australian Bureau of Statistics.

ABS (2019b) *Survey of Disability, Ageing and Carers, Household Questionnaire*, Canberra: Australian Bureau of Statistics.

ACQSC (Aged Care Quality and Safety Commission) (2024a) 'Aged care quality standards', *Aged Care Quality and Safety Commission*. Available from: https://www.agedcarequality.gov.au/providers/quality-standards [Accessed 6 February 2024].

ACQSC (2024b) 'Charter of aged care rights', *Aged Care Quality and Safety Commission*. Available from: https://www.agedcarequality.gov.au/older-australians/your-rights/charter-aged-care-rights [Accessed 6 February 2024].

AHRC (Australian Human Rights Commission) (2019) *A Human Rights Perspective on Aged Care*, Sydney: Australian Human Rights Commission.

AIHW (Australian Institute of Health and Welfare) (2019) 'Aged care', *Australian Institute of Health and Welfare*, Australia's Welfare Snapshots 2019, 28 June. Available from: https://www.aihw.gov.au/reports/australias-welf are/aged-care [Accessed 6 February 2024].

Allin, S., Grignon, M. and Le Grand, J. (2010) 'Subjective unmet need and utilization of health care services in Canada: what are the equity implications?', *Social Science & Medicine*, 70(3): 465–72.

Andresen, E.M., Rothenberg, B.M. and Kaplan, R.M. (1998) 'Performance of a self-administered mailed version of the Quality of Well-being (QWB-SA) Questionnaire among older adults', *Medical Care*, 36(9): 1349–60.

Baxter, R., Lövheim, H., Björk, S., Sköldunger, A., Lindkvist, M., Sjögren, K., et al (2019) 'The thriving of Older People Assessment Scale: psychometric evaluation and short-form development', *Journal of Advanced Nursing,* 75(12): 3831–43.

Blank, R.M. (2000) 'When can public policy makers rely on private markets? The effective provision of social services', *The Economic Journal*, 110(462): 34–49.

Bowling, A. (2009) 'The psychometric properties of the Older People's Quality of Life Questionnaire, compared with the CASP-19 and the WHOQOL-OLD', *Current Gerontology and Geriatrics Research*, 2009: 298950.

Bradshaw, J. (1972) 'A taxonomy of social need', *New Society*, 30(March): 640–3.

Brennan, D., Cass, B., Himmelweit, S. and Szebehely, M. (2012) 'The marketisation of care: rationales and consequences in Nordic and liberal care regimes', *Journal of European Social Policy*, 22(4): 377–91.

Brett, L., Georgiou, A., Jorgensen, M., Siette, J., Scott, G., Gow, E., et al (2019) 'Ageing well: evaluation of social participation and quality of life tools to enhance community aged care (study protocol)', *BMC Geriatrics*, 19(1): Article 78.

Butchard, S. and Kinderman, P. (2019) 'Human rights, dementia, and identity', *European Psychologist*, 24(2): 159–68.

Byrnes, A. (2020) 'Human rights unbound: an unrepentant call for a more complete application of human rights in relation to older persons – and beyond', *Australasian Journal on Ageing*, 39(2): 91–8.

Cardona, B., Fine, M., Stebbing, A., Duncan, C., Samsa, P. and Eagar, K. (2017) 'Measuring consumer outcomes: development and testing of the Australian Community Care Outcomes Measure', *Australasian Journal on Ageing*, 36(1): 69–71.

Cohen-Mansfield, J., Dakheel-Ali, M., Marx, M.S., Thein, K. and Regier, N.G. (2015) 'Which unmet needs contribute to behavior problems in persons with advanced dementia?', *Psychiatry Research*, 228(1): 59–64.

Corazzini, K.N., Anderson, R.A., Bowers, B.J., Chu, C.H., Edvardsson, D., Fagertun, A., et al (2019) 'Toward common data elements for international research in long-term care homes: advancing person-centered care', *Journal of the American Medical Directors Association*, 20(5): 598–603.

Counsel Assisting (2020) Counsel Assisting's Final Submissions, *Royal Commission in Aged Care Quality and Safety*, Adelaide: Commonwealth of Australia.

Culyer, A. and Wagstaff, A. (1993) 'Equity and equality in health and health care', *Journal of Health Economics*, 12(4): 431–57.

Davidson, B. (2011) 'Contestability in human service markets', *Journal of Australian Political Economy*, 68: 213–39.

Department of Health (2018) *My Aged Care Assessment Manual Version 1.1 June 2018*, Canberra: Commonwealth of Australia.

Department of Social Security (2019) *Carer Support Framework: Integrated Carer Support Service (ICSS) Version 1.0, December 2019*, Canberra: Commonwealth of Australia.

Dickson, D., Marier, R. and Dube, A.-S. (2022) 'Do assessment tools shape policy preferences? Analysing policy framing effects on older adults' conceptualisation of autonomy', *Journal of Social Policy*, 51(1): 114–31.

Edvardsson, D., Fetherstonhaugh, D., Nay, R. and Gibson, S. (2010) 'Development and initial testing of the Person-centered Care Assessment Tool (P-CAT)', *International Psychogeriatrics*, 22(1): 101–8.

Edvardsson, D., Baxter, R., Corneliusson, L., Anderson, R.A., Beeber, A., Boas, P.V., et al (2019) 'Advancing long-term care science through using common data elements: candidate measures for care outcomes of personhood, well-being, and quality of life', *Gerontology and Geriatric Medicine*, 5: 2333721419842672.

Ettema, T.P., Dröes, R.-M., de Lange, J., Mellenbergh, G.J. and Ribbe, M.W. (2007) 'QUALIDEM: development and evaluation of a dementia specific quality of life instrument: scalability, reliability and internal structure', *International Journal of Geriatric Psychiatry*, 22(6): 549–56.

Gingrich, J.R. (2011) *Making Markets in the Welfare State: The Politics of Varying Market Reforms*, Cambridge: Cambridge University Press.

Gobbens, R., van Assen, M., Luijkx, K., Wijnen-Sponselee, M. and Schols, J. (2010) 'The Tilburg Frailty Indicator: psychometric properties', *Journal of the American Medical Directors Association*, 11(5): 344–55.

Gobbens, R.J., Schols, J.M. and van Assen, M.A. (2017) 'Exploring the efficiency of the Tilburg Frailty Indicator: a review', *Clinical Interventions in Aging*, 12: 1739–52.

Grewal, I., Lewis, J., Flynn, T., Brown, J., Bond, J. and Coast, J. (2006) 'Developing attributes for a generic quality of life measure for older people: preferences or capabilities?', *Social Science and Medicine*, 62(8): 1891–901.

Harrison, F., Low, L.-F., Barnett, A., Gresham, M. and Brodaty, H. (2014) 'What do clients expect of community care and what are their needs? The Community care for the Elderly: Needs and Service Use Study (CENSUS)', *Australasian Journal on Ageing*, 33(3): 208–13.

Hill, T. (2022) 'Understanding unmet aged care need and care inequalities among older Australians', *Ageing & Society*, 42(11): 2665–94.

Hill, T., Cortis, N., Hamilton, M. and Pesiah, C. (2021) Unmet need for aged care: an interdisciplinary measurement approach. Discussion paper (Unpublished).

Hyde, M., Wiggins, R.D., Higgs, P. and Blane, D.B. (2003) 'A measure of quality of life in early old age: the theory, development and properties of a needs satisfaction model (CASP-19)', *Aging & Mental Health*, 7(3): 186–94.

Ignatieff, M. (1985) *The Needs of Strangers*, New York: Viking.

Kalisch, B.J. and Williams, R.A. (2009) 'Development and psychometric testing of a tool to measure missed nursing care', *JONA The Journal of Nursing Administration*, 39(5): 211–19.

Kasper, J.D., Black, B.S., Shore, A.D. and Rabins, P.V. (2009) 'Evaluation of the validity and reliability of the Alzheimer Disease-related Quality of Life Assessment Instrument', *Alzheimer Disease & Associated Disorders*, 23(3): 275–84.

Katz, S., Ford, A.B., Moskowitz, R.W., Jackson, B.A. and Jaffe, M.W. (1963) 'Studies of illness in the aged: the index of ADL: a standardized measure of biological and psychosocial function', *JAMA*, 185(12): 914–19.

Kröger, T. (2022) *Care Poverty: When Older People's Needs Remain Unmet*, Cham: Palgrave Macmillan.

Kröger, T., Mathew Puthenparambil, J. and Van Aerschot, L. (2019) 'Care poverty: unmet care needs in a Nordic welfare state', *International Journal of Care and Caring*, 3(4): 485–500.

Lawton, M.P. and Brody, E.M. (1969) 'Assessment of older people: self-maintaining and Instrumental Activities of Daily Living', *The Gerontologist*, 9(3 Part 1): 179–86.

Lister, R. (2010) *Understanding Theories and Concepts in Social Policy*, Bristol: Policy Press.

Low, L.-F., Fletcher, J., Gresham, M. and Brodaty, H. (2015) 'Community care for the elderly: Needs and Service Use Study (CENSUS): who receives home care packages and what are the outcomes?', *Australasian Journal on Ageing*, 34(3): E1–E8.

McIntyre, D., Mooney, G. and Jan, S. (2009) 'Need: what is it and how do we measure it?', in R. Detels, R. Beaglehole, M. Lansang and M. Gulliford (eds) *Oxford Textbook of Public Health* (5th edn), Oxford: Oxford University Press, pp 1535–48.

Meagher, G. and Baldwin, R. (2022) 'Making a profitable social service market: the evolution of the private nursing home sector', in G. Meagher, A. Stebbing and D. Perche (eds) *Designing Social Service Markets: Risk Regulation and Rent-seeking*, Canberra: ANU Press, pp 215–68.

Medicaid.gov (2020) 'CAHPS home and community based services survey', *Centers for Medicare & Medicaid Services*. Available from: https://www.medic aid.gov/medicaid/quality-of-care/quality-of-care-performance-meas urement/cahps-home-and-community-based-services-survey/index.html [Accessed 6 February 2024].

Netten, A., Burge, P., Malley, J., Potoglou, D., Towers, A.M., Brazier, J., et al (2012) 'Outcomes of social care for adults: developing a preference-weighted measure', *Health Technology Assessment*, 16(16): 1–166.

Onega, L.L. (2008) 'Helping those who help others: the Modified Caregiver Strain Index', *American Journal of Nursing*, 108(9): 62–9.

Palmore, E. (2004) 'Research note: ageism in Canada and the United States', *Journal of Cross-Cultural Gerontology*, 19(1): 41–6.

Peisah, C., Byrnes, A., Mitchell, W. and Bergman, A. (2023) 'Public health law, aged care and human rights', in B. Bennett and I. Freckelton (eds) *Australian Public Health Law: Contemporary Issues and Challenges*, Alexandria: The Federation Press, pp 457–82.

Power, M., Quinn, K., Schmidt, S. and WHOQOL-Old Group (2005) 'Development of the WHOQOL-Old Module', *Quality of Life Research*, 14(10): 2197–214.

Rabin, R. and de Charro, F. (2001) 'EQ-5D: a measure of health status from the EuroQol Group', *Annals of Medicine*, 33(5): 337–43.

Rabins, P.V., Kasper, J.D., Kleinman, L., Black, B.S. and Patrick, D.L. (1999) 'Concepts and methods in the development of the ADRQL: an instrument for assessing health-related quality of life in persons with Alzheimer's disease', *Journal of Mental Health and Aging*, 5(1): 33–48.

RCACQS (Royal Commission into Aged Care Quality and Safety) (2019a) *Interim Report: Neglect*, Adelaide: Commonwealth of Australia.

RCACQS (2019b) *A History of Aged Care Reviews Background Paper Number 8*, Adelaide: Commonwealth of Australia.

RCACQS (2021) *Final Report: Care. Dignity and Respect, Volume 1 Summary and Recommendations*, Adelaide: Commonwealth of Australia.

Repko, A. and Szostak, R. (2020) *Interdisciplinary Research: Process and Theory* (4th edn), Thousand Oaks: SAGE.

Resnick, B., Galik, E., Kolanowski, A., Van Haitsma, K., Boltz, M., Ellis, J., et al (2018) 'Reliability and validity testing of the Quality of Life in Late-Stage Dementia Scale', *American Journal of Alzheimers Disease & Other Dementias*, 33(5): 277–83.

Reynolds, T., Thornicroft, G., Abas, M., Woods, B., Hoe, J., Leese, M., et al (2000) 'Camberwell Assessment of Need for the Elderly (CANE): development, validity and reliability', *British Journal of Psychiatry*, 176(5): 444–52.

Robinson, B.C. (1983) 'Validation of a caregiver strain index', *Journal of Gerontology*, 38(3): 344–8.

SCRGSP (Steering Committee for the Review of Government Service Provision) (2023) *Report on Government Services 2023*, Canberra: Productivity Commission.

Sen, A. (1993) 'Capability and well-being', in M. Nussbaum and A. Sen (eds) *The Quality of Life*, Oxford: Oxford University Press, pp 30–53.

Shah, S., Vanclay, F. and Cooper, B. (1989) 'Improving the sensitivity of the Barthel Index for stroke rehabilitation', *Journal of Clinical Epidemiology*, 42(8): 703–9.

Smith, S. and Connolly, S. (2020) 'Re-thinking unmet need for health care: introducing a dynamic perspective', *Health Economics, Policy and Law*, 15(4): 440–57.

Smith, S.C., Lamping, D.L., Banerjee, S., Harwood, R.H., Foley, B., Smith, P., et al (2007) 'Development of a new measure of health-related quality of life for people with dementia: DEMQOL', *Psychological Medicine*, 37(5): 737–46.

Sopina, E., Chenoweth, L., Luckett, T., Agar, M., Luscombe, G.M., Davidson, P.M., et al (2019) 'Health-related quality of life in people with advanced dementia: a comparison of EQ-5D-5L and QUALID instruments', *Quality of Life Research*, 28(1): 121–9.

Spanier, B. and Doron, I. (2016) 'From well-being to rights: creating an International Older Persons' Human Rights Index (IOPHRI)', *Elder Law Journal*, 24(2): 245–92.

Spicker, P. (2014) *Social Policy: Theory and Practice*, Bristol: Policy Press.

Trigg, R., Skevington, S.M. and Jones, R.W. (2007) 'How can we best assess the quality of life of people with dementia? The Bath Assessment of Subjective Quality of Life in Dementia (BASQID)', *The Gerontologist*, 47(6): 789–97.

United Nations (1966) *International Covenant on Economic, Social, and Cultural Rights*, Treaty Series 999, 171.

United Nations (2006) *Convention on the Rights of Persons with Disabilities*. Available from: https://social.desa.un.org/issues/disability/crpd/convention-on-the-rights-of-persons-with-disabilities-crpd [Accessed 9 February 2024].

van Loon, M.S., van Leeuwen, K.M., Ostelo, R.W.J.G., Bosmans, J.E. and Widdershoven, G.A.M. (2018) 'Quality of life in a broader perspective: does ASCOT reflect the capability approach?', *Quality of Life Research*, 27(5): 1181–9.

Vlachantoni, A. (2019) 'Unmet need for social care among older people', *Ageing & Society*, 39(40): 657–84.

Vlachantoni, A., Shaw, R., Willis, R., Evandrou, M., Falkingham, J. and Luff, R. (2011) 'Measuring unmet need for social care amongst older people', *Population Trends*, 145: 1–17.

Weiner, M.F., Martin-Cook, K., Svetlik, D.A., Saine, K., Foster, B. and Fontaine, C.S. (2000) 'The quality of life in late-stage dementia (QUALID) scale', *Journal of the American Medical Directors Association*, 1(3): 114–16.

Westera, A., Snoek, M., Duncan, C., Quinsey, K., Samsa, P., McNamee, J., et al (2019) *The AN-ACC Assessment Model: The Resource Utilisation and Classification Study: Report 2*, Wollongong: Australian Health Services Research Institute, University of Wollongong.

Yu, S. and Byles, J. (2020) 'Waiting times in aged care: what matters?', *Australasian Journal of Ageing*, 39(1): 48–55.

5

Methods to match a novel concept: approaches to measuring care poverty

Márton Medgyesi, Ricardo Rodrigues and Eszter Zólyomi

Introduction

The concept of care poverty is still a relatively novel construct in the care literature (Kröger et al, 2019; Kröger, 2022) with a dearth of guidance about how to operationalise it. This raises issues as to the applicability of the concept, or the comparability of different estimates, and can ultimately limit the relevance of care poverty as a useful policy tool. This chapter aims to bridge this gap by reviewing and assessing the potential of different approaches to assess or measure care poverty, particularly from a comparative perspective both across time and space. We argue that the assessment of care poverty across different welfare states is of particular relevance, not only to compare outcomes of different policies, but also because the concept itself focuses on public policies as a potential determinant of care poverty (Kröger, 2022).

As its name implies, care poverty draws from the concept of (income) poverty insofar as it refers to a lack or insufficiency of resources that are necessary to fulfil one's potential (Kröger, 2022). Income poverty measures, of which there are several, are a well-established toolkit for the assessment of insufficiency of resources. This would make income poverty measures plausible candidates from which to build measures of care poverty. At the same time, and at its core, care poverty is about the (mis)match between care needs of older people and the care (formal and/or informal) that they receive (Kröger, 2022). In this sense, measuring care poverty could come to resemble or borrow from studies on inequalities in the distribution of long-term care use or unmet needs that take into consideration the distribution of needs across individuals (Rodrigues et al, 2018; Tenand et al, 2020a; 2020b). These two strands of literature, with their different measurement methodologies, provide the starting point for the review of possible care poverty measures which we will carry out in this chapter.

We begin by reviewing the basic distinctions used by poverty research (such as welfarist versus non-welfarist or relative versus absolute approaches) and applying them to the few approaches to the measurement of care poverty or unmet needs that have been proposed so far. In addition, we carry out a non-exhaustive review of methods for assessing inequalities in use of health and long-term care or unmet needs that could be relevant for the measurement of care poverty. In our discussion, we take into account the specificities of long-term care, such as difficulties in measuring care needs in an objective and comparable way across countries, as well as the differences in the institutional context and in the standards of care that are considered acceptable.

Concepts and measurement of poverty and care poverty

Basic approaches to poverty measurement

At a general level, poverty refers to situations when the well-being of an individual is considered low with respect to some reference value (a poverty threshold). The measurement of poverty involves two essential tasks: the identification of people in poverty and the aggregation of their poverty into an aggregate measure of poverty (Sen, 1983). Next, we will review approaches regarding the identification of people in poverty, which are related to the choice of some well-being measure to compare the situation of people and the choice of a poverty threshold.

Measuring well-being: welfarist versus multidimensional approaches

There are several approaches for measuring well-being. *The welfarist approach* aims to assess well-being in terms of 'utility' (Ravallion, 2016). As utility per se is unobservable in practical applications, this approach uses proxies for utility. One possibility is to use imperfect but objectively observable proxies for utility such as income or wealth. Another possibility is to use subjective measures such as satisfaction with life or satisfaction with financial situation of the household. Importantly, this approach assesses well-being in terms of overall utility and does not take into account which goods and services are consumed by the household.

The non-welfarist approaches acknowledge that there are multiple dimensions of well-being and prescribe that a minimum level should be attained on all (or at least on several) dimensions (Guio, 2018). One such approach (multiple deprivation approach) starts from a set of basic needs and defines minimum levels of the necessary inputs (such as food, shelter, sanitation) for well-being. Another non-welfarist approach regards 'functionings' as the constitutive elements of well-being. In contrast to basic needs, functionings are the outcomes in terms of well-being (being adequately nourished, being in good health, having self-respect, participating in community, and so on) (Sen, 1992).

The implementation of the non-welfarist approach starts with the choice of basic needs or functionings to be included in the analysis. This choice involves a trade-off between contextualising the choice of dimensions (in order to take into account the specific values prevailing in different societies) and the need for a certain degree of universality (Guio, 2018). There are several potential sources of information for a list of basic needs or functionings. Such lists can be based on normative assumptions or on experts' judgements, while approaches based on public consensus or some deliberative process are contingent on individual preferences regarding basic needs or functionings (Guio, 2018).

The choice of the poverty threshold: absolute, relative or subjective?

Absolute poverty refers to situations when the well-being of the individual is considered low compared to some externally given minimum level. To define an *absolute poverty threshold* in the welfarist approach, analysts might start with the definition of a set of basic needs and the description of a basket of goods which satisfies the predetermined level of basic needs. Then the poverty threshold is the minimum income that allows to buy this basket of goods (Ravallion, 2016). People in poverty are then those whose income is lower than this threshold. This approach thus does not identify people in poverty based on actual satisfaction of prescribed basic needs but identifies those who do not have sufficient resources to satisfy these needs (Sen, 1983). In this way this approach respects individual preferences and choices and tries to avoid a paternalistic approach to welfare measurement.

There are important informational requirements to implement this approach. The previously mentioned basic needs and basket of goods must be defined and compiled. When such a difficult exercise is done, it generally involves a large group of experts in each area of household consumption. Experts' work is sometimes contrasted with the opinion of everyday people (via focus groups or other deliberative methods). Other absolute poverty thresholds are purely conventional, for example, the World Bank uses a US$2.15/day threshold poverty line.

When defining an absolute threshold in case of a non-welfarist approach – after defining the dimensions of well-being to be considered – the analyst defines a cut-off level that determines whether someone is deprived on a given dimension, and the group of people in poverty is defined based on these deprivations. Two extreme possibilities for identifying people in poverty (Guio, 2018) are the 'intersection approach' (only those are in poverty who are deprived on all dimensions) and the 'union approach' (all people are in poverty who are deprived on at least one of the dimensions).

An intermediate solution is to define a minimum number of dimensions on which the individual has to be deprived to be considered poor (Alkire et al, 2015). The choice of the aggregation method implies assumptions about substitutability between the dimensions (Chakravarty and Chattopadhyay, 2018). The union approach assumes no substitutability between the dimensions, the arithmetical sum implies that dimensions are supposed to be perfect substitutes, while the intersection approach implies complementarity between the dimensions.

In contrast to absolute poverty, relative poverty refers to situations when people lack resources to satisfy their needs to the same extent as others typically do in the societies where they live (Townsend, 1979). In case of *relative poverty thresholds* low levels of well-being are defined with respect to the distribution of well-being prevailing in the given country. For measuring relative poverty in the welfarist approach, analysts most often specify an income threshold relative to typical incomes in the society (such as 60 per cent of the median equivalised household income). Relative poverty measures can be also used in case of multidimensional (non-welfarist) approaches (for example, depending on the distribution of the number of deprivations typically observed in the society).

In case of the absolute and relative poverty thresholds described earlier, the assessment of whether well-being is lower than the poverty threshold is made by a third person, who applies the same clearly defined criteria to all. In case of *subjective thresholds*, the individuals themselves decide whether they live in poverty or whether their needs are satisfied or not. Objective and subjective thresholds do not imply here a normative statement as we do not consider one of these approaches superior to the other. This terminology is used purely to differentiate between approaches on the basis of who is making the judgement about needs being unmet or being in poverty.

Based on the earlier discussion, we outline a typology of possible approaches to care poverty based on two aspects derived from poverty measurement (Table 5.1). The first aspect is about the dimensionality issue. In case of one-dimensional measurements, the assessment whether someone is in care poverty is done on a unique dimension, most frequently regarding having unmet needs in care in general. In case of multidimensional approaches, basic needs or functionings are measured in several dimensions and the assessment of whether needs are unmet is made separately in each dimension. Overall care poverty is then defined by some kind of aggregation of unmet needs measured on the separate dimensions. The second aspect is about the poverty threshold applied. In case of an objective threshold, the assessment is made by an external observer who applies the same clearly defined criteria to all. In case of subjective thresholds, the assessment is done by the respondent or a proxy (subjective by proxy approach).

Table 5.1: Typology of poverty approaches and examples of existing studies of care poverty

| | Care poverty threshold | | |
| | Objective | | Subjective |
	Absolute	Relative	
One-dimensional	Lagergren et al (2014), García-Gómez et al (2015), Carrieri et al (2017), Ilinca et al (2017), Rodrigues et al (2018), Hu et al (2024)	Tenand et al (2020a; 2020b)	Brimblecombe et al (2017)
Multidimensional	Davey et al (2013), Laferrère and Bosch (2015), Vlachantoni (2019)		Morrow-Howell et al (2001), Levy-Storms et al (2002), LaPlante et al (2004), Bién et al (2013), Kröger et al (2019), Kröger (2022)

The concept of care poverty

The concept of care poverty as proposed by Kröger refers to 'the deprivation of adequate coverage of care needs' (Kröger, 2022: 26) and as such results from the interplay between 'needs' and how they are met or covered (implicitly by care). Owning to an approach that also underpins studies on the distribution of health care use (Wagstaff and van Doorslaer, 2000), the definition of needs is thus the starting point of the concept of care poverty. Kröger (2022) posits that needs are multidimensional and proposes an approach that defines needs around three domains: personal care poverty related to limitations with Activities of Daily Living (ADLs), practical care poverty related to limitations with Instrumental Activities of Daily Living (IADLs) and socio-emotional care poverty related to loneliness, for example. When defining care poverty, the measure applies the 'union' approach, denying substitutability between the dimensions. This seems logical as unmet need in help with, for example, eating cannot be substituted with help received in other areas. Another central point of Kröger's concept of care poverty is the interaction between individual characteristics of older people and macro or societal-level factors impacting the availability and distribution of services (Kröger, 2022: 26). The union approach followed thus also highlights that the underlying causes of unmet needs may be different across the different domains.

In the measurement of care poverty, the assessment whether needs are unmet is made by the respondents themselves, despite objective approaches also being used elsewhere in the assessment of care needs (García-Gómez et al, 2015). In distinguishing between absolute and relative care poverty, Kröger (2022) departs somewhat from the terminology used in the poverty studies outlined earlier. In his work, absolute care poverty refers to those who receive no care whatsoever in relation to a given dimension of care poverty. His concept of relative care poverty refers to those who report unmet needs, including those whose needs are partially met. An argument in favour of using individuals' self-assessment in measuring relative care poverty is to anchor the replies of individuals to the specific context or distribution of care provision (or expectation of it) in their country or society (Kröger, 2022). This brings Kröger's relative care poverty closer to the concept of relative poverty defined earlier.

Measurement of care poverty: examples from the literature

In the subsequent discussion we present a partial review of studies of unmet needs in care and care poverty and situate them in the typology outlined in Table 5.1.

Examples of studies applying a subjective care poverty threshold

In addition to the aforementioned studies by Kröger et al (2019) and Kröger (2022), Morrow-Howell et al (2001) also present an example of a subjective approach to the measurement of unmet needs. The authors compared perspectives of care recipients and professionals on the sufficiency of home care received. Their findings show how role influences the assessment of sufficiency of care, with professionals reporting significantly lower ratings than older care recipients. The two dependent variables were: physical functioning ability, assessed by a multidimensional functional assessment questionnaire on seven ADLs and six IADLs (each measured with a three-level response) and sufficiency of care received from formal and informal sources rated specific to each area of functional need (measured on a four-point scale). The authors then calculated two summative scores, one for care recipients and one for care professionals, averaging the rated sufficiency of care across areas of functional dependence.

The study by Levy-Storms et al (2002) on unmet need among nursing home residents in the United States is one of the few examples in the literature that applies a subjective, preference-based approach to unmet need. They used three types of measures to identify unmet need on different ADL care domains: direct satisfaction, discrepancy between preferred and actual care received (both based on questions about the frequency or occurrence of ADL care), and whether the respondent wanted a change or not in the type of care received, drawing on residents' comments to open-ended questions.

The approach used by LaPlante et al (2004) to analyse unmet needs in the United States for personal care can also be considered a subjective multidimensional one, as individuals' unmet needs are assessed based on five ADL and ten IADL categories created by the researchers. Those who reported lack of help or need of more help in at least one I/ADL were then defined as having unmet need. Moreover, their study considers undermet need by estimating the shortfall of hours of help.

Bién et al (2013) apply a multidimensional approach to measuring unmet need as assessed not by the care recipient himself/herself, but by a proxy. Unmet needs are measured on eight need areas (such as health needs, mobility needs, physical/personal needs), each of which is assessed separately by the family carer. Care need was defined as unmet when the carer reported that they would like more help to meet the care recipient's need in the particular area. The authors then calculated the prevalence of unmet need for four separate need areas deemed most relevant, as well as the mean number of unmet needs for these four.

One example for a subjective approach using a single dimension is the study by Brimblecombe et al (2017) who examined perceived unmet needs in care dyads. Both care recipients and their carers were asked in their survey whether the service received was of the right amount or not, with the latter corresponding to a perceived need for any services.

Examples of studies applying an objective care poverty threshold

We differentiate between objective approaches depending on whether care poverty is assessed along single or multiple dimensions and according to the type of care poverty threshold used (absolute versus relative, as in the income poverty literature).

Objective multidimensional approaches using an absolute care poverty threshold

A good example for a multidimensional objective approach using an absolute threshold is the study of Davey et al (2013) that explores state-level variation of unmet need for formal and informal support in the United States. They assess unmet need separately for ADLs and IADLs and propose an overall measure of unmet need referring to those having unmet need for at least one functional limitation. A similar method is applied by Laferrère and Van den Bosch (2015) who compare patterns of unmet need in 12 European countries by creating and combining two indices, one for limitations with ADLs and one for IADLs, and differentiating between four different hierarchical levels of need based on number of ADLs and IADLs. They consider the use of three types of help, namely informal help, formal personal care and formal domestic help. Based on this, they define unmet need when people have one or more IADL limitations and receive neither formal domestic help nor informal help, or have one or more ADL limitations and receive neither formal personal care nor informal help. Another example is the analysis by Vlachantoni (2019), who studied unmet need for social care on data from the English Longitudinal Study of Ageing in England. In case of a selected number of ADLs, IADLs and mobility tasks, the survey asked those having difficulty whether they received support with that activity, with unmet needs referring to those who have not received any support (from any source) for that activity.

Objective one-dimensional approaches using an absolute care poverty threshold

Examples included here mainly concern studies from the care inequality literature that use regression techniques, decomposition analysis and concentration curves and indices to measure inequality and inequity (that is, inequalities that remain after accounting for different needs) in the use of care. It is important to note that in a number of these studies (see Tenand et al, 2020a; 2020b) care use is standardised according to need considering not only those with needs, which contradicts the definition of care poverty provided by Kröger whereby the concept should only apply to those who have needs and not to the whole population.

Lagergren et al (2014) provide an analysis of horizontal inequity (including both users and non-users of public care services) and vertical inequity (looking at only those receiving care services) to assess target efficiency in use of publicly provided long-term care. Their study builds on Swedish survey data using binary logistic regressions. Their measure of care need is operationalised as having at least one dependency in IADL or at least one dependency in ADL. In their study on horizontal inequity in long-term care in the Spanish context, García-Gómez et al (2015) suggest two alternative definitions of unmet needs: perceived need for care, but not received the service (a measure used generally in analysis of inequity in use of/access to care); and having minimum one limitation on ADL or IADL and not receiving the needed service (an objective measure).

Carrieri et al (2017) analyse needs-adjusted inequities in use of care services, building on data from the Survey on Health, Aging and Retirement and focusing on both paid domestic help and personal nursing care. By decomposing the concentration index (level of horizontal inequity), they measure the contribution of income, need (based on self-assessed health, number of activity limitations and number of symptoms) and non-need factors (education, marital status, area), also controlling for informal care received from children, to overall inequality. Ilinca et al (2017) use a similar decomposition analysis to analyse distributional fairness in the utilisation of long-term care by socioeconomic status. Two further examples using similar methods that apply an objective and absolute poverty approach are studies by

Rodrigues et al (2018), which focuses on inequity in different types of care use utilising two measures of socioeconomic status (income and wealth), and Hu et al (2024), which adopts a similar approach to investigate socioeconomic inequity by older people with and without dementia in England.

Objective one-dimensional approaches using a relative care poverty threshold

The two studies of Tenand et al (2020a; 2020b) that measure inequity and need-standardised care use in the Netherlands, specifically focusing on eligibility as need, provide cases for what would come close to the relative poverty concept as applied in the general poverty literature. Similar to other studies on horizontal inequity and those using concentration indices, care use is standardised against the use that would be expected for similar observed levels of need among the population.

Comparison of the different approaches

Objective poverty thresholds: absolute versus relative approaches

The difficulty of normative absolute poverty thresholds seems to be evident in the case of care poverty. The assessment of care needs by an independent observer proves difficult as needs carry an interpretational component (Kröger, 2022) and a relational component (Rodrigues, 2020). Therefore, absolute care poverty thresholds used in the literature tend to be purely conventional (for example, saying everyone with care needs who does not receive an hour of care is in unmet need).

The information requirements of applying a relative poverty threshold are less demanding compared to an absolute approach. If there is data about the distribution of care needs and care received in the population, relative poverty thresholds can be defined without further outside information. On the other hand, with relative thresholds it is more difficult to analyse the impact of a general decline or increase in availability of care services on care poverty. If the availability of services improves or declines similarly for everyone, a purely relative approach will not detect a change in care poverty.

Subjective care poverty thresholds: advantages and disadvantages

As obtaining professional judgement about unmet need of care for a large sample is very costly, a survey assessment of subjective unmet needs can be cost-effective (LaPlante et al, 2004; Smith and Connolly, 2020). In addition, the use of subjective information might also help in capturing the quality aspects of care (Levy-Storms et al, 2002). Smith and Connolly (2020) also argue that subjective measurement is consistent with the view that the care user is the best person to assess his/her care needs and the adequacy of care received. One disadvantage on the other hand with using subjective assessment of unmet need is that subjective measures might underestimate the problem if there is unperceived unmet need (Smith and Connolly, 2020).

When interpreting results of studies using a subjective threshold, it has to be kept in mind that individual judgements about the sufficiency or insufficiency of care might be formulated in comparison to some normative ideal but also in comparison to care typically received by other people in similar situations. The expectations of respondents about necessary and acceptable levels of care can be influenced by the country's level of development, the characteristics of the institutional context, social norms regarding the obligations of generations towards each other, and so on. In this sense, subjective thresholds are similar to some degree to a relative approach in which comparison to the actual, typical social context is of prime importance (Kröger, 2022).

Measuring the intensity of care poverty

Most approaches proposed to measure care poverty quantify only the percentage of those with unmet care needs (care poverty headcount ratio) and only a few take into account the intensity of care poverty. The intensity of poverty (or the depth of poverty) measures how far people in poverty are from the poverty threshold. One study applying such an approach is made by LaPlante et al (2004), who quantify the shortfall of hours of help that is associated with unmet care needs. However, simple poverty indices can be misleading. For example, a policy that redistributes income from the poorest to those just under the poverty line would reduce the headcount ratio, but at the expense of greater poverty intensity. The poverty literature has proposed more complex indices of poverty such as the Foster-Greer-Thorbecke-indices or the Sen-index, which take into account both these aspects (and also the distribution of incomes among people in poverty) to provide indices that are more useful for poverty research (see Seidl, 1988).

What measures of care poverty could help to derive policy implications?

In order to be useful for informing policy decisions, a measure of care poverty might have to go further than providing a simple percentage of those characterised by care poverty. One reason for this is based on the argumentation made in the previous section on the relevance of intensity of care poverty. Vlachantoni et al (2011) put forward another argument, as the group of those with unmet care needs might include people in very different situations, for example, those who have a low level of need but receive no assistance, those receiving formal support but who are unsatisfied with it or those who fall just below some formal needs assessment criteria. In order to target policy measures, one would preferably be able to identify those belonging to these subgroups separately. As well, Kröger (2022: 210) highlights the need to take the extent of needs into account when analysing care poverty.

A simple headcount measure of care poverty may also be of limited use for policy makers if it fails to disclose information on the possible reasons for unmet needs. Not all of these reasons may be relevant for policy makers (such as different preferences) and the policy responses may be quite different whether the mismatch is caused by lack of trust in the provider or insufficient resources to access care. It might thus be useful to distinguish different types of mismatch between need and care (see Allin et al, 2010). Smith and Connolly (2020), for example, take a dynamic perspective between three types of unmet need that could be useful to inform policy making: (1) needed but never demanded care; (2) delayed care; (3) demanded care but received suboptimal care. Similarly, Tenand et al (2020b) differentiate between inequalities that arise from eligibility criteria in the Dutch system and those that result from actual use of services.

Comparing care poverty across space

As mentioned earlier, comparing care poverty across different long-term care systems or countries holds a great potential for uncovering determinants of care poverty and possible policies to address them. This comparison, however, is affected by a number of challenges, reflected in the studies reviewed here with a comparative perspective. The first concerns difficulties in defining care needs across Europe. A recent study highlights the diversity of long-term care needs that are considered relevant in each country (Brugiavini et al, 2017). Similarly to income poverty, relative measures of care poverty may thus be better suited to be used in country comparisons. Few such relative measures or methods exist for now, though.

The second challenge concerns the metric used. Most studies reviewed relied on self-reported unmet need, which may be difficult to compare across countries as it is likely to be anchored around different expectations across countries as to what care is available. Conversely, Kröger (2022) argues that precisely because they reflect different expectations across countries, self-reported measures should be used as a measure of relative care poverty. What is clear is that comparisons of care poverty across countries should also consider the distribution of needs (Smith and Connolly, 2020; Tenand et al, 2020a).

The literature on care inequalities uses a methodological approach – inequity indices – which not only accounts for different distributions of need within countries but provides a metric that is comparable across countries (Rodrigues et al, 2018). The downside of this method is that it can only be used with ranking variables (such as net or gross income or wealth, but not with gender or even education). However, this difficulty may be overcome by applying methods that allow for the decomposition by population subgroups based on non-rank characteristics. Health care deprivation indices as proposed by Laudicella et al (2009) are one example of such alternative approaches, which are moreover compatible with a multidimensional view of care poverty.

Conclusion

Care poverty is a novel concept and indications regarding its measurement can be derived from a large body of literature on (income) poverty, unmet needs and inequalities in use of long-term care. Although we fall short of empirically applying the different methodologies reviewed here, we nonetheless suggest new approaches to the measurement of care poverty, each with possible strengths and caveats, particularly for the assessment of care poverty across countries or welfare states. Without this empirical testing, singling out one specific method was also beyond the remit of this chapter. We do highlight a number of principles that can be useful to guide future empirical assessment of care poverty, especially in a comparative perspective. It is particularly relevant to develop measures that are akin to the relative poverty thresholds used in the (income) poverty literature to enable cross-country comparisons. There are diverging opinions as to whether self-perceived unmet needs can be used across markedly different institutional and cultural concepts, but these measures do provide a 'voice' to those experiencing care poverty, who may otherwise feel disempowered. A key analytical dimension that is still missing is the intensity or degree of care poverty and how distant an individual may be from having their care needs met. Finally, it is worth considering that as with unmet needs for health care, not all mismatches between needs and care may have the same underlying mechanism and require the same policy intervention. A distinction between different types of needs left unmet may thus be particularly useful for policy makers.

One of the strengths of the nascent concept of care poverty is its multidisciplinary underpinning. In this chapter we attempted to do justice to this, by reviewing in a non-exhaustive manner a number of different studies that could contribute to a clearer operationalisation of care poverty. We believe that future developments and experiments on several measures of care poverty would be well-served by following a similar multidisciplinary approach.

References

Alkire, S., Foster, J., Seth, S., Santos, M.E., Roche, J.M. and Ballon, P. (2015) *Multidimensional Poverty Measurement and Analysis*, Oxford: Oxford University Press.

Allin, S., Grignon, M. and Le Grand, J. (2010) 'Subjective unmet need and utilization of health care services in Canada: what are the equity implications?', *Social Science & Medicine*, 70(3): 465–72.

Bień, B., McKee, K.J., Döhner, H., Triantafillou, J., Lamura, G., Doroszkiewicz, H., et al (2013) 'Disabled older people's use of health and social care services and their unmet care needs in six European countries', *European Journal of Public Health*, 23(6): 1032–8.

Brimblecombe, N., Pickard, L., King, D. and Knapp, M. (2017) 'Perceptions of unmet needs for community social care services in England: a comparison of working carers and the people they care for', *Health & Social Care in the Community*, 25(2): 435–46.

Brugiavini, A., Carrino, L., Orso, C.E. and Pasini, G. (2017) *Vulnerability and Long-term Care in Europe: An Economic Perspective*, Cheltenham: Palgrave Macmillan.

Carrieri, V., Di Novi, C. and Orso, C.E. (2017) 'Home sweet home? Public financing and inequalities in the use of home care services in Europe', *Fiscal Studies*, 38(3): 445–68.

Chakravarty, S.R. and Chattopadhyay, N. (2018) 'Multidimensional poverty and material deprivation: theoretical approaches', in C. D'Ambrosio (ed) *Handbook of Research on Economic and Social Well-being*, Cheltenham: Edward Elgar, pp 153–70.

Davey, A., Takagi, E., Sundström, G. and Malmberg, B. (2013) '(In)formal support and unmet needs in the National Long-Term Care Survey', *Journal of Comparative Family Studies*, 44(4): 437–53.

García-Gómez, P., Hernández-Quevedo, C., Jiménez-Rubio, D. and Oliva-Moreno, J. (2015) 'Inequity in long-term care use and unmet need: two sides of the same coin', *Journal of Health Economics*, 39(January): 147–58.

Guio, A.-C. (2018) 'Multidimensional poverty and material deprivation: empirical findings', in C. D'Ambrosio (ed) *Handbook of Research on Economic and Social Well-being*, Cheltenham: Edward Elgar, pp 171–92.

Hu, B., Read, S., Wittenberg, R., Brimblecombe, N., Rodrigues, R., Banerjee, S., et al (2024) 'Socioeconomic inequality of long-term care for older people with and without dementia in England', *Ageing & Society*, 44(7): 1597–617.

Ilinca, S., Rodrigues, R. and Schmidt, A.E. (2017) 'Fairness and eligibility to long-term care: an analysis of the factors driving inequality and inequity in the use of home care for older Europeans', *International Journal of Environmental Research and Public Health*, 14(10): Article 1224.

Kröger, T. (2022) *Care Poverty: When Older People's Needs Remain Unmet*, Cham: Palgrave Macmillan.

Kröger, T., Mathew Puthenparambil, J. and Van Aerschot, L. (2019) 'Care poverty: unmet care needs in a Nordic welfare state', *International Journal of Care and Caring*, 3(4): 485–500.

Laferrère, A. and Van den Bosch, K. (2015) 'Unmet need for long-term care and social exclusion', in A. Börsch-Supan, T. Kneip, H. Litwin, M. Myck and G. Weber (eds) *Ageing in Europe: Supporting Policies for an Inclusive Society*, Boston: De Gruyter, pp 331–42.

Lagergren, M., Sjölund, B., Fagerström, C., Berglund, J., Fratiglioni, L., Nordell, E., et al (2014) 'Horizontal and vertical target efficiency: a comparison between users and non-users of public long-term care in Sweden', *Ageing & Society*, 34(4): 700–19.

LaPlante, M.P., Kaye, H.S., Kang, T. and Harrington, C. (2004) 'Unmet need for personal assistance services: estimating the shortfall in hours of help and adverse consequences', *The Journals of Gerontology: Series B*, 59(2): S98–S108.

Laudicella, M., Cookson, R., Jones, A.M. and Rice, N. (2009) 'Health care deprivation profiles in the measurement of inequality and inequity: an application to GP fundholding in the English NHS', *Journal of Health Economics*, 28(6): 1048–61.

Levy-Storms, L., Schnelle, J.F. and Simmons, S.F. (2002) 'A comparison of methods to assess nursing home residents' unmet needs', *The Gerontologist*, 42(4): 454–61.

Morrow-Howell, N., Proctor, E. and Rozario, P. (2001) 'How much is enough? Perspectives of care recipients and professionals on the sufficiency of in-home care', *The Gerontologist*, 41(6): 723–32.

Ravallion, M. (2016) *The Economics of Poverty: History, Measurement, and Policy*, Oxford: Oxford University Press.

Rodrigues, R. (2020) 'Caring relationships and their role in users' choices: a study of users of Direct Payments in England', *Ageing & Society*, 40(7): 1469–89.

Rodrigues, R., Ilinca, S. and Schmidt, A.E. (2018) 'Income-rich and wealth-poor? The impact of measures of socio-economic status in the analysis of the distribution of long-term care use among older people', *Health Economics*, 27(3): 637–46.

Seidl, C. (1988) 'Poverty measurement: a survey', in D. Bös, M. Rose and C. Seidl (eds) *Welfare and Efficiency in Public Economics*, Berlin and Heidelberg: Springer, pp 71–147.

Sen, A. (1983) *Poverty and Famines: An Essay on Entitlement and Deprivation* (reprint edn), Oxford: Oxford University Press.

Sen, A.K. (1992) *Inequality Re-examined*, Cambridge, MA: Harvard University Press.

Smith, S. and Connolly, S. (2020) 'Re-thinking unmet need for health care: introducing a dynamic perspective', *Health Economics, Policy and Law*, 15(4): 440–57.

Tenand, M., Bakx, P. and van Doorslaer, E. (2020a) 'Equal long-term care for equal needs with universal and comprehensive coverage? An assessment using Dutch administrative data', *Health Economics*, 29(4): 435–51.

Tenand, M., Bakx, P. and van Doorslaer, E. (2020b) 'Eligibility or use? Disentangling the sources of horizontal inequity in home care receipt in the Netherlands', *Health Economics*, 29(10): 1161–79.

Townsend, P. (1979) *Poverty in the United Kingdom: A Survey of Household Resources and Standards of Living* (1st edn), London: Penguin.

Vlachantoni, A. (2019) 'Unmet need for social care among older people', *Ageing & Society*, 39(4): 657–84.

Vlachantoni, A., Shaw, R., Willis, R., Evandrou, M., Falkingham, J. and Luff, R. (2011) 'Measuring unmet need for social care amongst older people', *Population Trends*, 145: 56–72.

Wagstaff, A. and van Doorslaer, E. (2000) 'Measuring and testing for inequity in the delivery of health care', *Journal of Human Resources*, 35(4): 716–33.

PART III

Practice

6

Unmet care needs over time: social networks and persistent unmet needs

Athina Vlachantoni, Maria Evandrou,
Jane Falkingham and Min Qin

Introduction

Ensuring timely access to services and support necessary to maintain the functional ability that enables well-being in older age is a prerequisite for healthy ageing globally (Public Health England, 2019; WHO, 2020). Meeting older adults' social care needs is essential to older persons' capabilities for coping with daily challenges, and maintaining their health status, well-being and dignity (Allen et al, 2014). People who report unmet needs experience more challenges with their Activities of Daily Living (ADLs) (Komisar et al, 2005), use health care more often (DePalma et al, 2012; Xu et al, 2012) and have a higher mortality rate (He et al, 2015). Determining the extent and nature of unmet needs is, therefore, critical in assessing the effectiveness of social care provision and in identifying and quantifying the types of unmet needs that can help policy makers address them (Vlachantoni et al, 2011).

In England, social care includes physical and financial help, care, and support for individuals with diverse needs due to disability, illness, frailty and other life circumstances (DHSC, 2021). This includes home care, home adaptations and 24-hour care in care homes. Receiving and providing informal/family care depends upon individuals' needs, economic, physical and social resources, opportunities, and preferences (Litwin et al, 2008). Older persons' social networks constitute a major resource for personal care in later life (Ayalon and Levkovich, 2019). Understanding the relationship between different social networks and the dynamics of unmet need for social care can help pinpoint groups of individuals who face an elevated risk of experiencing persistent unmet needs, and inform policies aimed at supporting them. This chapter adds to the literature by investigating the dynamics of unmet need for social care across different domains and how this varies by social network typology, aiming to inform policy and practice.

Population ageing and challenges to meet social care needs

It is estimated that 14 per cent of people aged 60 years and over globally (142 million) are unable to perform their basic daily activities unassisted (WHO, 2020). Population ageing, especially the increase in the number of those aged 85 and over, is linked to an increase in health care and social care requirements (Jagger, 2015). In England, where around 1.5 million older people experience unmet needs for social care (Age UK, 2019), the support received by a person in need comes from a range of sources including informal, formal statutory publicly funded and/or self-paid sources. The most common source of informal care for older people is their partner or adult children (Pickard, 2015). However, population ageing and changes in intergenerational family structures have challenged how family carers provide care (Hoff, 2015). Increasing lifespans combined with lower fertility have led to more smaller family units that will need to support multiple generations. More women entering the workforce has changed the traditional division of labour within families (Irvine et al, 2022). Divorce and family forms such as 'living apart together' have also become more usual, resulting in a plurality of family forms (Haskey, 2005), and social risks in meeting the increasing demand for informal care.

The formal statutory social care system in England is means-tested and separate from the health care system (which is free at the point of need), with local government authorities being responsible for commissioning care, mostly from market providers (DHSC, 2021). Since 2008, the adult social care budgets of most local authorities have been cut (Ismail et al, 2014), resulting in many local authorities raising their eligibility thresholds. In practice, the allocation of publicly funded social care is strongly determined by the level of informal support and older persons' living arrangements (Fernandez et al, 2015), and more older people have to rely on their own resources to pay privately for care, or go without care (Maplethorpe et al, 2015).

Definitions and conceptual framework of unmet needs of social care and dynamics

There is no consensus regarding the definition and measurement of 'need' and 'unmet need' for social care. Much of the literature focusing on the need for assistance among older individuals highlights the link between need and one's difficulty with daily functions or activities, which determines the type of assistance required (Allin et al, 2010; Allen et al, 2014; Vlachantoni et al, 2015). Vlachantoni et al (2011) conceptualised unmet needs as being determined by the interaction between a person's type and level of need and the type and level of support they receive, and affected by their demographic, socioeconomic and health status characteristics. This framework was advanced by incorporating a temporal dimension to investigate the dynamics of met/unmet needs for social care over time (Vlachantoni et al, 2024). For the need for any type of care, five different dynamics were identified between two time points:

1. no longer have needs;
2. continued needs met;
3. newly arisen unmet needs;
4. delayed needs met; and
5. persistent unmet needs (Vlachantoni et al, 2024).

Kröger (2022) distinguished care needs under three different domains: personal care for ADL needs; practical care for Instrumental Activities of Daily Living (IADL) needs; and socio-emotional care needs for respect, love and belonging. This leads to a categorisation of three different domains for care poverty: personal care poverty (lack of coverage for ADL needs); practical care poverty (lack of help in meeting IADL needs); and unmet social and emotional needs, with loneliness as an expression. The concept of unmet need has been frequently used in gerontology and tends to focus on the micro-level of individuals' experiences and characteristics, whereas the concept of care poverty aims to capture both macro- and micro-level indicators, taking an interdisciplinary perspective and also focusing on inequalities. The present analysis adopts these three domains of care needs within a temporal perspective, combining the conceptual frameworks from Kröger (2022) and Vlachantoni et al (2024). Despite not being highlighted within England's social care system as a formal need, emotional care needs (loneliness) were included in this study as they impact on older adults' health (Macdonald et al, 2021). Loneliness differs from social isolation, as one can feel lonely even within a social network.

Social networks and social support

Previous studies have highlighted how informal social care receipt varies according to an older person's social network (Litwin and Landau, 2000). The social convoy model describes patterns of changing social networks and support as people age (Kahn and Antonucci, 1980), asserting that personal (for example, age) and situational factors (for example, role expectations) change over time and influence the quantity and quality of social relationships (such as a decrease in network size as one's own marital status changes). An alternate perspective is provided by the socio-emotional selectivity theory, arguing that as one ages, individuals become more selective and strengthen emotional ties, dissolving unimportant relationships and forming fewer, higher-quality ones (Carstensen, 1992).

Network types among older adults have been derived based on various criteria, including the availability of close kin, level of involvement of family, friends and neighbours, and geographic proximity, among others (Wenger, 1991; Litwin and Landau, 2000; Fiori et al, 2006). Common across different typologies, the network type significantly predicts social support and, in turn, impacts older people's well-being. Litwin and Landau (2000) found that the *Kin network* (mostly relatives/adult children) offers the most support, and the *Family-intensive* type (comprised overwhelmingly of adult children) the least. Fiori et al (2006) found that the *Diverse network* (likely to be married/have children, frequent contact with children, frequent attendance at meetings/religious services) had the best outcomes in depressive symptomatology and the *Non-family-restricted networks* (limited social ties, unlikely to be married or have children, limited contact) the worst.

Research objectives

There is limited evidence on the impact of heterogeneous network types on later-life care receipt and unmet needs. In most studies, social support scores reflect the relative supportiveness of respondents' networks, without distinguishing between care needs. This analysis examines the dynamics of three domains of unmet care needs (personal, practical and emotional) and their relationship with different social network types among older adults in England.

There are three specific objectives. First, we assess the dynamics of each domain of unmet care needs over two time points among older adults reporting needs at the baseline. Second, we derive a typology of social networks using demographic and social factors shown to be related to social network types. We expect that men, women and people of different levels of socioeconomic positions (SEP) and ages have different social network types. Third, we examine relationships between social network types and the dynamics of unmet social care needs in each domain. We anticipate that Diverse and Family incentive networks will be associated with better outcomes compared to Restricted or Friends-focused networks.

Methods

The English Longitudinal Study of Ageing (ELSA) began in 2002 and collects information on the physical and mental health and demographic and socioeconomic circumstances of a representative sample of the English population aged 50 and over living in the community (Banks et al, 2019). For this study the two most recent Waves 8 and 9 are employed (collected May 2016 to June 2017 and June 2018 to July 2019, respectively). The analytic sample includes respondents aged 65 and above who reported needing personal, practical or emotional social care in Wave 8 (baseline), and who participated in both Waves 8 and 9. A total of 4,075 respondents (mean age=74.0, SD=6.9, 54.4 per cent women) met the sample selection criteria for the emotional care needs analysis, assuming everyone has emotional needs; the same for 713 respondents (mean age=76.3, SD=7.9, 57.6 per cent women) with at least one ADL difficulty at Wave 8 for the personal care needs analysis; and 683 respondents (mean age=77.1, SD=8.0, 65.3 per cent women) with at least one IADL difficulty at Wave 8 for the practical care needs analysis. Among those needing personal care, 60.5 per cent also need practical care.

Measure

Dependent variables

The two waves of data included consistent questions about respondents' report of difficulties with ADLs (dressing, bathing, getting in/out of bed, walking across a room, using the toilet and eating) and IADLs (shopping for groceries, taking medications, house/garden work and managing money) and support receipt for such activities from informal/formal sources. The survey also collected information about loneliness ('How often one feels lonely').

Referring to three domains of care needs (Kröger, 2022) and the framework of unmet social care needs (Vlachantoni et al, 2011; 2024), in this study, at each wave, a person is defined as having 'unmet needs of personal care' when they reported any ADL difficulties but did not receive any support with such tasks from any source (formal or informal). A similar approach defines 'unmet needs of practical care', when respondents reported any IADL difficulties. Respondents are defined with 'unmet needs of emotional care' when they feel lonely sometimes or often.

Over the observation period, some older adults received help at Wave 8. Among these, at Wave 9, the majority continued receiving support which met their needs, as defined in this chapter (continued need met); a number of people reported no such difficulty anymore (no longer have needs); and a small number of people did not receive help anymore and thus now had unmet needs (newly arisen unmet needs).

Some older people had unmet needs at Wave 8. Among these, at Wave 9, some now received help which met their needs (delayed needs met); while some again did not receive any help (persistent unmet needs). Five different dynamics for each domain of care needs were identified, as described previously (Vlachantoni et al, 2024), to examine the relationship between the social networks type and unmet care needs.

In the descriptive analysis, the outcomes were personal care, practical care and emotional care unmet needs dynamics. In the multivariate statistical analyses, binary logistic regression was applied to hone in on each group, focusing on persistent unmet needs of:

1. personal care (not receiving help with at least one ADL difficulty at both waves);
2. practical care (similarly for IADL);
3. emotional care (feel lonely often or sometimes at both waves).

Type of social networks

This variable was measured at Wave 8. To construct the latent variable of the typology of social networks, 17 indicators were used regarding the family/non-family size, geographic proximity, physical and digital contact frequencies. Latent class analysis was applied. Each respondent was assigned a probability of social network membership in each latent class. Latent class analysis shows a five-class fitting the data best after comparing the Akaike Information Criterion (AIC), the Bayesian Information Criterion (BIC) and Entropy from four or five or six class analyses. The lower AIC and BIC, and the greater Entropy, the better the fit. The five-class social networks are named as:

1 *Friend-focused* (high frequency of contact with friends, both face-to-face and digital, children not living nearby, digital contact with children), accounting for 19.5 per cent out of 4,075 respondents.
2. *Diverse* (most extensive of all networks with a spouse, children, other family members and friends, both face-to-face and digital contact), accounting for 17.6 per cent.
3. *Couple-centred* (live with spouse/partner, low contact with other networks), accounting for 27.1 per cent.
4. *Children-centred* (children live nearby, high face-to-face contact, lower chance living with spouse/partner), accounting for 18.4 per cent.
5. *Restricted* (little social ties, not living with a spouse/partner, few/no children, low contact with friends), accounting for 17.4 per cent.

Covariates

Previous research has shown that several factors heighten the likelihood of experiencing unmet needs among older people, including their family, health and socioeconomic status (Vlachantoni, 2019). Age ranged from 65 to 90 and was coded as 0=65–74; 1=75–84; 2=85 and above. Self-reported gender was coded as 0=male; 1=female. Living arrangements were coded as 0=living with someone; 1=living alone, only partially overlapping with the variable used in constructing the social network typology (living with the spouse versus with others). The National Statistics Socio-Economic Classification

(NS-SEC), indicating a person's SEP, was coded as 0=professional; 1= intermediate; 2=routine. Routine reflects a low SEP. The wealth quintile was coded as 0=lowest quintile to 4=highest quintile. Self-rated health was coded as 0=excellent/very good; 1=good; 2= fair/poor.

Analytic plan

To construct the latent variable of social networks, the latent class analysis was conducted using Mplus8. To examine the associations between social network class membership and covariates with dynamics of different types of met/unmet needs (focusing on persistent unmet needs), multivariate analyses are presented applying logistic regression with STATA17.

Results

Dynamics of social care needs

Figure 6.1 shows the percentages of older persons in each dynamic for the personal, practical and emotional care needs under study. Taking personal care as an illustration, among those needing personal care in Wave 8 (N= 713), 24.6 per cent had met needs and 75.4 per cent had unmet needs. By Wave 9, 32.2 per cent of those with a care need in Wave 8 no longer had needs, 10.8 per cent continued to have their needs met, 7.9 per cent had new unmet needs, 10.3 per cent had their needs met with a delay, and 38.8 per cent had persistent unmet needs.

Older people needing personal care had the highest proportion of *persistent* unmet needs, followed by emotional and practical care needs. The proportions of older people with delayed needs met are similar across all three care domains, accounting for around one in ten who were in need. Around one-third of older adults with a need for personal or practical care in Wave 8 do not report having needs in Wave 9, indicating that their care needs have changed over time.

Social network types

Table 6.1 shows the distribution of social network types according to age, gender, socioeconomic classification, health status and living arrangements. Friends-focused networks are more common among younger ages, professionals, and individuals with excellent/very good health. Diverse networks are characteristic of younger persons, women, and those with excellent/very good health. Men dominate Couple-centred networks. Children-centred networks are featured among older ages, females, living alone and those in lower SEP. Restricted networks are characteristic of males, those living alone, and in higher SEP.

Figure 6.1: Dynamics of met and unmet personal, practical and emotional care needs (number and proportion of respondents in each of the defined categories)

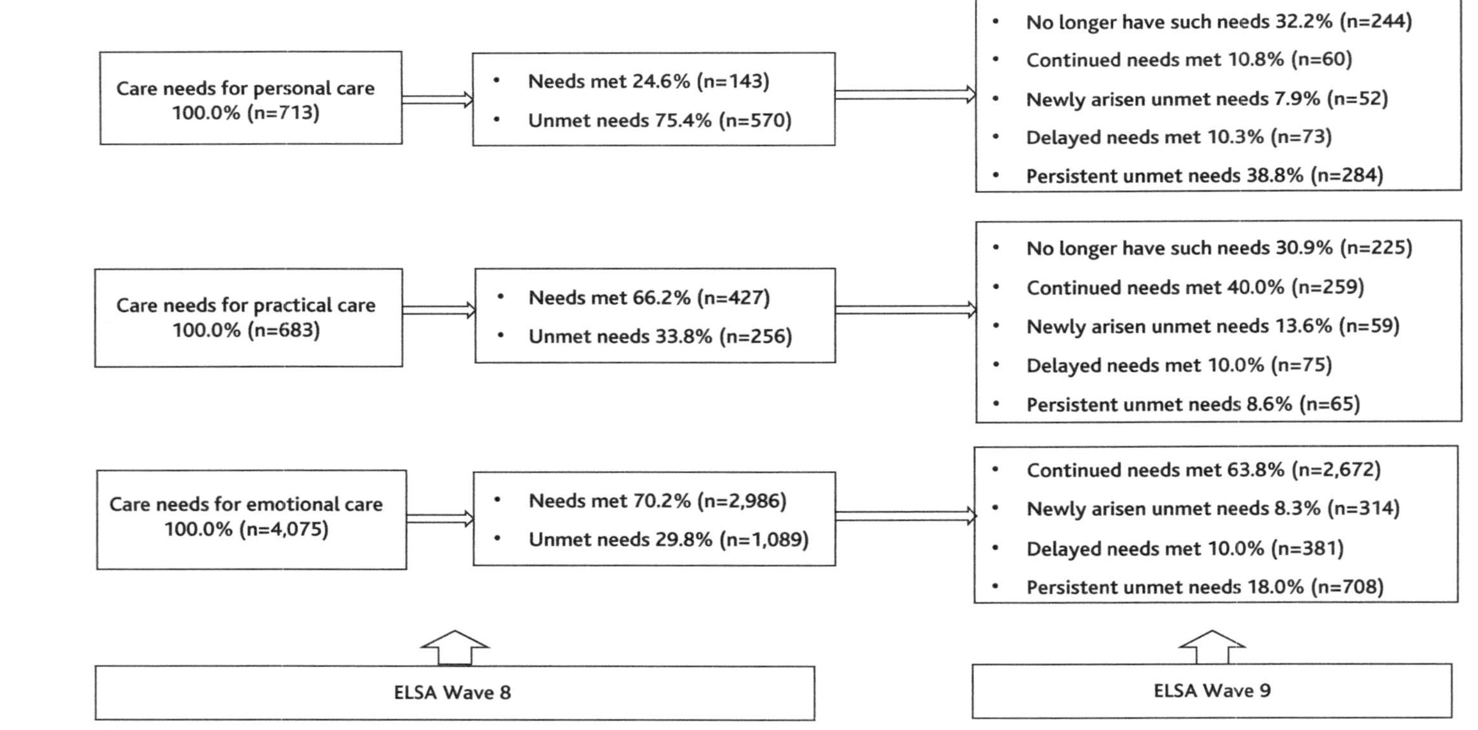

Source: Authors' analysis of ELSA (Waves 8 and 9).

Table 6.1: Respondents' characteristics and social networks (column percentages, N=4,075)

	Social networks					P-values	Total
	Friends-focused	Diverse	Couple-centred	Children-centred	Restricted		
Age						<0.001	
65–74	65.3	73.6	56.9	39.7	60.3		58.9
75–84	27.7	22.8	32.3	42.9	28.4		31.0
85+	6.9	3.6	10.7	17.4	11.2		10.1
Gender						<0.001	
Male	40.7	33.5	57.9	37.9	52.3		45.6
Female	59.3	66.5	42.1	62.1	47.7		54.4
NS-SEC						<0.001	
Professional	35.4	31.3	27.9	21.3	37.0		30.3
Intermediate	28.1	24.8	26.6	22.4	28.6		26.2
Routine	36.5	43.8	45.5	56.3	34.4		43.5
Self-reported health						<0.001	
Excellent/very good	42.8	42.9	32.2	27.8	36.4		36.1
Good	34.4	35.3	35.9	39.8	33.5		35.8
Fair/poor	22.8	21.8	31.8	32.4	30.1		28.1
Wealth quintile						<0.001	
Lowest	12.8	18.6	12.8	22.3	18.4		16.6
2nd	14.8	19.8	20.3	27.1	15.4		19.5
3rd	22.4	21.6	23.7	19.8	21.7		22.0
4th	21.9	20.4	21.4	19.0	23.2		21.2
Highest	27.6	19.2	21.0	11.6	20.5		20.7
Living arrangements						<0.001	
With someone	71.0	76.2	85.6	57.1	58.8		71.2
Alone	29.0	23.8	14.4	42.9	41.2		28.8
Number of ADL and IADL difficulties						<0.001	
0	80.5	77.8	72.0	65.6	69.3		73.0
1	8.2	9.5	11.3	14.9	11.9		11.1
More than 1	11.3	12.7	16.7	19.5	18.9		15.8

Source: Authors' analysis of ELSA (Waves 8 and 9).

Network types and dynamics of social care needs

The bivariate associations present the relationship between social network types and unmet social care needs dynamics (Table 6.2). Looking at personal care needs, a high proportion of those with Children-centred or Restricted networks experienced persistent unmet needs or delayed needs met. Those with Friends-focused networks also had a high level of delayed needs met. In contrast, those with Couple-centred networks had the lowest level for persistent and delayed unmet needs. Concerning practical care needs, respondents with Couple-centred networks had the highest proportion of persistent unmet needs. Those in Restricted networks had the highest proportion of delayed needs met, but those with Children-centred networks had the lowest. For emotional care needs, again, those with Children-centred or Restricted networks had a relatively high proportion of persistent unmet needs, while those with Diverse networks had the lowest. Overall, social network types are associated with practical and emotional but not personal care needs dynamics (Table 6.2), although bivariate associations may be confounded by other factors.

Table 6.3 presents the results of the logistic regression models predicting older people's persistent unmet needs for personal, practical and emotional care, respectively. As few respondents had delayed personal and practical care needs, this chapter only focuses on persistent unmet needs. Older people in Children-centred networks were more likely to have persistent unmet personal care needs than those in Diverse networks. Those with Couple-centred networks were more likely to have persistent unmet practical care needs. Older people with Couple-centred networks were more likely to have unmet emotional needs. Moreover, those living alone, or with fair/poor health were more likely to have persistent unmet personal care needs than their counterparts, while older persons or those in lower SEP were less likely to have such persistent unmet needs. The most elderly adults (over 85) and those from the richest households were less likely to have persistent practical unmet needs. Females, those living alone, with good or fair/poor health, and the lower NS-SEC were more likely to have unmet needs for emotional care. Older respondents were less likely to have such persistent unmet needs.

Interaction tests assessed whether other factors moderated the associations between social networks and persistent unmet needs (data not shown). Females who needed personal care and had Couple-centred networks had a lower likelihood of persistent unmet needs of such care, while those living alone who needed practical care and in Children-centred networks had a lower likelihood of persistent unmet needs of such care. The small number of respondents prevented similar analyses for delayed met needs.

Table 6.2: Binary relationship between social network type and dynamics of unmet needs (%)

	Social networks at Wave 8					P-value	Total
	Friends-focused	Diverse	Couple-centred	Children-centred	Restricted		
In need of personal care at Wave 8 (n=713)						0.219	
No longer have needs for social care	31.6	40.5	33.6	29.9	27.0		32.2
Continued needs met	11.4	11.9	14.8	5.1	10.4		10.8
Delayed needs met	10.1	7.1	5.4	8.5	9.6		7.9
Newly arisen unmet needs	7.6	7.1	14.1	8.5	11.3		10.3
Persistent unmet needs	39.2	33.3	32.2	47.9	41.7		38.8
In need of practical care at Wave 8 (n=683)						0.035	
No longer have needs for social care	37.5	41.8	28.9	26.3	30.9		31.7
Continued needs met	38.9	36.7	37.6	48.9	40.0		40.9
Delayed needs met	6.9	5.1	7.4	6.8	13.6		8.1
Newly arisen unmet needs	5.6	10.1	11.4	13.5	10.0		10.7
Persistent unmet needs	11.0	6.3	14.8	4.5	5.5		8.7
In need of emotional care at Wave 8 (n=4,075)						<0.001	
Continued needs met	68.5	66.9	65.9	53.6	62.7		63.8
Delayed needs met	6.9	9.3	10.5	13.9	9.2		10.0
Newly arisen unmet needs	7.8	9.1	7.6	10.3	7.0		8.3
Persistent unmet needs	16.8	14.7	16.0	22.2	21.1		18.0

Source: Authors' analysis of ELSA (Waves 8 and 9).

Discussion

This study observed significant unmet personal, practical and emotional care needs among older adults in England. The high level of *persistent* unmet personal care needs warrants more attention from policy makers and social care practitioners. Personal care combines a variety of forms of assistance for persons who require long-term help with basic ADLs. The widening gap between the need for social care and availability of support is reflected

Table 6.3: Logistic regression model predicting persistent unmet needs for personal, practical and emotional care

	Model 1 (N=713)		Model 2 (N=683)		Model 3 (N=4,075)	
	Persistent unmet needs of personal care		Persistent unmet needs of practical care		Persistent unmet needs of emotional care	
	OR	95% CI	OR	95% CI	OR	95% CI
Social networks type						
Diverse (ref)						
Friends-focused	1.24	0.70–2.19	2.26	0.82–6.24	1.07	0.80–1.44
Couple-centred	1.33	0.79–2.24	**2.68***	**1.09–6.60**	**1.46****	**1.10–1.95**
Children-centred	**1.95***	**1.12–3.39**	0.99	0.35–2.88	1.28	0.95–1.73
Restricted	1.07	0.62–1.84	1.42	0.51–3.95	1.21	0.90–1.62
Age						
65–74 (ref)						
75–84	0.76	0.53–1.09	0.94	0.52–1.69	**0.73****	**0.60–0.88**
85+	**0.56***	**0.34–0.93**	**0.38+**	**0.14–1.04**	**0.58****	**0.42–0.82**
Gender						
Male (ref)						
Female	1.03	0.74–1.44	0.81	0.45–1.43	**1.51****	**1.25–1.82**
Self-reported health						
Excellent/very good (ref)						
Good	1.14	0.61–1.45	0.45	0.14–1.47	**1.43****	**1.16–1.78**
Fair/poor	1.51	0.83–2.74	0.99	0.36–2.76	**2.02****	**1.58–2.57**
NS-SEC						
Professional (ref)						
Intermediate	0.94	0.62–1.45	0.82	0.37–1.81	0.95	0.75–1.19
Routine	**0.70+**	**0.47–1.04**	1.02	0.52–1.98	0.99	0.80–1.24
Wealth quintile						
Lowest (ref)						
2nd	0.75	0.47–1.21	0.69	0.32–1.47	1.04	0.78–1.38
3rd	0.95	0.55–1.46	0.93	0.42–2.02	1.03	0.78–1.38
4th	0.81	0.47–1.40	0.78	0.32–1.90	0.91	0.67–1.24
Highest	1.27	0.70–2.31	**0.24***	**0.06–0.92**	0.89	0.64–1.24
Living arrangements						
With someone (ref)						
Alone	**2.41*****	**1.66–3.51**	0.86	0.45–1.64	**4.24*****	**3.37–4.99**
Number of ADL and IADL difficulties	**1.15*****	**1.06–1.26**	0.90	0.77–1.04	**1.11*****	**1.05–1.18**

Source: Authors' analysis of ELSA (Waves 8 and 9).

Significance levels: + p<=0.1, * p<= 0.05, ** p <=0.01, *** p<=0.001.

in the magnitude of unmet care needs. The latest UK Census data show an overall decrease in the percentage of informal carers in the past decade, but a slightly higher percentage of people who provided intensive care (ONS, 2023). Meanwhile, the significant gap in the social care workforce remains (DHSC, 2021). Population ageing, particularly when the baby boom generations reach older ages after 2030, poses continuing challenges for policy makers in the provision of social care, not least because over a fifth of 'second baby boom generation' women (born in 1961–5) did not have a biological child (Evandrou and Falkingham, 2000).

We distinguished five social network types. Consistent with other studies, age, gender and SEP were linked to different network types (Stephens et al, 2011). As adults age, they may lose their ability to reciprocate instrumental support due to increased health and functional constraints and focus on close family members (Klein Ikkink and van Tilburg, 1999). Women have larger and more diverse networks (Fischer and Beresford, 2014), and people with lower SEP have smaller networks consisting mainly of family members (Antonucci et al, 2013).

Different networks have strengths and limitations vis-à-vis social care (Table 6.2). Diverse networks can meet all domains of care needs. Children-centred networks may meet practical care needs but are limited in meeting personal care demands. Couple-centred networks may meet personal care needs but are limited in meeting practical care needs, partly because such network relationships are embedded in normative expectations and obligations (Wenger, 1997) – spouses are more likely to provide emotional and physical support to the limit of their capacity, adult children to provide emotional support and instrumental help, while friends provide primarily expressive support or short-term emergency help. If there are no children, friends may provide more support. Our results support the social relations theories stressing the importance of multiple relationships and their functional specificity (Kahn and Antonucci, 1980; Carstensen, 1992).

The analysis uncovered that older adults in *Children-centred* or *Couple-centred* networks are relatively disadvantaged compared to those with *Diverse* networks in meeting social care needs over time regardless of their demographic, socioeconomic characteristics and health conditions (Table 6.3). It is widely believed that small dense family-based networks provide the most intensive personal care for the most extended periods, thereby avoiding unmet care needs. Nevertheless, since caregivers themselves are exposed to different stressors (such as other family responsibilities and work), their ability to meet the needs of older relatives may decrease over time (Pearlin et al, 1990). For older spousal carers, the decline in filial co-residence is likely to increase the intensity of care within the household (Beesley, 2006). Previous research found that family-intensive networks were the least supportive of all network configurations (Litwin and Landau, 2000), while the availability of informal care resources may limit opportunities to access formal social services (Fernandez et al, 2015). It is essential not to generalise the findings because country-specific features, such as eligibility rules for social care and individuals' preferences, impact decision-making about care (Bakx et al, 2015).

Interestingly, *Friend-focused* and *Restricted* networks are shown as resilient as *Diverse* networks in terms of minimising persistent unmet needs in all three domains once considering the confounders. Given the significant prevalence (37 per cent) of these two types of networks among older adults, further studies are needed to explore how individuals cope with their social care demands. Some scholars argue that, unlike family ties, friendships result from free choice, facilitating greater autonomy and integration into the wider community (Litwin and Landau, 2000).

Older adults without kin nearby may turn to state or private care services (Saloniki et al, 2019), or their family members living at a distance may reconcile work/other responsibilities to provide informal care (Brimblecombe et al, 2017). A previous study indicated that individuals without a partner are more inclined to use formal care, although regional differences were observed in social networks and formal care utilisation (Fernandez–Carro and Vlachantoni, 2019). The results also revealed that older persons with poor health and those living alone reported persistent unmet needs, even when controlling for the network type, which should concern policy makers.

There are several implications from our analysis. First, the number of informal *and* formal carers will have to increase to reduce unmet needs, which means that good quality social care services, especially personal care, need to be more widely available, accessible and affordable (Brimblecombe et al, 2017). Second, policies will need to provide targeted assistance to vulnerable networks like Children-centred or Couple-centred groups by offering additional caregiving resources, supporting persons to stay at home and be healthy (Carers Trust, 2015). Simultaneously, efforts should enhance social inclusion in diverse networks through intergenerational activities and community engagement. Recognising the resilience of Friend-focused and Restricted social networks, policies also need to explore the factors contributing to such resilience and implement interventions to bolster their ability to meet social care needs effectively. Finally, further research is required on how older adults with different networks, particularly baby boomers, mobilise their social resources to cope with emergent care needs.

This study focuses on social network typology measured at single point of time. While structural indicators like the presence of children, family and friends tend to remain stable over time, functional aspects such as physical and digital contact are dynamic, indicating changing social networks (Steijvers et al, 2022). Reverse causality is a potential issue, as individuals with unmet needs may have smaller social networks, while lonely individuals may lack strong social connections to access services, resulting in unmet needs (Chamberlain et al, 2023). Future research should consider social network changes and address reverse causality concerns.

References

Age UK (2019) *Estimating Need in Older People: Findings for England*, London: Age UK.

Allen, S.M., Piette, E. and Mor, V. (2014) 'The adverse consequences of unmet need among older persons living in the community: dual-eligible versus Medicare-only beneficiaries', *The Journals of Gerontology: Series B*, 69(Suppl 1): S51–8.

Allin, S., Grignon, M. and Le Grand, J. (2010) 'Subjective unmet need and utilization of health care services in Canada: what are the equity implications?' *Social Science & Medicine*, 70(3): 465–72.

Antonucci, T.C., Arjouch, K.J. and Birditt, K.S. (2013) 'The convoy model: explaining social relations from a multidisciplinary perspective', *The Gerontologist*, 54(1): 82–92.

Ayalon, L. and Levkovich, I. (2019) 'A systematic review of research on social networks of older adults', *The Gerontologist*, 59(3): e164–76.

Bakx, P., de Meijer, C., Schut, F. and van Doorslaer, E. (2015) 'Going formal or informal, who cares? The influence of public long-term care insurance', *Health Economics*, 24(6): 631–3.

Banks, J., Batty, G.D., Coughlin, K., Dangerfield, P., Marmot, M., Nazroo, J., et al (2019) 'English Longitudinal Study of Ageing: waves 0–9, 1998–2019', *UK Data Service* [Data collection]. Available from: http://doi.org/10.5255/UKDA-SN-5050-26 [Accessed 1 February 2023].

Beesley, L. (2006) *Informal Care in England*, London: King's Fund.

Brimblecombe, N., Pickard, L., King, D. and Knapp, M. (2017) 'Barriers to receipt of social care services for working carers and the people they care for in times of austerity', *Journal of Social Policy*, 47(2): 215–33.

Carers Trust (2015) *Caring about Older Carers*, London: Carers Trust.

Carstensen, L.L. (1992) 'Social and emotional patterns in adulthood: support for socioemotional selectivity theory', *Psychology and Aging*, 7(3): 331–8.

Chamberlain, S., Savage, R.D., Bronskill, S.E., Griffith, L.E., Rochon, P., Batara, J., et al (2023) 'Retrospective cross-sectional study examining the association between loneliness and unmet healthcare needs among middle-aged and older adults using the Canadian Longitudinal Study of Aging (CLSA)', *BMJ Open*, 13(3): e068769.

DePalma, G., Xu, H., Covinsky, K.E., Craig, B.A., Stallard, E., Thomas, J. III, et al (2012) 'Hospital readmission among older adults who return home with unmet need for ADL disability', *The Gerontologist*, 53(3): 454–61.

DHSC (Department of Health and Social Care) (2021) *The Adult Social Care Market in England*, London: Department of Health and Social Care.

Evandrou, M. and Falkingham, J. (2000) 'Looking back to look forward: lessons from four birth cohorts for ageing in the 21st century', *Population Trends*, 99: 27–36.

Fernandez, J., Snell, T. and Marczak, J. (2015) *An Assessment of the Impact of the Care Act 2014 Eligibility Regulations*, Canterbury: Personal Social Services Research Unit.

Fernandez-Carro, C. and Vlachantoni, A. (2019) 'The role of social networks in using home care by older people across Continental Europe', *Health and Social Care in the Community*, 27(4): 936–52.

Fiori, K.L., Antonucci, T.C. and Cortina, K.S. (2006) 'Social network typologies and mental health among older adults', *The Journals of Gerontology: Series B*, 61(1): 25–32.

Fischer, C.S. and Beresford, L. (2014) 'Changes in support networks in late middle age: the extension of gender and educational differences', *The Journals of Gerontology: Series B*, 70(1): 123–31.

Haskey, J. (2005) 'Living arrangements in contemporary Britain: having a partner who usually lives elsewhere and living apart together (LAT)', *Population Trends*, 122: 35–45.

He, S., Craig, B.A., Xu, H., Covinsky, K.E., Stallard, E., Thomas III, J., et al (2015) 'Unmet need for ADL assistance is associated with mortality among older adults with mild disability', *The Journals of Gerontology: Series A*, 70(9): 1128–32.

Hoff, A. (2015) *Current and Future Challenges of Family Care in the UK*, London: Foresight, UK Government Office for Science.

Irvine, S., Clark, H., Ward, M. and Francis-Devine, B. (2022) *Women and the UK Economy*, London: House of Commons Library.

Ismail, S., Thorlby, R. and Holder, H. (2014) *Focus On: Social Care for Older People*, London: The Health Foundation and Nuffield Trust.

Jagger, C. (2015) *Trends in Life Expectancy and Healthy Life Expectancy: Future of an Ageing Population Project: Evidence Review*, London: Foresight, UK Government Office for Science.

Kahn, R.L. and Antonucci, T.C. (1980) 'Convoys over the life course: attachment, roles, and social support', in P.B. Baltes and O.C. Brim (eds) *Life-span, Development, and Behavior*, New York: Academic Press, pp 254–83.

Klein Ikkink, K. and van Tilburg, T. (1999) 'Broken ties: reciprocity and other factors affecting the termination of older adults' relationships', *Social Networks*, 21(2): 131–46.

Komisar, H.L., Feder, J. and Kasper, J.D. (2005) 'Unmet long-term care needs: an analysis of Medicare-Medicaid dual eligibles', *Inquiry*, 42(2): 171–82.

Kröger, T. (2022) *Care Poverty: When Older People's Needs Remain Unmet*, Cham: Palgrave Macmillan.

Litwin, H. and Landau, R. (2000) 'Social network type and social support among the old-old', *Journal of Aging Studies*, 14(20): 213–28.

Litwin, H., Vogel, C., Kunemund, H. and Kohli, M. (2008) 'The balance of intergenerational exchange: correlates of net transfers in Germany and Israel', *European Journal of Ageing*, 5(2): 91–102.

Macdonald, M., Kulakiewicz, A. and Library Specialists (2021) *Tackling Loneliness*, London: House of Commons Library.

Maplethorpe, N., Darton, R. and Wittenberg, R. (2015) 'Social care: need for and receipt of help', *Health and Social Care Information Centre*. Available from: http://healthsurvey.hscic.gov.uk/media/33548/HSE2014-Ch5-Soc ial-care-need-and-receipt.pdf [Accessed 20 January 2023].

ONS (Office for National Statistics) (2023) 'Unpaid care, England and Wales: census 2021', *Office for National Statistics*. Available from: https:// www.ons.gov.uk/peoplepopulationandcommunity/healthandsocialcare/ healthandwellbeing/bulletins/unpaidcareenglandandwales/census2021 [Accessed 20 January 2023].

Pearlin, L.I., Mullan, J.T., Semple, S.J. and Skaff, M.N. (1990) 'Caregiving and the stress process: an overview of concepts and their measures', *The Gerontologist*, 30(5): 583–91.

Pickard, L. (2015) 'A growing care gap? The supply of unpaid care for older people by their adult children in England to 2032', *Ageing & Society*, 35(1): 96–123.

Public Health England (2019) *A Consensus on Healthy Ageing*, London: Public Health England.

Saloniki, E., Nizalova, O., Malisauskaite, G. and Forder, J. (2019) *The Impact of Formal Care on Informal Care for People over 75 in England*, Canterbury: Personal Social Services Research Unit.

Steijvers, L.C., Brinkhues, S., Tilburg, T.G.V., Hoebe, C.J., Stijnen, M.M., Vries, N., et al (2022) 'Changes in structure and function of social networks of independently living middle-aged and older adults in diverse sociodemographic subgroups during the COVID-19 pandemic: a longitudinal study', *BMC Public Health*, 22(1): Article 2253.

Stephens, C., Alpass, F., Towers, A. and Stevenson, B. (2011) 'The effects of types of social networks, perceived social support, and loneliness on the health of older people: accounting for the social context', *Journal of Aging and Health*, 23(6): 887–911.

Vlachantoni, A. (2019) 'Unmet need for social care among older people', *Ageing & Society*, 39(4): 657–84.

Vlachantoni, A., Shaw, R., Willis, R., Evandrou, M., Falkingham, J. and Luff, R. (2011) 'Measuring unmet need for social care amongst older people', *Population Trends*, 145: 60–76.

Vlachantoni, A., Shaw, R.J., Evandrou, M. and Falkingham, J. (2015) 'The determinants of receiving social care in later life in England', *Ageing & Society*, 35(2): 321–45.

Vlachantoni, A., Evandrou, M., Falkingham, J. and Qin, M. (2024) 'Dynamics of unmet need for social care in England', *Ageing & Society*, 44(6): 1247–65.

Wenger, G.C. (1991) 'A network typology: from theory to practice', *Journal of Aging Studies*, 5(2): 147–62.

Wenger, G.C. (1997) 'Social networks and the prediction of elderly people at risk', *Aging & Mental Health*, 1(4): 311–20.

WHO (World Health Organization) (2020) *Decade of Healthy Ageing: Baseline Report*, Geneva: World Health Organization.

Xu, H.P., Covinsky, K.E., Stallard, E., Thomas, J. III and Sands, L.P. (2012) 'Insufficient help for activity of daily living disabilities and risk of all-cause hospitalization', *Journal of the American Geriatrics Society*, 60(5): 927–33.

7

Care poverty and sources of care: formal services, informal care or a combination

Jiby Mathew Puthenparambil, Lina Van Aerschot and Teppo Kröger

Introduction

With the changes in health that old age brings, and a diminishing ability to do certain things, come increasing demands for care (for example, Sandberg et al, 2012; Døhl et al, 2016). Care needs can be met formally (through public, private or third sector care services), informally (via a spouse, children, in-laws, family or friends), or through any combination of these; yet all forms of support depend not only on their affordability and accessibility, but also whether such services are even available. In some cases, it might be the kind of welfare state an older person lives in that is more likely to shape the way they use formal care, while in others it is more likely to depend on family or friends willing and able to provide informal care. Combining both formal and informal forms of support becomes more common as care needs increase.

In Finland, older people are entitled to public care based on a needs assessment (Social Welfare Act 2014). Public services for older people in their own home focus on health-related needs and personal care and also provide support with daily activities like laundry, meals-on-wheels or transportation. Residential care is only available for the frailest; a recent study showed that most older people now going into residential care in Finland are more impaired and in worse health than before (Korhonen et al, 2023). Public authorities also provide support for informal – usually family – carers to provide care at home (FIHW, 2023).

Social care services for older people in Finland have undergone significant changes in recent decades, due to a number of factors that include stricter targeting and marketisation (see Kröger, 2019; Rostgaard et al, 2022). Targeting involves allocating public services more specifically to older people with intensive care needs by tightening the eligibility criteria. Needs-tested publicly funded care services are currently targeted at those older people that have particular physical or cognitive impairments and, in most cases, personal care needs, also known as Activities of Daily Living (ADLs). Older people with a need for help with other, more practical tasks – also known as Instrumental Activities of Daily Living (IADLs) – have to either purchase the services from the private market or receive care informally.

Although family members in Finland are not legally obliged to provide or pay for the care of older people, informal care does play a very important part (Verbakel, 2018; Eurocarers, 2023). Many older people with personal care needs receive a mixture of both publicly provided home care services and informal care, but the greater proportion is informal (Finne-Soveri et al, 2014). The tightening of criteria used in needs-testing has increased the importance of informal care and led to a situation in which care policies are predicated on the assumption that practical (IADL) assistance will be provided by informal carers together with social and emotional support (Kröger, 2019; Rostgaard et al, 2022). Informal care is encouraged by state support (Act on Support for Informal Care 2005), formalised through a commission agreement between public authorities, the older person and the caregiver that ensures a caregiver allowance, leave and additional assistance. However, such support is available only for caregivers who provide intensive continuous care. In a comparative study across 19 European countries, Verbakel (2018) found that Finland has the highest percentage of informal caregivers (44 per cent) providing care for older people – primarily offering support for less intensive care needs.

Older people frequently have difficulties getting their care needs met, often because they are complex, and also because care support may not be available, accessible or affordable (Brimblecombe et al, 2017; Vlachantoni, 2019; Kröger, 2022; Rostgaard et al, 2022). Not all older people have family or other informal networks willing or able to care for them; eligibility to public services (at least in the Finnish context) is complicated by the strict needs-assessment process; and using private services is often out of the question if people have low incomes (Mathew Puthenparambil, 2019).

People who find themselves ineligible for public services, with no informal care network available and unable to afford private care, thus risk being in the situation of not having all their care needs met – also known as 'care poverty'. Care poverty is a 'situation where, as a result of both individual and structural issues, people in need of care do not receive sufficient assistance from informal or formal sources, and thus have care needs that remain uncovered' (Kröger et al, 2019). In his book on the subject, Kröger (2022) looks extensively at the various individual and societal factors that affect care poverty among older people. Like others (LaPlante et al, 2004; Allin and Masseria, 2009; Casado et al, 2011), he notes that these unmet care needs can be attributed to insufficient quality of care or mismatched services (Kröger, 2022). Factors such as long waiting lists, being denied treatment or services due to stricter eligibility criteria, and bureaucratic red tape, not to mention the shortage of long-term care workers, may also increase the risk of care poverty occurring.

To better understand how care poverty arises, we need to look more closely at how older people arrange care for themselves – often from more than one source – and to what extent their care needs remain unmet. In this chapter, we thus ask:

1. whether older people get their care from formal care services, informal care or a combination of both;
2. the extent to which care poverty is present within each of these three user groups; and
3. what the individual and societal factors may be that contribute to care poverty in each user group.

By analysing data collected from a survey in Finland, we hope to better identify how care poverty has developed among service users and broaden our understanding of how older people's unmet care needs differ according to individual requirements and the availability of different kinds of care and support.

Individual and societal factors contributing to care poverty

We consider there to be three dimensions to the individual and societal factors contributing to care poverty among older people (Vlachantoni et al, 2015; Kröger, 2022). These are:

1. the individual's health and functional status;
2. their socio-demographic background; and
3. their access to care.

Taken together, these dimensions will determine an individual's care needs, the care services they use and the extent to which care poverty is present (Figure 7.1).

Perhaps the most essential dimension to understanding the extent of care poverty among old people is their *health and functional status* (Kröger et al, 2019; Vlachantoni, 2019; Aaltonen and Van Aerschot, 2021). These impact the level, amount, type and source of the care support received (Blomgren et al, 2008; Sandberg et al, 2012; Sigurdardottir and Kåreholt, 2014; Døhl et al, 2016). With age, the increasing likelihood of developing a chronic health condition, having severe impairments or experiencing functional limitations will mean older people's care needs inevitably multiply (Blomgren et al, 2008; Sandberg et al, 2012; Døhl et al, 2016). An individual's health

Figure 7.1: Framework for care poverty and sources of care

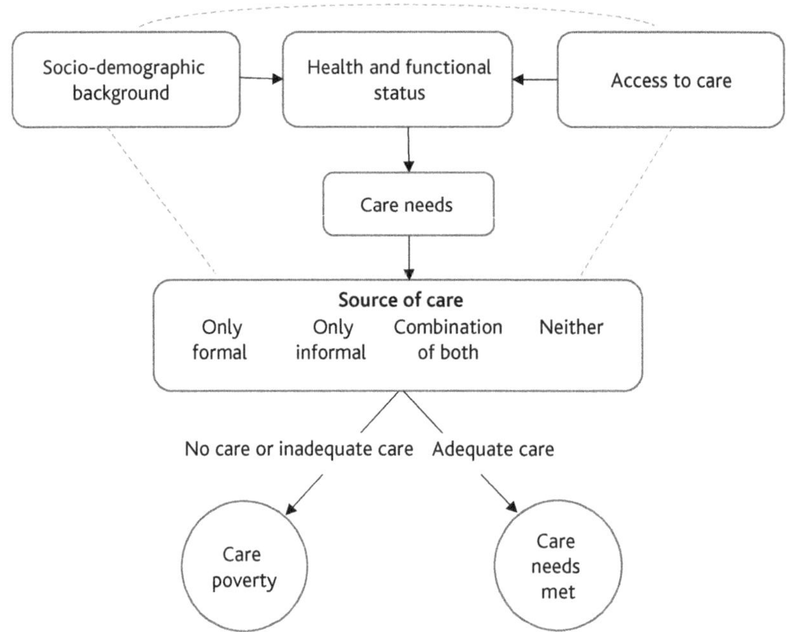

and functional status will also be influenced by the other two dimensions of their socioeconomic background and their access to care (for example, Matthews et al, 2005; Darin-Mattsson et al, 2017).

The *socio-demographic dimension* takes into account the background characteristics of individuals, such as their gender, age, level of education and household income (Figure 7.1) as these have been found to play a crucial role in shaping where care resources come from and how they are used (Blomgren et al, 2008; Sigurdardottir and Kåreholt, 2014; Døhl et al, 2016; Enroth et al, 2018; Chang et al, 2019; Brändström et al, 2022).

Finally, '*access to care*' refers to living arrangements (living alone or with someone), the area of residence, informal networks outside the household, and the affordability of care services. Each factor may play a role in determining whether individuals can access and use care resources (Geerlings et al, 2005; Sigurdardottir and Kåreholt, 2014; Døhl et al, 2016) and consequently whether some care needs go unmet. For example, an older person may be living alone without adequate social support or they may be living in a rural area with limited access to services. Finding adequate support may thus result from any number of factors linked to geographic location, cultural and social practices or a lack of financial resources to cover care costs when necessary (Eichler and Pfau-Effinger, 2009; Szebehely and Trydegård, 2012).

All three of the aforementioned dimensions – health and functional status, socio-demographic background, and access to care – are interconnected and together determine an older person's care needs, their access to care services and how they will use different sources of care. However, when any care needs are left unmet, it can lead to care poverty.

Data and methods

The research questions were examined using a nationwide survey dataset called DACO (Daily Life and Care in Old Age, or *Arki, apu ja palvelut* in Finnish). The survey was conducted between October and December 2020 among older people aged 75 or over living in their own homes or service housing across Finland.[1] Before this chapter (and Chapter 11 of this volume), findings from the 2020 wave of the survey have been reported in only one article (Chou et al, 2024). Results from previous (2010 and 2015) waves of the survey have been published earlier (see, for example, Kröger et al, 2019).

A survey questionnaire with a letter of informed consent was sent out to a sample of 6,000 participants, randomly chosen from the Finnish Digital and Population Data Agency and representing the age group from all parts of Finland. The consent letter described why data was being collected, assured recipients that the data would be anonymous, and informed them of their participation rights. In addition, we also included a pre-paid postage envelope to return the filled questionnaire. We received back 2,150 filled questionnaires in the first round of the survey, and after sending out a reminder to those who had not responded, a further 1,129 filled questionnaires came back to us. This meant that a total of 3,279 filled questionnaires were received back, so the overall response rate was 55 per cent. Most of the respondents were female (58 per cent) and many were living alone (42 per cent). The respondents' average age was 81 years (ranging from 75 to 103), and most lived in their own homes (96 per cent).

With our focus on care poverty, we asked the participants about the steps they were taking to manage their personal (ADL) and practical (IADL) care needs. The questionnaire had five items focusing on ADLs: *bathing, getting dressed, eating, getting into and out of bed*, and *using the toilet*. Meanwhile there were ten items covering IADLs: *cleaning, cooking, moving around inside the home, moving around outside the home, getting home help and other services, grocery shopping, managing bank affairs, minor home repairs and gardening, taking medication* and *transportation*. For each of the items, respondents could choose one of three responses:

1. I can cope without difficulty (which is equivalent to not having needs);
2. I do not cope by myself but I get enough help; and
3. I do not cope by myself and I need more help.

For the purposes of this chapter, the third option was taken to mean the care need was not being met.

As the focus of this chapter is on care poverty, we have only included those respondents (n=2,049) who chose the second or the third option for at least one daily activity – in other words, those who reported having care needs. We then categorised the source of care support for older people into three groups:

1. those using only formal care services;
2. those receiving only informal care; and
3. those receiving a combination of both.

The fourth group of respondents receiving neither formal nor informal support ('neither' in Figure 7.1) was excluded from the analysis because they were so few (n=5).

For the dimension of health and functional status, we used self-reported indicators to describe participants' overall health (good/fair or poor); long-term illness or impairment (none/one or several); the frequency of care received; and the number of care needs (Table 7.1). The frequency of care received served as a proxy variable and was measured dichotomously as either less frequently (monthly or less) or more frequently (daily or weekly). There were four variables in the socio-demographic dimension (Figure 7.1): gender was classified as male or female; age as 75–84 years or 85–105 years; education level as with a vocational/higher education or no vocational education; and household income as sufficient or insufficient/barely enough for essential needs.

There were also four variables in the access to care dimension. The first two were (1) living arrangements (alone or shared) and (2) area of residence (a larger city of 100,000 or more residents, including suburbs; a mid-sized town of 20,000–100,000 residents; or a rural area/small town of under 20,000 residents). The other two variables were (3) contact with an informal network, such as someone outside the respondent's household (on an occasional [monthly/less frequently] basis or frequent [daily/weekly] basis); and (4) affordability of user fees for public or private services (affordable or unaffordable). The aim was to see how these four dimensions – and the way they may interact – affect care poverty across the different service user groups.

We employed descriptive statistics, the Chi-Square test, and binary logistic regression to investigate the research questions. However, because the number of respondents who received only formal care was so small, we decided to drop the idea of using multinomial regression. Consequently, we decided to analyse each group separately with binary logistic regression. This resulted in us conducting three models of analysis using logistic regression for:

Table 7.1: Sources of care among participants according to background (column percentage, N=2,049)

	Total respondents in the study (N=2,049)	Source of care			P-values
		Formal care only (n=38)	Informal care only (n=1,026)	Combination (n=829)	
Sociodemographic background					
Gender					
Female	67.4	68.4	68.1	67.2	0.913
Male	32.6	31.6	31.9	32.8	
Age					
75–84 years	69.2	71.1	79.1	57.1	<0.001
85–105 years	30.8	28.9	20.9	42.9	
Education					
With vocational/higher	67.9	63.9	69.2	67.8	0.683
No vocational/higher	32.1	36.1	30.8	32.2	
Household income					
Sufficient	73.7	77.1	74.5	73.2	0.746
Insufficient/barely enough income for essential needs	26.3	22.9	25.5	26.8	
Health and functional status					
Health status					
Good/fair	80.7	81.6	85.4	73.2	<0.001
Poor	19.3	18.4	14.6	26.8	
Long-term illness or disability					
None/one	57.1	58.8	64.4	44.6	<0.001
Several	42.9	41.2	35.6	55.4	
Frequency of care received					
Less frequently	24.7	57.9	20.9	13.9	<0.001
More frequently	75.3	42.1	79.1	86.1	
Number of care needs					
1–3	59.8	73.7	70.8	40.9	<0.001
4–6	18.5	7.9	18.0	22.0	
6 or more	21.7	18.4	11.2	37.2	
Access to care					

(continued)

Table 7.1: Sources of care among participants according to background (column percentage, N=2,049) (continued)

	Total respondents in the study (N=2,049)	Source of care			P-values
		Formal care only (n=38)	Informal care only (n=1,026)	Combination (n=829)	
Living arrangements					
Alone	47.7	71.1	42.0	55.0	<0.001
Shared	52.3	28.9	58.0	45.0	
Area of residence					
Larger city/suburbs	31.4	44.7	29.5	32.2	0.021
Mid-sized city/town	36.0	28.9	39.6	33.2	
Smaller town/rural	32.6	26.3	30.9	34.6	
Contact with informal network					
Occasionally	8.0	23.7	6.1	7.4	<0.001
Frequently	92.0	76.3	93.9	92.6	
Affordability of user fees					
Unaffordable	21.5	18.4	22.5	22.0	
Affordable	78.5	81.6	77.5	78.0	0.818

Source: Authors' analysis of the DACO survey data.

1. met and unmet practical (IADL) care needs among users of informal care only;
2. met and unmet practical (IADL) care needs among combination users; and
3. met and unmet personal (ADL) care needs among combination users.

We refrained from analysing the unmet care needs of those receiving only formal care, and the personal care needs of those receiving only informal care due to the insufficient number of responses in either group. Prior to analysis, we assessed variables for multicollinearity using the collinearity diagnostics test. The result showed that the Variance Inflation Factor (VIF) fell within the range of 1–2, indicating the absence of collinearity issues in the model. The analyses were performed using IBM-SPSS 26.

Background of the respondents

Out of the total respondents in the study (N=2,049), the most were female (67.4 per cent), aged 75–84 years old (69.2 per cent) and had a vocational or higher education (67.9 per cent) (Table 7.1). Furthermore, a significant proportion of them reported having a sufficient income (73.7 per cent). Most also saw themselves as having good overall health and functional abilities and receiving care frequently (75.3 per cent). An equal number of respondents reported living alone or with someone else and respondents were equally spread between larger urban, mid-sized and smaller urban/rural settlements. Furthermore, most respondents (92 per cent) had regular informal contact with people outside their households.

When utilising different sources of care, older people who lived alone in larger cities or suburbs mainly used formal care. Those who were using a combination of formal and informal care were more likely to report poor health, multiple long-term illnesses or impairments and more care needs, and this group received more frequent care than the other two groups. Combination users and those who received informal care only also had more frequent contact with their informal network than those relying solely on formal care. All variables related to health status and access to care (except affordability of user fees) showed a statistically significant relationship with different sources of care (p<0.05). However, among the socio-demographic background variables, only age demonstrated a statistically significant result (p<0.05).

Care poverty among different user groups

Most respondents reported having practical (IADL) care needs (n=1,891) whereas a smaller proportion reported personal (ADL) care needs (n=347) (Figure 7.2). About 2.2 per cent (n=44) reported unmet personal care needs, while 17.6 per cent (n=361) reported unmet practical care needs. Only a small number of respondents with care needs (2 per cent; n=38) rely exclusively on formal care. Very few people (n=6) in this group reported

Figure 7.2: Met and unmet personal and practical care needs in different user groups (%)

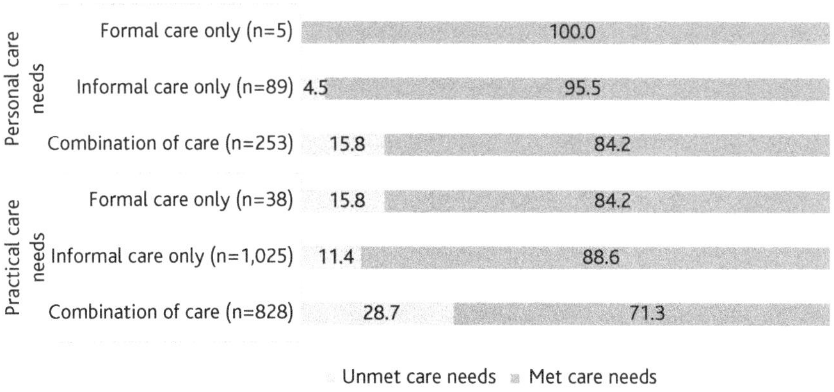

having unmet practical care needs and none had unmet personal care needs. Older people using a combination of care sources had the highest percentage (15.8 per cent) of unmet personal care needs (n=40) and the highest percentage (28.7 per cent) of unmet practical care needs (n=238), while the group with the highest percentage of practical care needs being met (88.6 per cent) was the group relying on informal care only – indicating that most people rely on informal care for help with IADLs. It is also worth noting that all those with personal care needs also reported having practical care needs, which would suggest that the total number of people with care needs (met or unmet across the different user groups) will be largely reflected in the figures for practical care needs.

We calculated care poverty rates for each user group in the form of a ratio representing the percentage of those with a particular care need who did not receive enough help to have that care need met. This follows the logic of measuring 'the share of those with unmet needs among those with long-term care needs' (Kröger et al, 2019: 490). Respondents in the user group of those receiving only informal care had the highest personal care poverty rates when it came to eating (16.7 per cent), getting into and out of bed (11.1 per cent) and using the toilet (8.0 per cent) (Table 7.2). With regard to practical care needs, the highest care poverty rates were for getting home help services (17.2 per cent), transportation (13.6 per cent) and moving around inside the home (11.1 per cent). In total, 8.7 per cent of this group had at least one unmet personal care need and the situation was rather the same for their unmet practical care needs (9.4 per cent).

In the group of those that received care from a combination of sources, the care poverty rate in personal care needs was highest for bathing (13.1 per cent), while in practical care needs, the highest care poverty rate was for moving around outside (28.7 per cent) and the lowest was for taking medications (10 per cent). Overall, 9.3 per cent of the combination group had at least one unmet personal care need and 16.2 per cent had at least one unmet practical care need. Notably, those in the combination group had substantially higher care poverty rates than those receiving only informal care in almost all practical care needs. We were not able to work out the care poverty rates for those receiving only formal care due to the small number of responses (n=6).

Logistic regression analysis of unmet care needs across the different groups showed that among those in the combination care user group, insufficient income (OR=3.51; p=<0.05) and poor health (OR=2.92; p=<0.05) were the only variables that significantly corresponded to unmet personal care needs (Table 7.3). However, when it came to predicting unmet practical care needs, insufficient income, poor health and number of care needs were significant (p=<0.05) in both the combination and informal-only user groups. This implies that older people with an inadequate income, poor health, and a greater number of care needs are more likely to experience

Table 7.2: Rates of care poverty for particular care needs within the different care user groups

	Formal care only (n=38) %	Informal care only (n=1,026) %	Combination (n=829) %
Personal care poverty			
Bathing	<1	3.8	13.1
Eating	<1	16.7	8.5
Getting into and out of bed	<1	11.1	8.1
Using the toilet	<1	8.0	9.4
Dressing	<1	4.0	7.6
Total	**<1**	**8.7**	**9.3**
Practical care poverty			
Transportation	<1	13.6	25.5
Moving around inside home	<1	11.1	12.3
Moving around outside home	<1	9.4	28.7
Grocery shopping	<1	6.3	10.7
Getting home help and other services	9.1	17.2	14.7
Managing bank affairs	<1	3.5	10.1
Small home repairs and gardening	13.8	8.3	19.1
Cleaning	7.4	10.4	16.6
Cooking	<1	4.9	14.4
Taking medications	<1	8.9	10.0
Total	**3.0**	**9.4**	**16.2**

Source: Authors' analysis of the DACO survey data.

practical care poverty, regardless of whether they combine both formal and informal care or rely purely on informal care alone.

Among those receiving only informal care, living alone and having less frequent informal contact increased the odds of practical care needs going unmet. In the combination group, unaffordable user fees (OR=1.75; p=<0.05) and frequency of care demonstrated significant results. Finally, across all groups, both unmet personal and practical care needs were found to correspond with poorer health and a greater number of care needs.

Discussion

The main focus of this chapter was to gain a deeper understanding of care poverty among older people, particularly when they rely on different sources

Table 7.3: Binary logistic regression: unmet care needs among different care user groups

	Practical care needs				Personal care needs	
	Unmet among receivers of informal care only (Ref: met care needs, n=893)		Unmet among receivers of combination care (Ref: met care needs, n=716)		Unmet among receivers of combination care (Ref: met care needs, n=214)	
	OR	95% CI	OR	95% CI	OR	95% CI
Socio-demographic background						
Male (Ref: female)	0.74	0.42–1.29	0.94	0.61–1.46	1.46	0.58–3.68
85–105 years (Ref: 75–84 years)	1.21	0.68–2.15	0.90	0.59–1.37	1.93	0.79–4.71
No vocational education (Ref: vocational/higher education)	0.70	0.41–1.18	0.70	0.45–1.08	1.39	0.60–3.21
Insufficient or barely enough income for essential needs (Ref: sufficient income)	1.90	1.13–3.20*	2.11	1.39–3.22**	3.51	1.51–8.16**
Health and functional status						
Poor health (Ref: good or fair health)	2.44	1.43–4.15**	2.46	1.60–3.78***	2.92	1.23–6.98**
Several long-term illnesses or disabilities (Ref: no/one illness)	2.09	1.24–3.51**	1.18	0.76–1.83	1.09	0.40–2.93
Frequency of care: more frequently (Ref: less frequently)	1.26	0.61–2.59	0.42	0.21–0.86*	(a)	(a)
4–6 care needs (Ref: <4 care needs)	3.50	1.96–6.25***	4.48	2.36–8.53***	(a)	(a)
6 or more care needs (Ref: <4 care needs)	6.35	3.26–12.4***	10.51	5.54–19.97***	(a)	(a)
Access to care						
Living with someone (Ref: living alone)	0.42	0.24–0.73**	0.96	0.62–1.48	1.18	0.47–2.93
Midsized city/town (Ref: larger city/suburbs)	0.63	0.35–1.13	0.73	0.45–1.19	0.94	0.35–2.57
Smaller urban area, town or rural area (Ref: larger city/suburbs)	0.89	0.5–1.60	0.79	0.49–1.27	1.02	0.37–2.77
More frequent contact outside household (Ref: less frequent)	0.34	0.15–0.76**	0.71	0.34–1.46	(a)	(a)
User fees unaffordable (Ref: affordable)	1.43	0.84–2.44	1.75	1.11–2.77*	0.88	0.36–2.16

Source: Authors' analysis of the DACO survey data. Significance levels: ***p<=0001, **p<=00.1, *p<=0.5; All models have Omnibus test <0.05; Homser and Lemeshow test >0.05. (a) Excluded because there were less than five responses in a cell.

of care. Among the participants with care needs (N=2,049), approximately 2.2 per cent reported personal care needs going unmet, and 17.6 per cent reported unmet practical care needs (Figure 7.2). This is in line with findings from a previous study conducted in two Finnish cities (Kröger et al, 2019) and would seem to indicate that unmet care needs among Finnish older people have remained relatively consistent. Furthermore, only a small percentage (n=38; <2 per cent) relied exclusively on formal care services and, remarkably, this group reported having all their personal care needs met. Nevertheless, caution is needed when drawing conclusions from this due to the small sample size.

Older people who require a high level of personal care often rely on a complex network of both informal and – where possible – formal support. When it comes to practical care needs, however, informal care seems to play a predominant role. Turning towards informal care for one's practical needs is not surprising, given that these needs tend to be less demanding and can be managed with less frequent support. Another contributing factor is that such care is nowadays only very rarely available from formal public services in Finland. The result corresponds with findings elsewhere (Sigurdardottir and Kåreholt, 2014; Vlachantoni et al, 2015; Chang et al, 2019), which indicate that older people turn to different sources of support according to the level of care required.

One interesting finding to emerge from this chapter, which holds true across all user groups, is that a poorer status of health and a greater number of care needs correspond with both personal and practical care needs not being met. Previous research has also demonstrated the close relationship between income and care poverty (for example, Kröger et al, 2019; Vlachantoni, 2019). The cost of care poses a considerable challenge for lower-income older people. Without sufficient formal public services, those from lower economic backgrounds face difficulties in covering the expenses which their personal and practical care otherwise require. Furthermore, even with public support, lower-income groups often struggle to afford the user fees for the services (Ilmarinen et al, 2024).

The affordability of services plays a pivotal role in determining people's access to care. We observed that those who considered user fees to be unaffordable in the combination care group were more likely to experience unmet care needs. Interestingly, however, we found no association between user fees and unmet personal care needs. In the Finnish context, the public sector no longer meets the practical care needs of older people, and they need to pay for care services offered by private for-profit providers (Mathew Puthenparambil, 2019) or use informal support. Unlike the less well-off, those older people with sufficient income are better positioned to afford services from private providers, often with tax reductions, which can even make them more affordable than paying the user fees for public services.

Yet it is disconcerting to observe that unmet care needs persist even among those using a combination of formal and informal sources of care. Formal and informal care may not be direct substitutes, especially for those with higher needs (Bonsang, 2009). Furthermore, inadequacies in the quantity or quality of care, as well as issues related to accessibility or affordability of services, may also be contributing factors.

The results from the regression analysis (Table 7.3) support some of these assumptions. Older people relying on a combination of formal and informal care, particularly those with less money and in poorer health, are clearly more likely to suffer from care poverty. Due to limited data regarding personal care needs, the results of this chapter primarily address the issue of unmet practical care needs. While several studies have focused on this subject, only a few have looked at the impact of these practical needs going unmet, even though practical care clearly has a very real impact on the everyday well-being of older people (see, however, Chapter 8). Both Allen et al (2014) and Beach et al (2018), for instance, conclude that when older people cannot get help with cleaning or with moving around when they are out, or with grocery shopping, their quality of life is seriously compromised.

In this study, six of our respondents with care needs reported not using any services at all – whether formal or informal – while approximately 150 others gave no information at all about how they received care. Consequently, we had to exclude them all from our analysis. Moreover, it became necessary to recategorise almost all independent variables to optimise the regression analysis. By recoding the categories, we could then increase the statistical power of our study as larger samples were obtained within each category. Although this helped simplify our interpretation of the results, we acknowledge that this approach may have resulted in losing finer distinctions captured by the original categories.

Furthermore, this study lacked adequate representation of participants with personal care needs, as most participants were healthy and required minimal care. This implies a potential exclusion of people with poor health and impairment from the sample pool (non-response rate was 45 per cent). Additionally, some respondents may have misidentified their care needs or responded inaccurately. Notably, approximately 9 per cent reported significant memory issues and around 6 per cent of responses were completed by someone else, which may have affected the accuracy of some responses. Since the data were collected during the COVID-19 pandemic, movement restrictions in Finland may have impacted older people's access to care services.

In a nutshell, the majority of older people with personal care needs use a combination of both formal and informal care, while those with practical care needs generally make do with just informal care. In most cases, however, even when older people receive care from a combination of formal and informal sources, this user group is the most likely to have unmet care needs.

Note

1   The survey and the writing of this chapter were funded by the Centre of Excellence in Research on Ageing and Care (CoE AgeCare), financed by the Research Council of Finland (grant no. 352735). CoE AgeCare also supported the Open Access publication of this book.

References

Aaltonen, M.S. and Van Aerschot, L.H. (2021) 'Unmet care needs are common among community-dwelling older people with memory problems in Finland', *Scandinavian Journal of Public Health*, 49(4): 423–32.

Allen, S.M., Piette, E.R. and Mor, V. (2014) 'The adverse consequences of unmet need among older persons living in the community: dual-eligible versus Medicare-only beneficiaries', *The Journals of Gerontology: Series B*, 69(Supplement 1): S51–8.

Allin, S. and Masseria, C. (2009) 'Unmet need as an indicator of health care access', *Eurohealth*, 15(3): 7–9.

Beach, S.R., Schulz, R., Friedman, E.M., Rodakowski, J., Martsolf, R.G. and James, A.E. (2018) 'Adverse consequences of unmet needs for care in high-need/high-cost older adults', *The Journals of Gerontology: Series B*, 75(2): 459–70.

Blomgren, J., Martikainen, P., Martelin, T. and Koskinen, S. (2008) 'Determinants of home-based formal help in community-dwelling older people in Finland', *European Journal of Ageing*, 5(4): 335–47.

Bonsang, E. (2009) 'Does informal care from children to their elderly parents substitute for formal care in Europe?', *Journal of Health Economics*, 28(1): 143–54.

Brändström, A., Meyer, A.C., Modig, K. and Sandström G. (2022) 'Determinants of home care utilization among the Swedish old: nationwide register-based study', *European Journal of Ageing*, 19(3): 651–62.

Brimblecombe, N., Pickard, L., King, D. and Knapp, M. (2017) 'Perceptions of unmet needs for community social care services in England: a comparison of working carers and the people they care for', *Health and Social Care in the Community*, 25(2): 435–46.

Casado, B.L., Van Vulpen, K.S. and Davis, S.L. (2011) 'Unmet needs for home and community-based services among frail older Americans and their caregivers', *Journal of Aging and Health*, 23(3): 529–53.

Chang, M., Geirsdottir, O.G., Sigurdarsdottir, S.H., Kåreholt, I. and Ramel, A. (2019) 'Associations between education and need for care among community dwelling older adults in Iceland', *Scandinavian Journal of Caring Sciences*, 33(4): 885–91.

Chou, Y.-C., Mathew Puthenparambil, J., Kröger, T. and Pu, C. (2024) 'Multidimensional care poverty among East Asian and Nordic older adults', *Innovation in Aging*, 8(9): igae076.

Darin-Mattsson, A., Fors, S. and Kåreholt, I. (2017) 'Different indicators of socioeconomic status and their relative importance as determinants of health in old age', *International Journal for Equity in Health*, 16: Article 173.

Døhl, Ø., Garåsen, H., Kalseth, J. and Magnussen, J. (2016) 'Factors associated with the amount of public home care received by elderly and intellectually disabled individuals in a large Norwegian municipality', *Health and Social Care in the Community*, 24(3): 297–308.

Eichler, M. and Pfau-Effinger, B. (2009) 'The "Consumer Principle" in the care of elderly people: free choice and actual choice in the German welfare state', *Social Policy & Administration*, 43(6): 617–33.

Enroth, L., Aaltonen, M., Raitanen, J., Nosraty, L. and Jylhä, M. (2018) 'Does use of long-term care differ between occupational classes among the oldest old? Vitality 90 + Study', *European Journal of Ageing*, 15(2): 143–53.

Eurocarers (2023) 'Finland', *Eurocarers*, 2 March [Country profiles]. Available from: https://eurocarers.org/country-profiles/finland/ [Accessed 19 October 2023].

FIHW (Finnish Institute for Health and Welfare) (2023) 'Informal care and adult foster care', *Finnish Institute for Health and Welfare*. Available from: https://thl.fi/en/web/ageing/older-people-services-undergoing-a-change/informal-care-and-adult-foster-care [Accessed 20 October 2023].

Finne-Soveri, H., Heikkilä, R., Mäkelä, M., Asikainen, J., Vilkko, A., Andersson, S., et al (2014) 'Mitä on huomioitava vanhusten laitoshoitoa vähennettäessä' [What needs to be taken into account when decreasing residential care for older people], in A. Noro and H. Alastalo (eds) *Vanhuspalvelulain 980/2012 toimeenpanon seuranta: tilanne ennen lain voimaantuloa vuonna 2013* [Monitoring the Implementation of the Act 980/2012 on Services for Older People: Situation before the Act Entered into Force in 2013], Helsinki: Terveyden ja hyvinvoinnin laitos, pp 56–70.

Geerlings, S.W., Margriet Pot, A., Twisk, J.W.R. and Deeg, D.J.H. (2005) 'Predicting transitions in the use of informal and professional care by older adults', *Ageing & Society*, 25(1): 111–30.

Ilmarinen, K., Van Aerschot, L. and Kröger, T. (2024) 'Not free at all: home care user fees in a Nordic care system', *Social Policy and Society*, 23(3): 513–28.

Korhonen, K., Moustgaard, H., Murphy, M. and Martikainen, P. (2023) 'Why is care use declining? Changes in residential long-term care between 1999 and 2018 in Finland', *European Journal of Public Health*, 33(Supplement_2): ckad160.671.

Kröger, T. (2019) 'Looking for the easy way out: demographic panic and the twists and turns of long-term care policy in Finland', in T.K. Jing, S. Kuhnle, Y. Pan and S. Chen (eds) *Aging Welfare and Social Policy: International Perspectives on Aging*, Cham: Springer, pp 91–104.

Kröger, T. (2022) *Care Poverty: When Older People's Needs Remain Unmet*, Cham: Palgrave Macmillan.

Kröger, T., Mathew Puthenparambil, J. and Van Aerschot, L. (2019) 'Care poverty: unmet care needs in a Nordic welfare state', *International Journal of Care and Caring*, 3(4): 485–500.

LaPlante, M.P., Kaye, H.S., Kang, T. and Harrington, C. (2004) 'Unmet need for personal assistance services: estimating the shortfall in hours of help and adverse consequences', *The Journals of Gerontology: Series B*, 59(2): S98–108.

Mathew Puthenparambil, J. (2019) *Marketisation of Care Within the Nordic Context: Private Care Provision for Older People in Finland*, Jyväskylä: University of Jyväskylä.

Matthews, R.J., Smith, L.K., Hancock, R.M., Jagger, C. and Spiers, N.A. (2005) 'Socioeconomic factors associated with the onset of disability in older age: a longitudinal study of people aged 75 years and over', *Social Science & Medicine*, 61(7): 1567–75.

Rostgaard, T., Jacobsen, F., Kröger, T. and Peterson, E. (2022) 'Revisiting the Nordic long-term care model for older people: still equal?', *European Journal of Ageing*, 19(2): 201–10.

Sandberg, M., Kristensson, J., Midlöv, P., Fagerström, C. and Jakobsson, U. (2012) 'Prevalence and predictors of healthcare utilization among older people (60+): focusing on ADL dependency and risk of depression', *Archives of Gerontology and Geriatrics*, 54(3): e349–63.

Sigurdardottir, S.H. and Kåreholt, I. (2014) 'Informal and formal care of older people in Iceland', *Scandinavian Journal of Caring Sciences*, 28(4): 802–11.

Szebehely, M. and Trydegård, G.-B. (2012) 'Home care for older people in Sweden: a universal model in transition', *Health and Social Care in the Community*, 20(3): 300–9.

Verbakel, E. (2018) 'How to understand informal caregiving patterns in Europe? The role of formal long-term care provisions and family care norms', *Scandinavian Journal of Public Health*, 46(4): 436–47.

Vlachantoni, A. (2019) 'Unmet need for social care among older people', *Ageing & Society*, 39(4): 657–84.

Vlachantoni, A., Shaw, R., Evandrou, M. and Falkingham, J. (2015) 'The determinants of receiving social care in later life in England', *Ageing & Society*, 35(2): 321–45.

8

Unmet need and care poverty: new patterns of distribution in Danish home care for older people

Tine Rostgaard

Introduction

In the Nordic countries, long-term care for older people is often said to constitute a perfect example of the 'public service model' (Anttonen and Sipilä, 1996). This partly refers to the main responsibility for the organisation, provision and financing of care lying with the public sector, largely the local authorities. Universalism is another defining feature of this model (Anttonen et al, 2012), with access to benefits being based on citizenship rather than contributions or merit. In the case of long-term care services, access is also dependent on need. A final characteristic of the Nordic public service model, as argued by Vabø and Szebehely (2012), is that care services are attractive, affordable and flexible so as to meet diverse needs and preferences, explaining why they are generally used across social class divides with no stigma associated. In other words, there is a shared cultural and political understanding of the importance of sufficiently meeting the needs of the older population.

As an example, home care for frail older people in Denmark is free of charge and has long been generously awarded. During its heyday in the 1990s, personal care and/or cleaning services were provided for up to one fifth of the population aged 65 and above (Rostgaard and Fridberg, 1998). Worldwide, Denmark was one of the first countries to redirect away from institutional long-term care in favour of providing extensive home care, thus enabling a policy of 'ageing in place'. However, more recently, the coverage rate for home care has dropped considerably, providing for 11 per cent of the 65+ population in 2020 (Rostgaard et al, 2022).

This chapter investigates possible causes of this fall in coverage, specifically, examining whether it can be explained by factors such as healthy ageing and the recent introduction of reablement. Or, by contrast, whether it indicates a development towards a targeted approach to needs assessment and service allocation, prioritising those with highest need. To this end, the first analytical section investigates policy changes in assessment for and allocation of home care in reference to national registry data. Following which, survey data is used to investigate this shift in recipients of home care, controlling for changes in individual characteristics. It also explores whether the decline in home care is accompanied by differences in the help provided from other sources, such as family or privately purchased help. Finally, the chapter discusses the possible consequences of unmet needs, and eventually care poverty.

Method

The analysis is based on high-quality registry and survey data. Registry data are collected annually by Statistics Denmark and are based on national, population-based registers. The survey data are from the Danish Longitudinal Study of Ageing (DLSA), a nationally representative longitudinal survey. This survey is designed as a prospective cohort study and includes around 10,000 respondents aged 52 and above, sampled among all individuals residing in Denmark. Data have been collected every five years since 1997, mainly by telephone. In 1997, the oldest cohort was 77 years old and, in 2017, 97 years. There is a high response rate (74.5 per cent in 2007 and 67.3 per cent in 2017) but, as is the case in most surveys, the most vulnerable in the population may be under-represented. The 20-year attrition rate is high, with 28.6 per cent of baseline respondents participating in the 2017 survey (Kjær et al, 2019). This chapter uses survey data from 2007 and 2017, includes the 67–87 age group and analyses the data from a cross-sectional perspective. The chapter also utilises register data of income and educational level.

Included in the analysis are respondents who live at home and are defined as being frail according to Shanas' validated index of functional ability in daily activities (Shanas et al, 1968; Shanas, 1972). The index measures ability to independently conduct three Activities of Daily Living (ADLs): cutting toenails, washing/bathing and dressing/undressing; and four Instrumental Activities of Daily Living (IADLs): climbing stairs, walking outdoors, walking around indoors and shopping/carrying groceries home. The analysis only includes respondents who say they are unable to perform one or more of these tasks without help. Such individuals are considered, to varying degrees, to need help and assistance in daily activities. The activities are related to physical mobility and may therefore not capture social, cognitive or physiological incapacity, unless such conditions result in the inability to carry out daily activities; for example, dementia may limit the person in organising shopping and so on. A summed index with values 0–7 is applied, according to the number of limitations, and respondents are classified into two groups: those with one functional limitation (slight limitation) and those with two or more functional limitations (more severe limitations).

Using the index measures, our initial analysis of the data reveals a larger proportion of older people in the 67–87 age group that have had no functional limitations in recent years, from 80.2 per cent in 2007 to 85.3 per cent in 2017. There is also a declining share that have two or more functional limitations, from 9.1 per cent in 2007 to 4.6 per cent in 2017, which means that, over time, fewer older people have experienced moderate to severe functional limitations. This decline in functional limitations could be caused by the small decline in response rates over time, as persons with functional limitations are generally less likely to participate in surveys. The proportion with less severe limitations (those with only one functional limitation) remains stable, at 10.8 per cent in 2007 and 10.2 per cent in 2017. In the following, the analysis includes only the two groups in the survey who have either one or two or more functional limitations (n=829 in 2007 and n=713 in 2017).

The analysis of formal home care use applies a number of variables to control for development over the years within this sub-population, such as the aforementioned functional limitations, as well as gender, marital status, education, income, whether the person has children, and whether they live alone or with others. The analysis is focused on formal home care assistance with *practical tasks* only, as it is not possible to compare the home care provision of *personal care* over time, due to a change in the way questions have been asked in the survey. Practical tasks cover daily household tasks, such as cleaning, laundry, shopping and/or cooking, which are all components of free home care services in Denmark.

Unmet needs and care poverty – conceptual notions

The understanding of unmet needs in the chapter is inspired by the definition set out by Williams et al (1997: 102): 'unmet need occurs in long-term care when a person has disabilities for which help is needed, but is unavailable or insufficient'. This includes all sources of help, formal as well as informal, and refers to the person's subjective assessment of need, and whether such needs are met with the current form of help and assistance.

In this chapter, unmet needs are operationalised as respondents having stated in the survey that they are unable to independently perform one or more daily activity, and also having stated that no one helps with these activities, whether family or other sources, such as municipal home care. Therefore, the concept of unmet need is based on a subjective understanding of needs and whether assistance is provided. In its binary form, the concept can be argued to be conservative as it does not consider cases where help and assistance is indeed provided but perhaps in an insufficient manner. In this way, this application of the concept differs slightly from the approach of Williams et al (1997).

Also, the individual phenomenon of unmet need is seen in relation to long-term care policies. This allows us to apply the theoretical framework of care poverty, defined as inadequate coverage of care needs, stemming from an interplay between individual and societal factors (Kröger et al, 2019; Kröger, 2022). The operationalisation of the concept of care poverty thus combines the micro and macro levels, as it sees individual experience in light of the (changing) policy context.

As well as policies, it can be said that cultural setting is another important part of societal structures (Pfau-Effinger, 2005), in that the culture of care may influence the actual understanding of what constitutes needs, how these are best met, and when are they considered to be (in)adequately met. Cultures of care are embedded in the whole complex of values, institutional traditions and institutional practices of the welfare state and to which relevant actors refer, explicitly or more implicitly (Pfau-Effinger, 2005). In the case of the welfare arrangements in the Nordic countries, this would include generalised principles of universalism, generosity and mediating in inequalities between gender and social classes. As such, cultures of care may frame the norms, obligations and expectations at the societal level which will modify the individual evaluation of the impact of policies.

Therefore, the application of the concept of care poverty assesses the outcome of long-term care policies seen from the individual perspective but situated in a particular policy and cultural setting that influences which resources should be available and whether these are considered adequate for meeting individual needs.

A pioneer in de-institutionalisation and active home care

To understand the particular cultural and policy setting that shapes the expectations for meeting needs, it should be noted that Denmark was among the first countries worldwide to introduce home care as a policy of de-institutionalisation in long-term care for older people (WHO, 2019). This policy was introduced in the early 1970s and favoured care in the home over care in an institution. Since then, policy priority has been providing (free) home care so that many older people who wish to remain in their own homes can do so, as well as providing a more cost-efficient alternative to institutional care. Home care covers the need for personal care, practical assistance and, in later years, medical needs.

This development towards de-institutionalisation in long-term care for older people was strongly influenced by various reports from the National Commission on Ageing in the 1980s, which recommended active care that could facilitate self-care (*hjælp-til-selvhjælp*) in old age, and in this way encourage a more preventive and rehabilitative approach (Boll Hansen et al, 1991; Rostgaard, 2007). The Commission reports also introduced principles of continuity and normalisation. This meant that, regardless of need, the provision of care should aim at ensuring the continuation of the older person's preferred way of living and ensure that they could remain in their own home for as long as possible (*længst muligt i eget hjem*), which became a popular slogan for de-institutionalisation.

A Home Care Commission in 2013 established that active care, or more precisely, reablement, was the preferred way forward for designing home care intervention. This was presented as an alternative to the traditional home care approach, which was seen to be passive and offered no opportunities for engaging the user (Social– og Integrationsministeriet, 2013). Reablement implies a focused, short-term multidisciplinary intervention in the home, often by a team of social care workers and occupational therapists, with the aim of increasing functional ability in everyday activities, and is based on the older person's goals. It focuses on changing daily routines of living, home modifications, using assistive devices and improving functional ability through individualised physical exercises. In essence, it is a way of providing active care with the long-term aim of making the person less or entirely independent of care (Aspinal et al, 2016; Rostgaard et al, 2023).

Since 2007, more and more Danish municipalities have introduced reablement, making Denmark one of the pioneers in the world. Since 2015, it has been part of the legislation, obliging all municipalities to first consider whether the older person has so-called potential for reablement, requiring the person to be motivated and willing to change daily routines. Traditional home care services are offered only if the older person is not able or willing to participate in reablement or does not regain physical capacity.

Changes in need assessment and service allocation

The de-institutionalisation policy stands strong even today in Denmark and care at home continues to be favoured as the first policy response. There is a legal right to be assessed within a reasonable period of time, and entitlement to both home care and a nursing home place is based entirely on need; and, in the case of reablement, on the aforementioned willingness to engage in a transformative intervention.

The home care service includes help with housekeeping and personal care. These may be IADL tasks, such as cleaning, laundering, bed making, meal preparation and shopping, but it may also entail various ADL tasks, such as assistance with using the toilet, dressing, bathing and hair combing. A person in need of care is entitled to receive home care, irrespective of their age, financial means, income or family situation. As such, long-term care remains an individualised and universal care service, as traditionally portrayed in the literature on the Nordic care model (Anttonen et al, 2012; Vabø and Szebehely, 2012). Nonetheless, with the ageing of the population, there are

Figure 8.1: Older persons (80+) living in a nursing home or receiving home care in Denmark, 2008–22

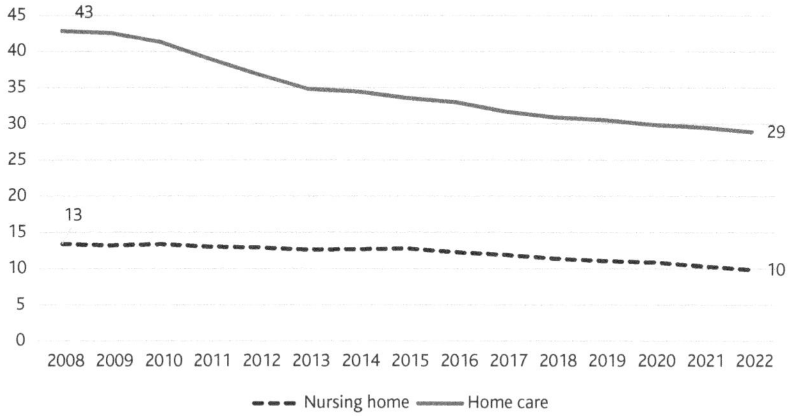

Source: NOSOSCO (2024); Statistics Denmark (nd).

indications that the principles behind assessment for and allocation of home care have changed over time in Danish municipalities, with prioritisation and targeting as the result.

First, there has been a substantial reduction in both the number of home care recipients as well as their share of the older population since 2008, despite a general increase in the older population during the same period. Figure 8.1 presents the change in the proportion receiving home care: 29 per cent of older people aged 80+ received home care services in 2020 compared to 43 per cent in 2008. Meanwhile, the proportion of older people living in institutional care has not increased to compensate for this decline; rather, this figure has also dropped slightly from 13 to 10 per cent in the same period. Second, a change is seen in those who receive home care and how much support is given. The number of people aged 65 and above in the population in receipt of practical care or a combination of practical care and personal care has declined by 34,000 since 2007, while the number of persons receiving personal care has remained stable (not shown in figure) (Rostgaard and Matthiessen, 2019). Taken together, this means that the overall proportion of people receiving home care has declined, especially in relation to practical care (such as cleaning the home). There is also a considerable decline in the average number of hours delivered (Rostgaard and Mathiessen, 2019; Houlberg and Foged, 2023). This is not a nationally formulated strategy but has been applied locally as a means of coping with rising demand. As a result, it is usual to receive help with domestic tasks only fortnightly or only every third week and often only for half an hour (Houlberg and Foged, 2023).

Third, the organisation and provision of home care has changed fundamentally since the introduction of reablement in 2015. In 2017, 3.6

per cent of people aged 65 and above received a reablement intervention according to registry data. However, there is no systematic documentation of precisely what these reablement interventions entailed, nor of the outcomes. A few local evaluations have been conducted, at times as a comparison across municipalities (for example, Petersen et al, 2017), but not as randomised or case-controlled designs (for information on the international evidence on outcomes of reablement, see Rostgaard et al, 2023). If reablement is successful, one would expect the need for home care to be reduced as functional ability improves in the target population, which would explain the drop in home care. Likewise, a general improvement in frailty as part of healthy ageing could also contribute to explaining the changes in the use of home care.

In line with this, the common understanding and national and local policy explanation for the decline in use of home care, as described earlier, has been that need has changed due to healthier ageing and the introduction of reablement, which has caused an accommodation of daily routines and resulted in less frailty.

There is indeed some indication of healthy ageing, as described earlier in the chapter, where the survey data support a tendency for the older population to maintain their independence in daily activities. However, there are other indications with more mixed support for the healthy ageing argument. This includes a drop in healthy life years for the population aged 65 and above in Denmark during 2010–18 (European Commission, 2021). This is in line with the international literature, where there is evidence for compression of morbidity and a reduction in severe disability (Lindgren, 2016), but also for the increase in functional limitations as we age (Heger and Kolodziej, 2016).

An indication that the changes in the provision of home care, or long-term care more generally, have not followed the needs of the ageing society, or at least the expectation in the general population on how needs should be met, is to be found in a recent Organisation for Economic Co-operation and Development survey (OECD, 2021). Here, Denmark comes out as the least worried country with regards to social risks overall. However, the risk that concerns Danes the most is not being able to access quality long-term care services for older family members. In all, 43.3 per cent of respondents report this concern. This concern corresponds well with how Danes typically prioritise long-term care for older people in surveys running up to local elections, and in competition with other municipal policy areas. It is only in recent years that climate change has been more important to local voters. Prior to the election in 2021, 56 per cent cited climate change as the most important local policy issue, compared to 36 per cent who prioritised long-term care (Rostgaard, 2023). In this way, we see a persistent cultural understanding of the importance of sufficiently meeting the needs of the older population, as well as a worry that needs are not being met.

Recalibration of Danish home care?

The following analysis of the survey data will first investigate whether the changes in use of home care for practical tasks reflect a recalibration of the Danish home care system, rather than an outcome of less frailty or healthy ageing.

Table 8.1 presents change over time in the number of frail older people receiving assistance with practical tasks from various sources (those aged 67–87 that identify as having at least one functional limitation). The proportion of frail older people receiving home care in the survey has in the period 2007–17 been reduced from 43 to 25 per cent (Table 8.1), while there has been no significant change in the assistance from other sources in the period. That is, around one in five of frail older people in the sample have received assistance with practical tasks from a spouse or partner and/ or children and other family members. Around one in ten have purchased private help, and around 3 per cent have received help from friends and/ or acquaintances.

Overall, the change is to be found only in the proportion of frail older people who receive assistance from public home care, while help from other sources has remained stable. The decline in home care for practical tasks is in accordance with the development shown in Figure 8.1 and could be an indication of healthy ageing and therefore an ageing population with less need for care (although a decline in other sources of care could be expected also).

A separate analysis of the full sample (not shown here), including those who are not categorised as 'frail' (that is, with no functional limitation) and looking at changes in the background variables, confirms that some

Table 8.1: Proportion of frail older people (67–87 years) receiving assistance with practical tasks from various sources, 2007 and 2017 (%)

	2007	2017
Home care	42.82	24.62***
Spouse/partner	17.01	18.27
Children/other family	16.77	13.48
Friends/acquaintances	3.15	3.46
Privately purchased help	8.69	11.62
N	829	713

Note: T-tests have been conducted to test significance between 2017 and 2017: *<0.05, **<0.01, ***<0.001. The figures are based on all frail older people (67–87 years) in the sample with at least one functional limitation. It is possible to receive help and assistance from more than one source and the percentages do not sum to 100.

Source: DLSA.

Table 8.2: Logistic regression estimating the difference in likelihood for receiving home care for practical assistance among frail older people (67–87 years) from a given source of help, 2017 compared to 2007 (odds ratio)

	Home care	Spouse/ partner	Children/ other family	Friends/ acquain- tances	Privately purchased assistance
Development 2007–2017	0.49***	1.12	0.95	1.30	1.18

Note: Logistic regression for frail older people with at least one functional limitation. N=1,530. Controlled for changes in age, gender, education, income, children, living alone. Not controlled for spouse/partner as there is complete correlation with living alone. Odds ratios 2007 and 2017 and t-test: *<0.05, **<0.01, ***<0.001.

Source: DLSA.

healthy ageing has taken place in the general population in this age group since 2007. Most importantly, since 2007, fewer respondents have severe functional limitations (2+) and more often share a household with others who may assist them. As this may influence the results, a regression analysis is conducted, here controlling for all changes in background variables.

The regression analysis shows that the odds ratio for receiving home care has dropped from 1.00 to 0.49 between 2007 and 2017 when controlling for change in background characteristics (Table 8.2). Parallel to this, there has been no significant change in the odds ratio for receiving assistance with practical tasks from either a spouse/partner, children/other family, friends/acquaintances, and nor was there any change in the odds ratio for purchasing private care.

If these were shown in percentages, this is the equivalent to a likelihood of 36 per cent in 2007 for a frail older person to receive home care with practical tasks, and 25 per cent in 2017; that is, a reduction of 11 percentage points when controlling for all changes in the background variables (Figure 8.2). Figure 8.2 also shows the likelihood in percentage for receiving practical assistance from other sources of help. Only the change over time in home care is significant.

Targeting towards the most vulnerable

There are patterns in these changes that suggest targeting at the most vulnerable (those with two or more functional limitations). From a separate analysis, over time, this group has a higher likelihood of receiving home care for practical tasks. However, even among this group, there is a reduced likelihood of receiving practical home care (51 per cent received home care in 2007 compared to 43 per cent in 2017). In comparison, among those with one functional limitation, 31 per cent received home care in 2007 and 16 per cent in 2017.

Figure 8.2: Likelihood for receiving practical assistance for frail older people (67–87 years) from various sources, 2007 and 2017

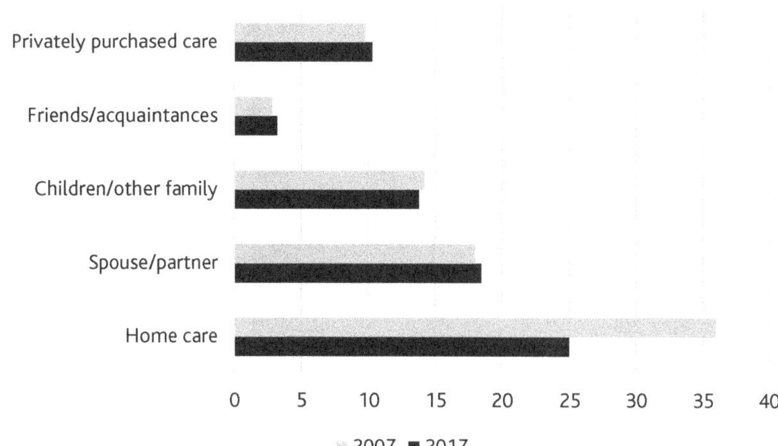

Additionally, there is an increased likelihood for those in the lowest income bracket to receive assistance from a spouse/partner, even though they are less likely overall to have a spouse/partner than those in the other income brackets. For those in the higher income brackets, the strategy used to compensate for the fall in public home care seems to be the purchase of private, for-profit home care. Among those in the third income quartile, the proportion that purchases private care thus increased from 5 per cent in 2007 to 10 per cent in 2017. In the fourth quartile, one fifth (20–21 per cent) purchased such assistance.

Combinations of sources of assistance

The following analysis looks further at how frail older people combine assistance from various sources. This is illustrated in Figure 8.3, looking separately at those who have only one functional limitation and those who have two or more. All possible combinations of sources of assistance are included but only those combinations that appear most frequently in the dataset are named. Across both years and levels of functional limitation, the most likely and sole source of assistance is home care from the municipality, but the drop in the proportion of frail older people receiving practical assistance from the municipality is apparent. Otherwise, a relatively large proportion of frail older people report that they receive assistance only from their spouse/partner. In contrast to the change in home care, there are no apparent (nor significant) changes in the proportions of frail older people who receive care from spouse/partner or (combinations of) other sources.

Figure 8.3: Share of frail older people (67–87 years) receiving specific combinations of assistance with practical tasks in 2007 and 2017

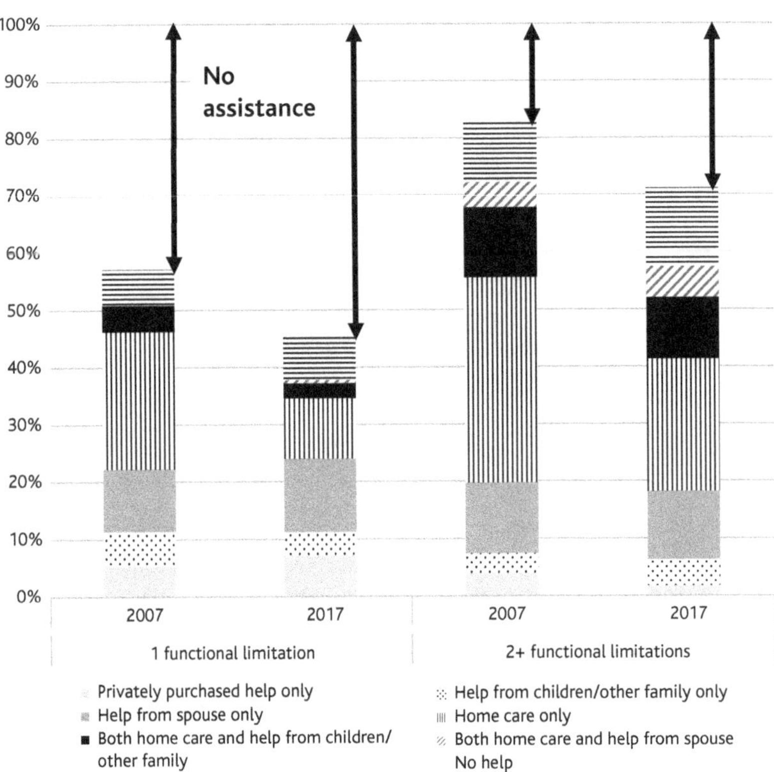

Increase in proportion of frail older people without assistance

What is apparent, however, is the increase in the proportion of frail older people who have no one to assist them, as indicated in Figure 8.3 by the arrows (and in the columns reducing in size over time). For frail older people with one functional limitation, there is an increase in the proportion who report that they receive no assistance from 43 per cent in 2007 to 54 per cent in 2017. For the most frail (the group with two or more functional limitations), the proportion with no assistance increases from 17 per cent in 2017 to 29 per cent in 2017.

The change may again be explained by a development in background characteristics. In Table 8.3, the change in odds ratios for not receiving assistance with practical tasks is shown, controlling for such a development. As indicated, the risk of not receiving assistance is 1.72 times higher in 2017 than in 2007. Recalculated into percentages, this is the equivalent of 35 per cent in 2007 and 47 per cent in 2017. The probability of frail older people not receiving assistance with practical tasks has thus risen by 12 percentage points.

Table 8.3: Logistic regression estimating the difference over time among frail older people (67–87 years) for not receiving assistance from one single source or combinations of sources of help, 2017 compared to 2007 (odds ratio)

	No assistance
Development 2007–2017	1.72***

Note: Logistic regression for frail older people with one or more functional limitation. Controlled for all background variables. Comparison of odds ratios based on a t-test: *<0.05, **<0.01, ***<0.001. N=1,530.

Source: DLSA.

Further analysis suggests that the change in likelihood of not receiving assistance has occurred across the whole sub-population of frail older people, and thus regardless of differences in age, income, and so on. However, some subgroups are at particular risk. The probability of being without assistance thus increases more for men over time than women (from 30 per cent in 2017 to 53 per cent in 2017). Also, frail older people of higher educational background experience a particular increase (from 25 per cent to 46 per cent).

Unmet need

The analysis so far has shown a decline in the likelihood of receiving home care, and no apparent substitution from other sources, resulting in a larger proportion of frail older people without assistance. The question remains as to whether this corresponds to actual unmet needs. A final focus for the analysis is therefore whether the respondents find that they have unmet needs. In this case, the data allows for looking at everyday chores related to both ADLs and IADLs. The respondents include both those that indicate receiving assistance from home care, family or others, and those who indicate that they receive no assistance. Table 8.4 shows the proportion of frail older people indicating they need (more) assistance according to level of functional limitations.

Overall, and regardless of the level of functional limitation, the IADL task for which respondents most often report an unmet need is heavy cleaning, which includes hoovering, washing the floor and similar strenuous tasks (14 per cent among those with one functional limitation and 20 per cent among those with two or more limitations). Some respondents also indicate unmet need in the preparation of meals (7 per cent and 6 per cent) and shopping, especially among respondents with higher needs (1 per cent and 6 per cent). This corresponds to earlier findings showing the declining likelihood of receiving practical care. However, unmet need is also found in ADL chores, such as showering and bathing. Again, this is more often among those with two or more functional limitations (1 per cent and 4 per cent).

Table 8.4: Proportion of frail older people with 1 and 2+ functional limitations indicating need for (more) assistance in daily activities in 2017 (%)

	1 functional limitation	2+ functional limitations
Preparing meals	6.45	5.67
Heavy cleaning	14.05	19.58
Shopping	0.91	5.55**
Laundry	1.50	3.97
Going outdoor	0.41	3.41
Climbing stairs	1.51	1.83
Walking around indoor	0.17	0.96
Showering/bathing	0.86	3.99**
Getting dressed	0.38	1.29

Note: T-test for difference between levels of functional limitations: *<0.05, **<0.01, ***<0.001. N=1,530.

Source: DLSA.

Conclusion

The analysis in this chapter suggests a fundamental recalibration in the distribution of home care within Denmark in recent decades. For those who are frail and unable to carry out one or more daily activities without assistance (15 per cent of the 65+ population in 2017), there is a clear and significant change in the ways that they receive assistance with daily activities. Controlling for changes in background characteristics, there is a considerable reduction in the likelihood of receiving home care for practical tasks, which cannot be explained solely by healthy ageing or by the success of reablement.

This recalibration of home care means that there is a substantial increase in the proportion of frail older persons who have no one to help them. Today, more than half of those with mild functional limitations, and one in three of those with more severe functional limitations, indicate that they receive no assistance. The likelihood of receiving assistance from family and friends has not changed, while support from public home care is significantly lower today, resulting in unmet needs. These unmet needs concern ADL as well as IADL tasks, and especially help with heavy cleaning. This development particularly affects men, who are more often without home care or support from others, indicating a new vulnerable group. And, overall, there are patterns of social inequality, as those with economic means increasingly appear to compensate by purchasing care on the private market, while those with lower incomes rely on their partner.

It is also noteworthy that these changes have taken place in a cultural setting where long-term care for older people continues to have high priority among voters, and where there is a concern in the population for the inadequacy of provision of care. The changes have also taken place in a policy setting where the political discourse, at least at the national level, continues to support the generous provision of assistance for frail older people, and where there have been no national reforms advocating changes in assessment and allocation of home care. This suggests a transformation by stealth, as witnessed in other Nordic countries (for example, Kröger and Leinonen, 2012), where fundamental changes have taken place at the local level. As such, this is not on the basis of political ideology but on an inability to let resources follow the ageing of the population.

All in all, our results show an inadequate coverage of care needs, stemming from an interplay between individual and societal factors, where local political priorities clash with a generalised cultural understanding of how needs are best met. It indicates a substantial change with implications for the core elements of the public service model, in regard to generosity and universalism. The results also suggest that there is reason to discuss the extent of the phenomenon of care poverty and the inequalities it entails.

References

Anttonen, A. and Sipilä, J. (1996) 'European social care services: is it possible to identify models?', *Journal of European Social Policy*, 6(2): 87–100.

Anttonen, A., Häikiö, L., Stefansson, K. and Sipilä, J. (2012) 'Universalism and the challenge of diversity', in A. Anttonen, L. Häikiö and K. Stefánsson (eds) *Welfare State, Universalism and Diversity*, Cheltenham: Edward Elgar, pp 1–15.

Aspinal, F., Glasby, J., Rostgaard, T., Tuntland, H. and Westendorp, R.G. (2016) 'New horizons: reablement – supporting older people towards independence', *Age and Ageing*, 45(5): 574–8.

Boll Hansen, E., Jordal-Jørgensen, J. and Kock, A. (1991) *Fra plejehjem til hjemmepleje* [From Care Homes to Home Care], København: Amterne og Kommunernes Forskningsinstitut.

European Commission (2021) *The 2021 Ageing Report: Economic & Budgetary Projections for the EU Member States (2019–2070)*, Brussels: Publications Office.

Heger, D. and Kolodziej, I.W.K. (2016) *Changes in Morbidity over Time: Evidence from Europe*, Dortmund: University of Duisburg-Essen.

Houlberg, K. and Foged, S.K. (2023) 'Færre hjemmehjælpstimer til ældre, især uden for hovedstadsområdet' [Fewer home help hours for older people, especially outside the metropolitan area], *VIVE*. Available from: https://www.vive.dk/da/udgivelser/faerre-hjemmehjaelpstimer-til-aeldre-isaer-uden-for-hovedstadsomraadet-yz25k0z1/ [Accessed 15 February 2024].

Kjær, A.A., Siren, A., Seestedt, M.H., Fridberg, T. and Casier, F. (2019) 'Cohort profile: the Danish Longitudinal Study of Ageing (DLSA)', *International Journal of Epidemiology*, 48(4): 1050–50g.

Kröger, T. (2022) *Care Poverty: When Older People's Needs Remain Unmet*, Cham: Palgrave Macmillan.

Kröger, T. and Leinonen, A. (2012) 'Transformation by stealth: the retargeting of home care services in Finland', *Health and Social Care in the Community*, 20(3): 319–27.

Kröger, T., Mathew Puthenparambil, J. and Van Aerschot, L. (2019) 'Care poverty: unmet care needs in a Nordic welfare state', *International Journal of Care and Caring*, 3(4): 485–500.

Lindgren, B. (2016) 'The rise in life expectancy, health trends among the elderly, and the demand for care: a selected literature review', *National Bureau of Economic Research*. Available from: https://doi.org/10.3386/w22 521 [Accessed 15 February 2024].

NOSOSCO (Nordic Social Statistical Committee) (2024) 'Services to elderly people', *Nordic Health and Welfare Statistics*, 26 February. Available from: https://nhwstat.org/welfare/old-age/services-elderly-people/servi ces-elderly-people [Accessed 28 February 2024].

OECD (Organisation for Economic Co-operation and Development) (2021) *Main Findings from the 2020 Risks that Matter Survey*, Paris: OECD.

Petersen, A., Graff, L., Rostgaard, T., Kjellberg, J. and Kjellberg, P.K. (2017) *Rehabilitering på ældreområdet: Hvad fortæller danske undersøgelser os om kommunernes arbejde med rehabilitering i hjemmeplejen?* [Reablement for Older People: What do Danish Studies Tell Us about Municipalities' Work with Reablement in Home Care?], København: KORA.

Pfau-Effinger, B. (2005) 'Culture and welfare state policies: reflections on a complex interrelation', *Journal of Social Policy*, 34(1): 3–20.

Rostgaard, T. (2007) *Begreber om kvalitet i ældreplejen: Temaer, roller og relationer* [Concepts of Quality in Care for Older People: Themes, Roles and Relationships], København: SFI.

Rostgaard, T. (2023) 'Ældreplejen i en brydningstid: justering eller egentlig krise?' [Care for older people in a time of change: adjustment or actual crisis?], *Økonomi & Politik*, 96(3): 28–45.

Rostgaard, T. and Fridberg, T. (1998) *Caring for Children and Older People: A Comparison of European Policies and Practices*, Copenhagen: The Danish National Institute of Social Research.

Rostgaard, T. and Matthiessen, M.U. (2019) 'Hjælp til svage ældre' [Help for frail elderly people], *VIVE*. Available from: https://www.vive.dk/da/udg ivelser/hjaelp-til-svage-aeldre-lxmb05vd/ [Accessed 15 February 2024].

Rostgaard, T., Jacobsen, F., Kröger, T. and Peterson, E. (2022) 'Revisiting the Nordic long-term care model for older people: still equal?', *European Journal of Ageing*, 19(2): 201–10.

Rostgaard, T., Parsons, J. and Tuntland, H. (eds) (2023) *Reablement in Long-term Care for Older People: International Perspectives and Future Directions*, Bristol: Policy Press.

Shanas, E. (1972) 'Health status of older people: cross-national implications', *American Journal of Public Health*, 64(3): 261–4.

Shanas, E., Townsend, P., Wedderburn, D., Friis, H., Milhøj, P. and Stehouwer, J. (1968) *Old People in Three Industrial Societies*, New York: Atherton Press.

Social- og Integrationsministeriet (2013) *Rapport fra Hjemmehjælpskommissionen* [*Report from the Home Care Commission*], København: Social- og Integrationsministeriet.

Statistics Denmark (nd) Statistikbanken [Bank of statistics], *Statistics Denmark*. Available from: https://www.statistikbanken.dk/statbank5a/default.asp?w= 1920 [Accessed 15 February 2024].

Vabø, M. and Szebehely, M. (2012) 'A caring state for all older people?', in A. Anttonen, L. Häikiö and K. Stefánsson (eds) *Welfare State, Universalism and Diversity*, Cheltenham: Edward Elgar, pp 121–43.

WHO (World Health Organization) (2019) *Denmark: Country Case Study on the Integrated Delivery of Long-term Care*, Copenhagen: World Health Organization.

Williams, J., Lyons, B. and Rowland, D. (1997) 'Unmet long-term care needs of elderly people in the community: a review of the literature', *Home Health Care Services Quarterly*, 16(1–2): 93–119.

9

Pathways to and through caring: family care, socioeconomic differences and care poverty

Tjaša Potočnik, Maša Filipovič Hrast,
Miriam Hurtado Monarres and Valentina Hlebec

Introduction

Informal caregiving represents a bulk of caregiving across different care regimes (Leitner, 2003; Saraceno, 2016). It is most prevalent in socioeconomically disadvantaged households, often indicating a lack of other resources to meet the needs of older people (Carmichael and Ercolani, 2016; Rodrigues et al, 2018; Quashie et al, 2022). Furthermore, research emphasises that (especially intensive) caregiving can also negatively affect caregivers' health, well-being and social participation (Roth et al, 2015; Carmichael and Ercolani, 2016). Care, therefore, has a specific cost for the caregiver in terms of time, labour market participation, investment in non-caring segments of life, family relationships and emotional well-being (see Daly and Lewis, 2000). It is important to observe how potentially disproportionally this cost is divided within society and how social policy and the availability of formal care provisions shape these inequalities.

Care poverty is an expression of unequal outcomes of social policy, an insufficient level of care services and inadequate resources or opportunities in terms of organising care (Kröger et al, 2019; Kröger, 2022). In this chapter we will use *the relative approach to care poverty*, which is based on self-reported unmet needs and encompasses situations in which formal or/and informal care that the older adult receives is inadequate or insufficient (Kröger, 2022). Looking at informal caregivers of older people who combine informal care with formal home care services, we are interested in how the socioeconomic status (SES) of the caregiving dyad shapes family carers' pathways to care (how they assume the caregiving role) and through care (how they navigate caring obligations in everyday life), and its consequences for family carers in terms of choices, well-being and (unmet) needs.

Prevalence and consequences of relative care poverty are likely to be unevenly distributed among care dyads, particularly across those of different SES. Addressing the issue of social inequality in pathways to and through informal family caregiving is therefore of crucial importance for understanding the process that can lead to care poverty, as it identifies individual and contextual factors that increase/decrease the risk of relative care poverty (Kröger, 2022).

In Chapter 7 it was emphasised that older people combining formal and informal care turned out to have considerable unmet needs in terms of both personal and practical care. This chapter aims for a deeper understanding of processes and situations that can lead to unmet needs in informal–formal care arrangements. Therefore, in this chapter we will observe the institutional and social policy context of Slovenia and how it frames the care choices of care dyads concerning their use of formal and informal care, with specific attention to socioeconomic differences.

Socioeconomic inequalities, unmet needs and care poverty

In the past years, studies of the association between SES and caregiving focused predominantly on the relationship between, on the one hand, quality of life of either older people or informal caregivers and, on the other hand, different socioeconomic determinants/measures of SES, such as education (Rodrigues et al, 2022), income and wealth (Rodrigues et al, 2018), employment (Carmichael and Ercolani, 2016; Van Houtven et al, 2013) as well as gender (Daly, 2020). Recently, life-course scholars (Fast et al, 2021) have stressed the importance of studying family care from a life-course perspective.

As research has shown, SES is an important factor when care is negotiated, thus transitions into caregiving may result from a cumulative process of advantages or disadvantages (Crystal et al, 2017). Given that low SES is a risk factor for poorer health (Roth et al, 2015; Brandt et al, 2022), the demand for care is higher in low SES families, resulting in an increased likelihood of informal caregiving (Quashie et al, 2022). Less wealthy individuals and individuals with lower education are more likely to transition into informal care (Rodrigues et al, 2018; Quashie et al, 2022), while families in higher socioeconomic groups have financial resources with which they can more easily afford formal care services and meet the needs of older people (Rodrigues et al, 2022). Therefore, less affluent individuals are more likely to provide informal care, provide more intensive care and consequently report a higher care burden (Brandt et al, 2022).

Women are disproportionally represented among informal caregivers, especially those from lower SES and marginal social groups who are additionally disadvantaged in pathways to and through caregiving (del Río-Lozano et al, 2013). Accumulation of disadvantages among women from lower socioeconomic groups might be connected to a lack of choice in the transition to caregiving as consumerisation allows choice only to the individuals who can afford to pay for care on the market (Yeandle et al, 2012; Quashie et al, 2022).

Furthermore, lack of choice in becoming an informal caregiver could have detrimental consequences for the caregiver's as well as the care receiver's quality of life. Schulz et al (2012) emphasise that caregivers who report lack of choice in the transition into caregiving experience higher levels of emotional stress and are more likely to report physical strain from caregiving. Additionally, lack of choice is also highly likely to affect the quality of care provided, as burdened and distressed caregivers more likely engage in potentially harmful behaviours towards the care receiver (Schulz et al, 2012). This can lead to care receivers feeling less satisfied with the care provided and therefore more likely to report unmet needs (Zhu, 2015).

Lack of financial means, lack of choice and information about the care system along with accumulated disadvantages can prevent access to formal care services among individuals from low SES, increase care burden and potentially lead to more unmet needs. However, even though some studies have revealed a connection between lower income and a higher probability to have unmet needs (Burchardt et al, 2018), Kröger (2022: 156–60) underscores that the correlation between income and unmet needs is contingent upon the country's policy context.

Contextual framework: care for older people in Slovenia

As the care poverty concept emphasises contextual and policy embeddedness of care choices and consequent inequalities and unmet needs, it is important to present the context in which we have studied the care dyads. Slovenia is a country that predominantly relies on family care and its care regime can be therefore characterised as *implicit familialism* (Saraceno, 2016; Filipovič Hrast et al, 2020). This means that family care is dominant, assumed and prescribed by a legal obligation to financially support the costs of formal care in cases where the older person's income is insufficient. Formal home care services in Slovenia have predominantly a supplementary role in mostly informal care arrangements and are provided to about 1.7 per cent of people aged 65 and over (Kovač et al, 2022). The provision of subsidised home care is limited to 20 hours per week and its financing is divided between the municipality, contributing at least 50 per cent and typically more than 70 per cent of the overall expenditures, and the private out-of-pocket contributions of users or their family members.

The level of co-funding and out-of-pocket contributions are decided by municipalities, resulting in high geographical variation in costs and accessibility of home care services. For example, the out-of-pocket contribution in the municipality with the highest such contribution is six times that of the municipality with the lowest contribution. Furthermore, a study by Hlebec et al (2016) on the unmet needs for care services among older people revealed that in Slovenia around 4 per cent of the 65+ population with severe functional limitations (two or more limitations with Activities of Daily Living or Instrumental Activities of Daily Living) living in the community do not receive any kind of care (formal or informal) (Hlebec et al, 2016). They found that unmet needs increase with age and among individuals living in rural settings.

Data and methods

Data for this study were collected in Slovenia, using semi-structured face-to-face interviews with dyads of self-identified primary family caregivers (that is, partners, children, children-in-law or grandchildren) and older persons living in the community and receiving home care services. Recruitment of participants was supported and facilitated by providers of home care services across Slovenia. All interviewees received an information sheet about the study and their participation was voluntary. Family caregivers and care receivers were interviewed separately, predominantly at the interviewees' residence. Sometimes care receivers requested that their caregivers were present during the interview and in those cases caregivers were also interviewed at the care receiver's residence. Ethical approval for the qualitative fieldwork was obtained from the ethical committee at the Faculty of Social Sciences, University of Ljubljana (2016-01/KERFDV). All interviews were recorded, transcribed verbatim and analysed using NVivo 12 software. In accordance with the process of thematic analysis, as described by Braun and Clarke (2006), data were coded iteratively using deductive reasoning to establish the structure of themes, and then enriched with inductive reasoning by using themes stemming from the interviews. We have analysed interviews of 54 dyads of caregivers and care receivers using home care services.

Following the terminology used by Rodrigues et al (2022) and based on the criteria of self-reported income, formal education and work status, we classified caregivers and care receivers into three different classes – high, middle or low SES. Under high SES we have categorised the interviewees that had high self-rated income, university or high school education and were employed in leading-position jobs (for example, director of a company or a manager). Under middle SES we have categorised the caregivers and care receivers who had middle self-reported income, high school or vocational school education and were employed in a non-leading position (for example, a physiotherapist or a teacher). Under low SES we categorised those with low income, high school or primary school education and who were employed in a non-leading position or unemployed.

This classification resulted in nine different categories according to caregivers' and care receivers' SES, which we then used to analyse the data. As economic, social and human capital is shared and compensated between caregiver and care receiver (with great awareness of intra-category heterogeneity and differences), we assessed the SES of the dyads and not individuals. Those dyads in which both had low SES or one was assessed as middle and one as low SES were categorised as low SES dyads and similarly those where both had high SES or one was assessed as middle and the other as high SES, were categorised as high SES dyads (for further information see Daly, 2020). Remaining combinations of the dyads of older people and their caregivers – middle-middle SES, low-high and high-low SES combinations – were categorised as middle SES dyads

Based on this classification there were eight dyads with high SES, 26 with middle SES and 20 with low SES. The SES of the dyads was used only as an informative observation framework through which we analysed differences in pathways to and through care. There are limitations to this framework, due to variations between the dyads, reality of resource sharing and differences between those that co-reside and those that do not.

Pathways to and through caring in Slovenia

In this section, we first examine pathways to informal care through caregivers' decision for and motivation to care. After that, pathways through care are analysed on the basis of the organisation of informal and formal care and potentially existing unmet needs. The concept of pathways is defined as a dynamic life-course process within broader family constellations, linking family caregiving in later life with events and processes in earlier life stages, relationships with others (such as siblings and other family members) and contextual factors, such as public policies and cultural norms (Rodrigues et al, 2022). As caregiving is a process of dyadic interdependence, informal caregivers' and care receivers' perceptions of unmet needs, combined with individual and contextual factors that influence the organisation of care, are important as they can potentially create inequalities between caregiving dyads and lead to situations that increase the risk of care poverty.

Cohabitation, support and motivation: pathways to caring

Cohabiting is a common characteristic in Slovenia among low SES dyads. Some caregivers have moved back in with the care receivers, in some cases because they became unemployed or have separated from their partner and had nowhere else to go, or it was deemed financially beneficial.

Interviewer: Oh. So in year 2011 you moved back with your parents.
Interviewee: Yes. ... Simply, wife and I got separated ... I first worked in Celje and had only a basic salary. The

> apartment costed €500 a month – the rent and the costs. I was making €800. If you are alone … you are barely surviving. (Caregiver 15, middle-low SES dyad)

Furthermore, caregivers from middle and high socioeconomic dyads frequently chose to move in with the care receivers for their own convenience, in order to avoid the costs associated with maintaining their own separate residence or due to the care receiver's larger dwelling. Some have moved back to ensure that the care receivers could stay at home. In certain situations, caregivers have chosen to move in with care receivers in order to provide care for them, as they were no longer able to care for themselves or because their partner was no longer capable of providing adequate care. This decision to move back home was driven by the necessity to ensure that the care receiver can remain in a familiar and comfortable environment while receiving the necessary care.

Interviewee:	Then I got retired and … because mother got seriously ill, moved up. That was 4–5 years ago.
Interviewer:	So, this affected your life in the way that you had to move back home?
Interviewee:	Yes, yes, I moved. It is a kind of a shock. (Caregiver 85, middle-low SES dyad)

The choices available to caregivers in these situations were often constrained by various factors. On the one hand, some caregivers found themselves compelled to move in with the care receiver or unable to move out due to financial limitations (for example, they could not pay for formal care or the family caregiver was unemployed). This was especially common among low-low and low-middle/middle-low dyads. In those care dyads that involved unemployed or partially retired caregivers, the assumed availability of these individuals frequently led other family members or relatives to impose the responsibility of care upon them: 'Seven years, yes. … I am the only one currently unemployed and everyone said that in this case I can take care of her … and now everyone is using this as an excuse' (Caregiver 19, low-low class dyad).

Caregivers emphasised that there was no one else available to provide care. Most caregivers did not have a choice when it came to making a decision on becoming a caregiver or not. This was either due to a lack of alternative caregivers, for example, not having a sibling or other close family members, or to having a family that lives far away or does not have the time to provide care (usually due to work obligations) or with which they do not have a good relationship: 'So, concerning that my job is very flexible. My brother is currently still working in three shifts. That is, in the morning, in the afternoon and in the night. And then we basically adapt' (Caregiver 4, high-high SES dyad).

Along with the evidently different pathways to care and more limited life choices that have been characteristic of low SES dyads, we have also identified some differences in motivations for care. Based on the analysis, three themes stood out as important reasons to transition into caring among all caregivers: feelings of duty or obligation (caring for parents as part of filial duty and societal norm); reciprocity (caring as a return of gratitude because the parent cared for them); and personal satisfaction: 'But from a moral standpoint, it's right. Considering that parents raise you, financially support you, and educate you. ... Then in old age, it's only fair that you take care of them' (Caregiver 15, middle-low SES dyad).

We are aware that due to the nature of qualitative research, it is hard to generalise data, however there were some differences among care dyads related to the motivation for care. Among high SES dyads, reciprocity and personal satisfaction were often mentioned as reasons to provide care, while obligation/responsibility was rarely mentioned. In middle SES dyads, no particular reason stood out as the main reason for the decision to provide care: all causes were regularly mentioned, with reciprocity as the most common reason, followed by feelings of obligation and duty and personal satisfaction. The interviewees justified caregiving as a reciprocal relation, but this is also part of the norm. Taking care of parents is something normal in society but it is also linked to reciprocal relationships in the past – parents also took care of their children when they were young – and to personal satisfaction, as something they enjoy doing because they can see their parents are happy. Similarly, in low SES dyads, no particular reason stood out as all three causes – reciprocity, duty and personal satisfaction – were cited.

Navigating pathways through caring and unmet needs

When talking about unmet needs, the majority of caregivers and care receivers from all SES dyads frequently emphasised that home care services were not available to the extent and at the times that they were needed (either due to organisational factors or a lack of staff). They highlighted the challenges posed by the lack of accessible formal home care services, particularly concerning older persons with moderate to high care needs. Even though home care users are in Slovenia entitled by law to 20 hours of home care per week, the amount of formal home care available to them is often lower: 'The fact is that they don't have enough staff ... for her to practically have around 20 hours of home care. ... Currently, we have resolved this with our own private caregivers' (Caregiver 43, middle-middle SES dyad).

This situation often compels caregivers to either hire a private care worker (paid out of their own pocket), a choice more common among care dyads from middle and upper SES, or to increase their provision of family care, a situation predominantly seen among care dyads from lower SES. In the latter case additional burden was placed on family caregivers. Due to unavailability or inadequacy of formal home care services, combined with low income that prevented dyads from being able to afford private care, unmet needs were a risk particularly among low SES dyads.

> Formal care – we would need more of it. Then you need to hire some informal, private help as well. So, it is complex to coordinate, because it's not possible to cover all needs with formal services alone. … Now, usually someone is always at home. Now, if somehow someone isn't there, we hire someone for that time, a care worker. (Caregiver 5, middle-middle SES dyad)

Even co-paying for publicly subsidised home care was a problem for care dyads from lower SES, so they usually could not afford to pay for private care services, either: 'Maybe if we were financially more, you know, situated. Then we would hire private help' (Caregiver 44, not available-low SES dyad). Modest pensions received by care recipients, especially in low SES dyads, appear to be a significant risk factor for care poverty, particularly when caregivers themselves come from lower or middle SES and lack informal support from family members or cannot afford private care services to supplement the insufficient home care services. Furthermore, caregivers from middle and low SES often stressed that having to pay rent for their own house or debt was frequently a barrier to be able to financially support care receivers: 'Not socially, but the financial situation has [changed]. Both of them receive home care, so in the end, it all adds up. The issue is more of a financial nature. I mean, I would need a care worker in the afternoon, but financially, it's just not feasible' (Caregiver 28, middle-middle SES dyad).

Among care dyads where the caregiver was classified as high SES and the older person as low SES, the caregiver's better socioeconomic position seemed to cover the gap between needed and received support, as they could financially contribute to buy services – public as well as private services and also to cover other expenses of the older person (bills, food): 'When she said that she wouldn't go to a retirement home, I presented her with this option [home care]. But I told her, "Mom, you'll have to make an effort because these care workers are expensive … we do not have such bad salaries, but we have some loans"' (Caregiver 23, middle-low SES dyad).

Furthermore, working hours and availability of formal care workers were frequently stressed as issues, especially by care dyads from middle and low socioeconomic categories. Caregivers frequently emphasised that home care services were not available at weekends and national holidays, or that formal caregivers' schedules did not suit care receivers' daily routine. Care dyads from lower SES and those with high care needs also frequently reported that care was not available at the onset of care needs, so they had to wait:

> It has happened several times that we asked them [to increase the provision of care], and we know that you are entitled to a certain number of hours per week. That means two visits per day. But they couldn't provide it. They said, 'We don't have caregivers, and you can't get them'. (Caregiver 5, middle-middle SES dyad)

Caregivers from all social classes often complained that formal care workers were not allowed to provide certain care tasks (like nail clipping, bandaging the legs, and so on). Consequently, these responsibilities were often left to informal caregivers to handle: 'They are not allowed to change the stoma bag. Which is funny because they claim it is a medical thing, but on the other hand they change diapers' (Caregiver 4, high-high SES dyad).

The lack of information about the availability and accessibility of services was also highlighted as a problem, particularly by caregivers with low SES. They emphasised the need for professional help for caregivers to which they can turn for information about the caregiving situation and how they can help the care receiver: 'Sometimes I feel like I would need some professional help to educate myself on how to deal with an elderly person if they fall, if they vomit … in that sense. How to react and in what way to react' (Caregiver 30, middle-low SES dyad).

The most frequently expressed unmet need identified by care receivers from all SES was lack of company, social interaction and socialising activities for the older person. Care receivers often emphasised that they feel socially isolated and lonely. Caregivers from low SES, who did not have support from their family/social network and who could not afford to pay for private home care, were the most burdened. Conversely, caregivers from higher SES had considerably more choices and options available to address the needs of care receivers:

> And here you actually have to drive. And this ride takes a lot of time. … In the end, when you calculate twice, thrice, and it all starts to accumulate. So now we are working on moving them somewhere closer to my brother so that he can have them in the walking distance. … Now he found one practically next to his house that was on sale and he bought it. So now the plan is that we renovate the house, enlarge it and move them there. (Caregiver 4, high-high SES dyad)

As most caregivers were still active in the labour market, caregiving responsibilities had to be reconciled with paid work:

> Even though you can work from home; you have to do it after 10 pm when the grandmother goes to sleep. If I am alone with her, if my parents are not at home, then after 10 pm I can start working for my job, until 2 am. You adapt a bit. (Caregiver 5, middle–middle SES dyad)

Balancing paid work and family caregiving was more difficult for caregivers from the middle SES, and especially from the low SES, that do not have flexible schedules. These workers need more coordination when balancing work and caregiving, as their strategies depend more on external factors, such as fixed schedules, employers' good will and co-workers' support. It was frequently emphasised that they needed to coordinate their absence with their employers:

> I am here as much as I possibly can, but I have such a job that I am absent a lot. But in the past, I have set my schedule so that I work from 9 to 13 and I get home. … Back then [before the onset of the need for care] I worked the same as now but for more hours. Now I shortened the hours and adapted my schedule to 9–13. (Caregiver 11, high–low SES dyad)

Discussion

In our study, we found that the choice of caregivers to transition into caring in Slovenia aligns with the cost–benefit calculation mentioned by Carmichael and Ercolani (2016): pathways to informal care among lower SES caregivers were related to the financial and practical aspects of cohabitation and the availability/lack of choice to provide care. This in turn was conditioned by the institutional organisation of home care services in Slovenia as well as by available housing options. On the other hand, pathways to family care provision of middle and especially higher SES caregivers were characterised by more alternatives at their disposal and the ability to make choices.

Inadequate supply of formal home care services affected the organisation and navigation of care obligations in everyday life, with SES emerging as a crucial determinant. Care dyads from middle and higher SES were able to supplement the deficient public home care supply with private care services. In contrast, lack of financial resources among care dyads from lower SES prevented such an option. It seems that care poverty overlaps with (income) poverty, as low-income caregivers frequently reported feeling trapped and overburdened in their role, which could negatively affect the quality of care (Schulz et al, 2012) and lead to an increase in unmet needs for both the caregiver and the older adult.

However, an important contribution of our study is also the emphasis on other factors (beside income) that might contribute to unmet needs of caregiving dyads. Regional inequality in care organisation in Slovenia is putting care dyads in an unequal position, as the organisation of care and everyday life of care dyads differ in different municipalities. The Slovenian care system does not adequately address the care needs of older people and their caregivers, but rather creates inequalities in access to care services and thus co-produces care poverty.

Financial resources enable high and most middle SES dyads to have different strategies to close the gap between publicly available care and older people's needs. Low SES dyads, especially those with care recipients with high care needs, often struggle with out-of-pocket payments for publicly subsidised home care services, and therefore have to fill the care gap by increasing the family care provision. This illustrates how insufficient level of care services and inadequate resources result in unequal outcomes not only for older people, but also for their family caregivers. It reinforces the call for the development of home care services as well as financial support for low-income care receivers to enable them to meet their care needs and decrease the risk of care poverty. Furthermore, the need to address and involve caregivers in long-term care policies was identified as important, because inadequate or insufficient support for care needs from formal and informal sources affects their living arrangements, well-being and labour market participation.

References

Brandt, M., Kaschowitz, J. and Quashie, N.T. (2022) 'Socioeconomic inequalities in the wellbeing of informal caregivers across Europe', *Aging and Mental Health*, 26(8): 1589–96.

Braun, V. and Clarke, V. (2006) 'Using thematic analysis in psychology', *Qualitative Research in Psychology*, 3(2): 77–101.

Burchardt, T., Jones, E. and Obolenskaya, P. (2018) 'Formal and informal long-term care in the community: interlocking or incoherent systems?', *Journal of Social Policy*, 47(3): 479–503.

Carmichael, F. and Ercolani, M.G. (2016) 'Unpaid caregiving and paid work over life-courses: different pathways, diverging outcomes', *Social Science & Medicine*, 156: 1–11.

Crystal, S., Shea, D.G. and Reyes, A.M. (2017) 'Cumulative advantage, cumulative disadvantage, and evolving patterns of late-life inequality', *The Gerontologist*, 57(5): 910–20.

Daly, M. (2020) *Gender Inequality and Welfare States in Europe*, Cheltenham: Edward Elgar.

Daly, M. and Lewis, J. (2000) 'The concept of social care and the analysis of contemporary welfare states', *The British Journal of Sociology*, 51(2): 281–98.

del Río-Lozano, M., García-Calvente, M., Marcos, J., Entrena-Durán, F. and Maroto-Navarro, G. (2013) 'Gender identity in informal care: impact on health in Spanish caregivers', *Qualitative Health Research*, 23(11): 1506–20.

Fast, J., Keating, N., Eales, J., Kim, C. and Lee, Y. (2021) 'Trajectories of family care over the lifecourse: evidence from Canada', *Ageing & Society*, 41(5): 1145–62.

Filipovič Hrast, M., Hlebec, V. and Rakar, T. (2020) 'Sustainable care in a familialist regime: coping with elderly care in Slovenia', *Sustainability*, 12(20): Article 8498.

Hlebec, V., Srakar, A. and Majcen, B. (2016) 'Determinants of unmet needs among Slovenian old population', *Zdravstveno varstvo*, 55(1): 78–85.

Kovač, N., Istenič, A. and Petrič, M. (2022) *Spremljanje izvajanja storitev storitve pomoči za družino: Pomoč na domu − Analiza stanja v 2021* [Monitoring the Implementation of the Family Support Service: Home Help − Analysis of the Situation in 2021], Ljubljana: Inštitut Republike Slovenije za socialno varstvo.

Kröger, T. (2022) *Care Poverty: When Older People's Needs Remain Unmet*, Cham: Palgrave Macmillan.

Kröger, T., Mathew Puthenparambil, J. and Van Aerschot, L. (2019) 'Care poverty: unmet care needs in a Nordic welfare state', *International Journal of Care and Caring*, 3(4): 485–500.

Leitner, S. (2003) 'Varieties of familialism: the caring function of the family in comparative perspective', *European Societies*, 5(4): 353–75.

Quashie, N.T., Wagner, M., Verbakel, E. and Deindl, C. (2022) 'Socioeconomic differences in informal caregiving in Europe', *European Journal of Ageing*, 19(3): 621–32.

Rodrigues, R., Ilinca, S. and Schmidt, A.E. (2018) 'Income-rich and wealth-poor? The impact of measures of socio-economic status in the analysis of the distribution of long-term care use among older people', *Health Economics*, 27(3): 637–46.

Rodrigues, R., Filipovič Hrast, M., Kadi, S., Hurtado Monarres, M. and Hlebec, V. (2022) 'Life course pathways into intergenerational caregiving', *The Journals of Gerontology: Series B*, 77(7): 1305–14.

Roth, D.L., Fredman, L. and Haley, W.E. (2015) 'Informal caregiving and its impact on health: a reappraisal from population-based studies', *The Gerontologist*, 55(2): 309–19.

Saraceno, C. (2016) 'Varieties of familialism: comparing four Southern European and East Asian welfare regimes', *Journal of European Social Policy*, 26(4): 314–26.

Schulz, R., Beach, S.R., Cook, T.B., Martire, L.M., Tomlinson, J.M. and Monin, J.K. (2012) 'Predictors and consequences of perceived lack of choice in becoming an informal caregiver', *Aging and Mental Health*, 16(6): 712–21.

Van Houtven, C.H., Coe, N.B. and Skira, M.M. (2013) 'The effect of informal care on work and wages', *Journal of Health Economics*, 32(1): 240–52.

Yeandle, S., Kröger, T. and Cass, B. (2012) 'Voice and choice for users and carers? Developments in patterns of care for older people in Australia, England and Finland', *Journal of European Social Policy*, 22(4): 432–45.

Zhu, H. (2015) 'Unmet needs in long-term care and their associated factors among the oldest old in China', *BMC Geriatrics*, 15(1): 1–11.

10

Needs and unmet needs of family carers: an intersectional approach to long-term care in Germany

Simone Leiber and Daniela Brüker

Introduction

In recent years, research interest in inequalities in long-term care has grown considerably, with a particular focus on the unmet needs of older adults in need of care (for an overview, see Hill, 2022; Kröger, 2022). Family carers are often considered as alternative or complementary respondents in surveys of unmet needs in long-term care (for example, Brimblecombe et al, 2017). However, since the end of the 1980s, there has also been interest in the needs and unmet needs of family carers themselves (for example, Nolan and Grant, 1989).

It should be noted that the needs of care recipients and their informal carers are closely linked. Indeed, Kröger (2022: 26) uses the concept of care poverty to refer to 'the deprivation of adequate coverage of care needs resulting from an interplay between individual and societal factors'. Furthermore, care poverty is described as 'a situation where people in need of care do not receive sufficient assistance from either informal or formal sources' (Kröger, 2022: 26; see also Chapter 1 of this volume). The extent to which and how care poverty arises and can be prevented depends largely on the well-being of family carers and whether they themselves have unmet needs that affect their ability to support the individuals they care for. Focusing on the unmet needs of carers is particularly important in welfare states with a high degree of familialism (Leitner, 2003).

In Germany, family carers are the main source of care for older adults and formal care still plays a subordinate role in long-term care provision (Geyer et al, 2023). Research shows that caring for a person with complex long-term care needs can be associated with increased physical or mental illness, issues with work–life balance and financial constraints (Denham et al, 2020; Brandt et al, 2022). Recognising *carers' own support needs* is, thus, important from both an individual and societal perspective if the need for care among the growing population of older adults is to be met and if care poverty is to be prevented.

This chapter gives a brief summary of current international research on the (unmet) needs of carers and highlights existing research gaps, as well as presenting the results of two empirical projects on family carers in Germany. German studies in the field of long-term care under the heading of 'unmet needs' are generally scarce and are non-existent in relation to 'care poverty'.

First, this chapter presents empirical results from the project PflegeIntersek,[1] which was carried out in the region of North-Rhine-Westphalia in Western Germany between 2016 and 2018. The central aim of PflegeIntersek and of this chapter is to apply an *intersectional perspective* to informal care. It is assumed that carers differ in their coping strategies according to categories of social difference. Based on prior literature on German carers, this study focused on gender, socioeconomic status (SES), employment status and ethnicity, while remaining open to other categories that emerged inductively from the interview material.

Second, to capture more recent developments under the revised German long-term care insurance scheme, as well as potential differences between German regions, these perspectives are complemented by another qualitative study carried out in 2022 and 2023 with a focus on family carers in Eastern Germany. Based on these two studies, this chapter examines the needs and unmet needs of carers in Germany from a perspective of intersectional inequality, the existence of important differences between Eastern and Western Germany, and policy implications.

Family carers and care policies in Germany

Family carers in Germany are predominantly women (60 per cent). They have always been and remain the central pillar of long-term care provision in Germany (Geyer et al, 2023). This importance of family carers has been supported by familialistic care policies in general (Leitner, 2003) and the strong emphasis placed on family responsibility by the German long-term care insurance scheme. According to the Federal Statistical Office, there are currently around five million people in Germany in need of care, of whom almost 75 per cent are cared for by their relatives *alone* (Statistisches Bundesamt, 2022). Notably, carers in Eastern Germany use professional home care services for support more frequently than those in Western Germany, which makes the German example an interesting case for an in-depth analysis of the unmet needs of family carers.

With the introduction of the German long-term care insurance in 1995, people in need of care have the choice between cash benefits and benefits in kind, or a combination of both. *De jure*, cash benefits are intended for the person in need of care and not the carer, although in reality, the cash benefit is often at least partially transferred to the carer. However, for many carers, the care allowance does not even exceed the level of social assistance, as the allowance depends on the level of care to which the person in need of care is classified. Therefore, the benefit often does not grant independent income security. Currently, unlike in the area of childcare, there is no substantial publicly funded wage replacement scheme for carers of older people. In addition, professional services that are financed via the long-term care insurance system are often not sufficient for time-intensive care and, especially in residential care, are accompanied by a high private financial contribution (Geyer et al, 2023).

Until recently, the needs of people with dementia were poorly addressed by the public system. However, this changed with the 2017 reform of the long-term care insurance system, which significantly broadened the definition of long-term care needs to include cognitive and mental impairments and introduced a new needs assessment tool. In terms of policies *explicitly targeting carers*, existing schemes are not well known or widely used, and they are not very attractive to low-income earners as they provide time rights without money.

An intersectional approach to the needs and unmet needs of carers

A broad range of international studies focus on the economic and living conditions, health and well-being of informal carers, also from a perspective of social inequalities (for example, Brandt et al, 2022; Brimblecombe and Cartagena Farias, 2022). Concomitantly, there is also a growing research interest in the needs and unmet needs of carers, specifically for people with dementia (for example, Alves et al, 2020; Clemmensen et al, 2021; Chapter 11 in this volume).

However, what the 'needs' of informal carers really are and who should determine them still seem to be controversial issues. Some attempts have been made to develop needs assessment tools for carers (Aoun et al, 2018) with a variety of different categorisations of needs and unmet needs, but in this context reconciling paid work and care has largely been ignored (but see Alves et al, 2020). Additionally, the support needs of cultural minorities have been rather neglected (Clemmensen et al, 2021: 694). Therefore, we included data on cultural minorities in a high-income country (in particular, carers with a family history of migration from Turkey living in Germany). From a social policy perspective, this chapter considers both individual and structural conditions, such as policies to reconcile paid work and care. We also explicitly seek to address issues of intersectional inequality in relation to carers' unmet needs. Finally, differences between Eastern and Western Germany are examined, highlighting the importance of cultural values in relation to caring.

Intersectionality has become an important reference point for research that examines the complex interactions between inequality-generating categories of difference and highlights the consequences of these interactions in terms of inclusion versus exclusion (McCall, 2005; Walgenbach, 2012). A focus on intersectionality aims to analyse and enhance the visibility of complex power relations. Intersectional analyses differ from diversity concepts, for example, in that the analysis is not based on a cumulative understanding of multiple discriminations using a set of structural categories but rather on interactions between the categories (Walgenbach, 2012: 1). Through an intersectional approach, structural inequalities in care can be uncovered and addressed.

Data and methods

This chapter presents selected findings from the PflegeIntersek project, based on an analysis of 20 in-depth semi-structured qualitative interviews with family carers from an intersectional perspective. The sample comprises carers of working age, some of whom had a Turkish background. The interviewees were selected according to a predefined qualitative sampling plan following an intra-categorical approach (McCall, 2005). In particular, priority was given to classifying the individuals based on their high, medium or low SES, conceptualised in this work in terms of income and education levels. In addition to the qualitative information from the interviews on the financial aspects of the care arrangement, the carer's net monthly household income, the number of persons living in the carer's household, the highest educational qualification and the highest professional qualification were recorded using a standardised short questionnaire. Any receipt of social benefits was also noted. The educational and professional status of the caregiver's spouse, if present, was also noted. SES classifications were determined based on an overall review of the elements. In most cases, income and educational status were congruent. When this was not the case, the indicator that was more relevant to coping with the care situation was given priority in the sample plan.

It was decided that SES would be central to examining interactions with the three other structural categories, namely gender, employment status and ethnicity. A binary conceptualisation of gender was used. Moreover, in the PflegeIntersek project we focused on care for older parents or parents-in-law because most carers in this target group are still of working age and are likely to be balancing work and care. To ensure that coping strategies were examined in demanding care situations, we only included persons in need of care who had dementia or were classified at least at level two (pre-2017 system) or grade three (new system) in the long-term care insurance system. Finally, 'ethnicity' distinguishes carers with a family history of migration from Turkey (the largest migrant group in Germany) from those without such a family history.

The interviews were analysed in a two-stage process: first, by means of theme-centred coding (Schmidt, 2012), and second, by means of an intersectional analysis based on the work of Walgenbach (2012). The sample included seven male and 13 female carers. Overall, eight had a family history of migration, 11 were employed and 11 had high SES. A wide variety of category combinations were achieved (Table 10.1).

The information from the PflegeIntersek study does not fully capture the impact of the 2017 long-term care reform. The study was also limited to urban areas in the most populous state in Western Germany. Therefore, additional interviews from a second study are included in the analysis. Specifically, between 2022 and 2023, ten semi-narrative interviews were conducted with family carers of East German origin, mainly from rural areas. Their place of socialisation was in the former German Democratic Republic (GDR), meaning these carers were all born in the former GDR and they or their parents had lived there for a substantial part of their lives. These individuals mostly cared for their parents, parents-in-law or grandparents; one interviewee was caring for her husband, and another was caring for her adult daughter. Two carers had already retired during the course of care, one of them took over care when he was already retired and all the others were of working age. Four East German interviewees were male, seven lived in rural areas and six had high SES (Table 10.1). The data were examined by means of qualitative content analysis (Kuckartz and Rädiker, 2022).

Four types of needs have been identified in the literature (Bradshaw, 1972): felt, normative, comparative and expressed needs. While recognising that carers may find it difficult to recognise and discuss their own needs, we focus on expressed needs (needs that carers are able to articulate themselves) and normative needs (needs that are assessed by third-party experts, in this case, social scientists). The analytical perspective adopted made it possible not only to identify the needs expressed by the carers during the interviews (self-perception, explicit needs) but, with a further interpretive step, to elaborate implicitly emerging normative needs along the categories of difference (third-party assessment, implicit needs).

Results

Unmet needs of family carers in Western Germany

In previous publications of the PflegeIntersek project, a typology of caring was developed, comprising five different types of family carers with similar strategies for coping with and providing care (Auth et al, 2023). The dimensions of the typology are based on the interrelations of the four structural categories of SES, gender, employment status and ethnicity, with an inductively derived dividing line referring to the 'self-care orientation' of the carers. The term self-care is understood here as the carers' concern for themselves and their own needs (for example, their own need for rest, time for themselves or the opportunity to pursue their own life plans). Three

Table 10.1: Interview sample

No.	Socioeconomic status L (low) M (medium) H (high)	Gender F (female) M (male)	Employment status NE (non-employed) E (employed)	Ethnicity M (family history of migration) NM (no family history of migration)	Region U (urban) R (rural) U/R (urban/rural mix)
Sample West Germany (N=20)					
1	L	F	NE	M	U
2	L	F	NE	NM	U
3	L	F	NE	NM	U
4	L	F	E	NM	U
5	L	F	E	NM	U
6	L	F	E	M	U
7	L	M	E	M	U
8	L	M	NE	NM	U
9	L	M	NE	M	U
10	H	F	NE	NM	U
11	H	F	NE	M	U
12	H	F	E	M	U
13	H	F	NE	NM	U
14	H	F	E	NM	U
15	H	F	E	NM	U
16	H	F	E	M	U
17	H	M	E	M	U
18	H	M	NE	NM	U
19	H	M	E	NM	U
20	H	M	E	NM	U
Sample East Germany (N=10)					
21	L	M	NE	NM	U
22	M	F	E	NM	R
23	M	F	E	NM	R
24	M	M	E	NM	R
25	H	F	E	NM	U/R
26	H	F	NE	NM	R
27	H	F	E	NM	R
28	H	F	E	NM	R
29	H	M	NE	NM	U
30	H	M	E	NM	R

Table 10.2: Coping with family care: a typology

'Rather successful' coping			'Rather precarious' coping	
Type 1 'Care organised around gainful employment'	*Type 2* 'Active use of family resources'	*Type 3* 'Sense of purpose'	*Type 4* 'Struggling for control'	*Type 5* 'No alternative'

Source: Based on Auth et al (2023).

types of family carers could be assigned to a group with 'rather successful' coping, and two types were assigned to a group with 'rather precarious' coping (Table 10.2).

In the following paragraphs, the constellations of 'rather precarious coping' are explored as these arrangements show the highest prevalence of unmet needs (for further detail about types one to three, representing 'rather successful' coping, see Auth et al, 2023). However, we also summarise the common unmet needs that emerged across all five types.

The 'relative success' or 'precariousness' (based on the well-being of the carer) of coping with care responsibilities showed no simple relationships with the four selected structural categories, which is why the typology was developed. Indeed, although SES was prioritised in the sampling process, it did not prove to be as crucial to successful coping as expected. Even against a background of high SES, carers' needs were often unmet.

Here 'success' and 'precariousness' refer primarily to the well-being of the carer, based on family carers' descriptions regarding the care arrangements and their coping within the situation. Carers were classified in the 'precarious' coping group if they subordinated their life plans almost completely to the needs of the person in need of care. Accordingly, these individuals have higher heteronomy and limited agency. For these carers, coping with the caring task is perceived as minimally or not at all controllable. Social recognition by the family or the person in need of care is usually lacking and the situation is subjectively perceived as highly burdensome and more or less inescapable. Overall, eight out of the 20 carers in the sample fell into this category. This subsample included carers with high and low SES and both with and without a family history of migration. All of these carers were female; however, due to the qualitative approach of the study, this gendered pattern requires further investigation. Finally, the carers in type four continue to work while caring, while those in type five are not employed.

The caring situation in type four, 'Struggling for control', is characterised by the fact that the carers have some options to manage their care responsibilities, maintain employment, are mindful of their own needs and actively practice self-care. Despite this, they are in a constant struggle to maintain control over their own life plans, and specific conditions cause these carers to be exposed to a very high and involuntary burden of care, which is often described as emerging in a gradual process.

In a caring context that has been largely forced upon them, these individuals perceive their options for coping as limited. Support from external care services is possible in cases with high SES, but this support can be only partially applied to the person in need and, thus, provides only minor respite. A permanent struggle takes place either with third parties imposing care responsibilities (often in a conflictual relationship with other family members) or when managing the expectations and needs of the person being cared for, who, for example, may refuse care from non-family members. Against this background, staying in employment is considered particularly important for these carers. However, the reconciliation of carrying out both gainful employment and caring is not always successful to the desired extent and may cause stress. The material thus shows an unmet need for professional support for guiding carers in managing their role as a carer and their ambivalent feelings in decision-making situations.

In addition to these 'inner conflicts', there are often 'external conflicts' present in these arrangements. These conflicts can be triggered by the person in need of care if the fulfilment of their care needs (for example, due to dementia) or their care expectations cannot be reconciled with the wishes and needs of the carer. For type four, in particular, the migrant background of the person in need of care may also have an aggravating effect on 'successful' coping. Caring relatives with a family history of migration have to shape their self-care orientation in a field of tension between different generational and cultural norms. In addition, even if the family agrees on an arrangement and is willing to make use of professional care, culturally sensitive and Turkish-speaking support services are difficult to find in Germany, as in Ms Yüksel's[2] case:

> Even in respite care, there was no Turkish staff to give support or translate. One or two cleaners were there in the mornings, who might have provided a little support. But the language is a great, a very great loss. A big gap. I mean that there is so little on offer regarding that point. (Ms Yüksel, no. 16)

This unmet need leaves the main responsibility with the family, with few options other than shifting the responsibilities *within* the family.

This is also true for the case of Ms Cordes, who emigrated to Germany together with her grandmother, mother and three siblings when she was ten years old and is married to a German. She was categorised as belonging to type five, 'No alternative', at the end of her 'caring career'. For this type, even a high SES does not bring advantages for coping with caring because other stress factors overshadow its possible benefits, such as a lack of culturally sensitive services: 'Germany is full of Turks or people of Turkish origin or Turkish-speaking people. But if you need support at home, there is no professional care service with Turkish-speaking people' (Ms Cordes, no. 11).

Irrespective of whether there is a family history of migration, family carers classified as type five refer to potentially forced care orientations that are influenced not only by religious beliefs but also by individual family constellations and are always a matter of conscience. Self-caring is not possible for family carers of this type and self-care orientation is low. For this type, there is often a striking perceived dependence in the relationship to the person being cared for, which reveals itself either financially or emotionally. These carers are also characterised by a value set that does not permit any kind of alternative to not taking on the main care responsibility, even when additional services are available to provide respite from caring.

For example, Ms Kessler's mother suffered from advanced dementia. Although she was entitled to benefits according to the highest care level (5) of the long-term care insurance, Ms Kessler had been providing care completely on her own for several years. One reason for this is that her mother did not accept food or fluids from other people and Ms Kessler was, thus, only able to leave the house rarely and for short periods. Her social contacts had suffered greatly as a result: 'Either let mum die or look after mum myself. Yes. And I've been in this situation for a total of four years now. ... Today I'm alone from Monday to Sunday. ... And this loneliness ... is very hard for me' (Ms Kessler, no. 3).

Ms Kessler was also financially dependent on her mother, as she gave up her job to care for her. Ms Kessler's dependency and her underlying values of family responsibility severely limited her orientation to self-care to the point of completely negating any other options. The rather resigned attitude and passivity with which caring relatives endure such highly stressful care requirements also indicate an unmet need for professional support. Carers in such situations, who perceive having 'no alternative', are particularly dependent on their needs becoming visible.

In addition to these *type-specific* unmet needs, three particularly central unmet needs emerged from the material *across all types*:

1. Unmet needs related to *information obstacles*: across all phases of the caring process, needs for care-relevant information are apparent. Those with a higher level of education or better integration into existing low-threshold care-sensitive structures (for example, employers, health actors, care counselling) are more likely to be able to navigate the long-term care system. However, carers across different types and situations complained about difficulties in receiving adequate information. In several cases, finding the right contact points was described as 'exhausting'. Too much initiative was often needed to obtain the relevant information and support.

2. Unmet needs related to *access to culturally sensitive care infrastructure and adequate housing*. This was an issue not only for carers with Turkish roots in types four and five but was a common theme across all types. Another common unmet need, particularly for carers who take their older parents into their own households, is the issue of adequate and affordable housing. In one case, the housing situation forced the family into a situation where the mother in need of care could not leave the home:

> [T]he next thing I have to do now is look for a flat. I don't know how long my mother will live. I live on the third floor without a lift. I can't get her down anymore. We tried on Sunday and had real difficulties. ... I have already cancelled doctor's appointments because I can't do it alone. (Ms Aslan, no. 1)

This lack of adequate housing is not only an issue for migrant families. Another daughter gave up her own (not barrier-free) flat, stored her furniture at a cost and moved in with her mother to enable her to receive care at home. In another case, a grandmother had to move into her daughter's flat and the children had to give up their rooms. This situation was only made easier again when a son moved out.

3. Unmet needs related to *coping with life after care*: after the death of a cared-for relative, an empty space in everyday life may arise. In this context, carers' coping strategies for moving on with their lives depend primarily on their retrospective evaluation of the care experience and on care-related changes in their own life plans. In the interview material, carers rarely explicitly expressed a need for support at this stage. However, unmet support needs were implicitly revealed when some of the carers described the difficult situations they faced after the death of their older family member. These experiences showed an unmet need for targeted counselling and guidance in the post–care phase of life.

Unmet needs of family carers in Eastern Germany

Studies in the field of family policy suggest that there are still differences in attitudes and practices between Eastern and Western Germany with regard to the division of formal and informal work between men and women (Schiefer, 2017), the participation of parents in the labour market and the use of public support structures. However, whether this is also the case in long-term care remains an open empirical question. In the former GDR, both men and women were integrated into the labour market and the right and duty of women and men to work were enshrined in the GDR constitution (Schmidt and Ostheim, 2007).

Against the background of the accumulation of ageing, emigration and weakness of support structures, informal care in Eastern Germany faces particular challenges (BMFSFJ, 2017). The problems of undersupply of home care services in rural areas were clearly confirmed in the interview material. For example, some providers refuse to provide care for people living in remote areas for economic reasons, meaning these families do not receive any support.

The interview data show that reconciling paid work and care is a key issue for these carers. Most of them reported working full-time or almost full-time in addition to caring, and neither SES nor gender differences affected this strong orientation towards the adult worker model. In cases where men provided care, their wives were relieved from caring duties, and the male carers supported their employment. This finding differs from studies on male carers in West Germany, where wives are regularly involved in caring for their in-laws (Auth et al, 2016).

The difficult labour market situation in Eastern Germany means that some carers must travel very long distances to and from work. In this study, the carers mentioned the need for homeworking, which could help to combine work and care in these circumstances. However, one carer, who worked in a small business, reported that her boss was very reluctant to allow her to work from home. Furthermore, her request to leave the company two years before her official retirement date to care for her parents was not granted due to staff shortages: 'I wanted to stop working then. Two years ago. And then a colleague of mine quit because she knew that the office would close in two years. She found a job that suited her and then resigned. Then the boss said, I can't let you go now' (Ms Auerbach, no. 22).

Even when working from home, there are still challenges to overcome, particularly when caring for a relative with dementia. For example, the carers reported interruptions when working from home. The need for constant supervision of the family member means that neighbourhood help, live-in care by migrants from Central and Eastern Europe, or day care is required, as otherwise it is difficult to combine employment and caring. However, not all families have the financial means to pay for such support and the German long-term care insurance system provides only limited funding for professional home care services.

For the carers in rural areas, long journeys to doctors and therapists are another burden, and these carers expressed a need for relief. Accompanying the individual in need of care to these appointments leads to several hours of absence from work and, in the context of full-time employment, this can only be arranged if flexible working hours are available. Work is then either done early in the morning or made up in the evening, resulting in a lack of rest and sleep. One carer proposed that special leave should be granted for such tasks, but a right for such a leave does not exist in Germany. Furthermore, reducing working hours raised concerns about maintaining an independent livelihood. Finally, the need for wage-replacement benefits was articulated by the carers, as the care allowance of the long-term care insurance scheme does not secure the standard of living.

The high employment rate of carers in East Germany (TNS Infratest Sozialforschung, 2017) also meant that grandchildren were involved in caring for their grandparents, as they compensated for the time constraints and work-related absences of their parents. All three grandchildren in the sample accepted this task, but they also reported a lack of time as teenagers as well as restrictions on partnerships and starting a family: 'And it's very, very hard, I have to say, because I actually completely miss those teenage years that you have, because that's when the care actually started' (Ms Hutschenreuther, no. 27). There was little understanding of the caring situation among peers, as most of their friends had not had their own caring experiences, thus leading to the loss of friendships and a lack of socio-emotional support.

In addition, the issue of pensions was a dominant theme in most of these interviews, much more than in the PflegeIntersek sample. Indeed, female carers from East Germany seemed very much aware of the impact of caring on their pension provision. For example, a female carer who had reduced her working hours expressed the need for more pension points for the care of her family members: 'And the next thing is the issue of pension points. You do get a few pension points for caring, but it's actually not much. Where I think that should be accounted for in a completely different way' (Ms Hutschenreuther, no. 27).

Overall, most East German carers in the sample were very employment-centred, and it seemed more common than in the West to use professional services if the families could afford them. Almost all the interviewees used in-kind services, sometimes despite the resistance of the person in need of care. Personal care was mostly seen as a task that could be outsourced to professional home care services and this attitude persisted across gender and SES. However, the carers also stressed many structural challenges that were mostly related to the risk of old-age poverty, the lack of support to reconcile caring and employment and the lack of home care in rural areas. Even after the major German long-term care reform in 2017, these structural deficits have remained.

Conclusion

This chapter has shown that not only people in need of care but also carers are at risk of having unmet needs. The intersectional approach did not reveal simple dividing lines along classical structural categories. Instead, the analysis identified different type-specific unmet needs along an intersectional typology of coping with caring, as well as overarching unmet needs across the coping types. In addition, this chapter found indications in the qualitative sample that there are still differences in coping with caring between West and East Germany. These differences may be related to structural deficits in rural areas in the East, but also to, for example, the high level of employment despite caring responsibilities and the higher use of professional care services regardless of gender and SES of the carer.

The phrase 'care for carers' emphasises the relevance of an independent policy perspective on family carers and highlights approaches for public intervention to secure their respective living situations. Informal carers should be protected against health risks and the risks of poverty, including in old age. In Germany, researchers have highlighted the low level of compensation for caring, in comparison to childcare, in the pension insurance system and the resulting poverty risk for women (Knauthe and Deindl, 2019), which was also a theme in the East German sample.

Functioning family relationships continue to be an important resource for carers in many situations but cannot be entirely relied upon. Therefore, it is important to have and further develop an encompassing, flexible, low-threshold, culturally sensitive, tailored public and private social support system that places the needs of family carers on an equal footing with those of people in need of long-term care. Differences between urban and rural areas should also be countered by special programmes (for example, shuttle services, expansion of online support).

In general, carers in Germany would benefit from more comprehensive case management structures as well as outreach support and counselling, including during the post-death phase. Finally, regarding reconciling care and paid work, raising awareness in companies and introducing more comprehensive paid care leave structures would represent a major step forward. Particularly in welfare states with a strong tradition of familialism, better addressing the unmet needs of family carers through such policies appears to be an important condition for reducing the risk of care poverty in the future.

Notes

[1]   The project was carried out by the University of Duisburg-Essen, the Cologne University of Applied Sciences and the Bielefeld University of Applied Sciences, funded by the German research institute Forschungsinstitut für gesellschaftliche Weiterentwicklung NRW. We are grateful to our project colleagues who have contributed to the results presented here.

[2]   All names have been changed. The numbers of respondents refer to Table 10.1.

References

Alves, S., Ribeiro, O. and Paúl, C. (2020) 'Unmet needs of informal carers of the oldest old in Portugal', *Health and Social Care in the Community*, 28(6): 2408–17.

Aoun, S.M., Toye, C., Slatyer, S., Robinson, A. and Beattie, E. (2018) 'A person-centred approach to family carer needs assessment and support in dementia community care in Western Australia', *Health and Social Care in the Community*, 26(4): 578–86.

Auth, D., Dierkes, M., Leiber, S. and Leitner, S. (2016) 'Trotz Pflege kein Vereinbarkeitsproblem? Typische Arrangements und Ressourcen erwerbstätiger pflegender Söhne' [No reconciliation problem despite caring? Typical arrangements and resources of working caring sons], *Zeitschrift für Sozialreform*, 62(1): 79–110.

Auth, D., Leiber, S. and Leitner, S. (2023) 'Contestations in coping with elderly care: an intersectional analysis addressing family caregivers in Germany', *European Journal of Politics and Gender*, 6(2): 222–39.

BMFSFJ (Bundesministerium für Familie, Senioren, Frauen und Jugend) (2017) *Siebter Altenbericht: Sorge und Mitverantwortung in der Kommune* [Seventh Report on Older People: Care and Shared Responsibility in the Community], Berlin: Bundesministerium für Familie, Senioren, Frauen und Jugend.

Bradshaw, J. (1972) 'Taxonomy of social need', in G. McLachlan (ed) *Problems and Progress in Medical Care: Essays on Current Research*, London: Oxford University Press, pp 71–82.

Brandt, M., Kaschowitz, J. and Quashie, N.T. (2022) 'Socioeconomic inequalities in the wellbeing of informal caregivers across Europe', *Aging and Mental Health*, 26(8): 1589–96.

Brimblecombe, N. and Cartagena Farias, J. (2022) 'Inequalities in unpaid carer's health, employment status and social isolation', *Health and Social Care in the Community*, 30(6): 6564–76.

Brimblecombe, N., Pickard, L., King, D. and Knapp, M. (2017) 'Perceptions of unmet needs for community social care services in England: a comparison of working carers and the people they care for', *Health and Social Care in the Community*, 25(2): 435–46.

Clemmensen, T.H., Hein Lauridsen, H., Andersen-Ranberg, K. and Kaae Kristensen, H. (2021) 'Informal carers' support needs when caring for a person with dementia: a scoping literature review', *Scandinavian Journal of Caring Sciences*, 35(3): 685–700.

Denham, A.M.J., Wynne, O., Baker, A.L., Spratt, N.J., Turner, A., Magin, P., et al (2020) 'An online survey of informal caregivers' unmet needs and associated factors', *PLoS One*, 15(12): e0243502.

Geyer, J., Börsch-Supan, A., Haan, P. and Perdrix, E. (2023) *Long-term Care in Germany*, Cambridge, MA: National Bureau of Economic Research.

Hill, T. (2022) 'Understanding unmet aged care need and care inequalities among older Australians', *Ageing & Society*, 42(11): 2665–94.

Knauthe, K. and Deindl, C. (2019) *Altersarmut von Frauen durch häusliche Pflege* [Old-age Poverty Among Women Due to Domestic Care], Berlin: Sozialverband Deutschland e.V.

Kröger, T. (2022) *Care Poverty: When Older People's Needs Remain Unmet*, Cham: Palgrave Macmillan.

Kuckartz, U. and Rädiker, S. (2022) *Qualitative Inhaltsanalyse: Methoden, Praxis, Computerunterstützung* [Qualitative Content Analysis: Methods, Practice, Computer Support], Weinheim and Basel: Beltz Juventa.

Leitner, S. (2003) 'Varieties of familialism: the caring function of the family in comparative perspective', *European Societies*, 5(4): 353–75.

McCall, L. (2005) 'The complexity of intersectionality', *Journal of Women in Culture and Society*, 30(3): 1771–800.

Nolan, M.R. and Grant, G. (1989) 'Addressing the needs of informal carers: a neglected area of nursing practice', *Journal of Advanced Nursing*, 14(11): 950–61.

Schiefer, K. (2017) *Familienleitbilder in Ost- und Westdeutschland* [Family Models in East and West Germany], München: Ergon Verlag.

Schmidt, C. (2012) 'Analyse von Leitfadeninterviews' [Analysis of guided interviews], in U. Flick, E. von Kardoff and I. Steinke (eds) *Qualitative Forschung: Ein Handbuch* [Qualitative Research: A Handbook], Hamburg: Reinbeck, pp 447–56.

Schmidt, M.G. and Ostheim, T. (2007) 'Sozialpolitik in der Deutschen Demokratischen Republik' [Social policy in the German Democratic Republic], in M.G. Schmidt, T. Ostheim, N.A. Siegel and R. Zohlnhöfer (eds) *Der Wohlfahrtsstaat: Eine Einführung in den historischen und internationalen Vergleich* [The Welfare State: An Introduction to Historical and International Comparison], Wiesbaden: VS Verlag, pp 173–92.

Statistisches Bundesamt (2022) *Pflegestatistik: Pflege im Rahmen der Pflegeversicherung* [Long-term Care Statistics: Care within the Framework of Long-term Care Insurance], Wiesbaden: Statistisches Bundesamt.

TNS Infratest Sozialforschung (2017) *Abschlussbericht: Studie zur Wirkung des Pflege-Neuausrichtungs-Gesetzes (PNG) und des ersten Pflegestärkungsgesetzes (PSG I)* [Final Report: Study on the Impact of the Care Reorganisation Act (PNG) and the First Care Strengthening Act (PSG I)], München: TNS Infratest Sozialforschung.

Walgenbach, K. (2012) *Intersektionalität – eine Einführung* [Intersectionality: An Introduction], *Portal Intersektionalität*. Available from: http://portal-intersektionalitaet.de/theoriebildung/ueberblickstexte/walgenbach-einfuehrung/ [Accessed 7 January 2024].

11

People with dementia and their informal carers: at particular risk of care poverty

Mari Aaltonen, Päivi Eskola and Lina Van Aerschot

Introduction

This chapter discusses the unmet care needs of community-dwelling persons with dementia and their informal carers. The chapter builds on our previous research based on quantitative survey data and qualitative interviews collected from older people living in the community in Finland. We draw the results of these studies together and discuss why people with dementia and their carers are at particular risk of unmet needs and care poverty.

Focusing on people with dementia when discussing unmet needs is essential because the number of people with dementia is increasing worldwide as the population ages (Cao et al, 2020; GBD, 2022). Old age is a major risk factor for dementia (Ngandu and Kivipelto, 2018). In addition, a high need for care is common among people with dementia. Previous research shows that higher care needs regularly entail unmet needs and that people with dementia often have unmet care needs (Kerpershoek et al, 2018; Zhou et al, 2018; Khanassov et al, 2021). *Unmet needs* have been defined as a situation in which an older person has 'insufficient care to fulfill [their] basic requirements for food, warmth, cleanliness or security' and a situation where 'care was provided only at the cost of the undue strain of relatives' (Isaacs and Neville, 1976). Another more general definition is that unmet needs occur in long-term care when a person has disabilities for which help is needed, but it is unavailable or insufficient (Williams et al, 1997: 102). *Care poverty* combines the perspective of lacking care at the societal and population level with the individual situation in which a person has unmet needs (Kröger et al, 2019; Kröger, 2022). Thus, care poverty refers to the social and socio-political question of persons with care needs who do not receive sufficient assistance and care. As a concept, care poverty differs from 'unmet needs' by interpreting the problems of unmet needs at the level of care policies, service systems and the welfare state.

To better understand the nature of the needs and symptoms of dementia at the individual and population level, it is necessary to understand what dementia is and what it means. Dementia is not a uniform disease but results from a variety of diseases and injuries that primarily or secondarily affect the brain (WHO, 2023), such as Alzheimer's disease. Dementia, caused by neurodegenerative diseases, is both chronic and progressive. Due to the different underlying causes of dementia, the spectrum of its symptoms varies, but they also vary according to the stage of the condition (Kolanowski et al, 2018). Dementia often includes symptoms such as changes in behaviour, memory problems, cognitive decline and restlessness, and eventually leads to cognitive and physical impairment. The diversity of symptoms of dementia and individual differences pose challenges to adequate and timely recognition of needs and care planning (Khanassov et al, 2021). In individual care planning, getting to know the person with dementia, their condition, preferences, experiences, and needs is crucial (Fazio et al, 2018).

Dementia affects not only the individual living with the condition but also the daily life of family members, relatives and other close people such as friends and neighbours. Family members and relatives are often the main providers of care and help (Verbeek-Oudijk et al, 2014; Eurocarers, 2023). When care needs increase due to progressing dementia, and if care services that support, top-up or replace informal care are insufficient to meet those needs, the strain on relatives may become too heavy. In a study by Khanassov et al (2021), people with dementia, and especially their family carers, reported a wide range of unmet needs. It is also possible that informal carers face an undue strain when they provide extensive care (Isaacs and Neville, 1976; Brodaty and Donkin, 2009; Wennberg et al, 2015; Connors et al, 2020), leading to a situation in which the carers face and cover a major share of unmet needs. For instance, the informal carer's poor health, excessive strain and 'burden' predict that the person with dementia will move into a care home (Luppa et al, 2008; Kuzuya et al, 2011; Nunez, 2021). In Finland, family members or other relatives do not have any legal obligation to take care of their older relatives. However, a substantial share of older people with care needs receive help from families or other informal carers (Omaishoitajaliitto, 2021). About 20–30 per cent of Finnish adult persons provide informal care for a person living outside their household (Kauppinen et al, 2013; Erhola et al, 2018).

In this chapter, we focus on the nature and diversity of unmet needs of people with dementia and their informal carers. To better grasp the nature and root causes of unmet needs and care poverty of people with dementia, we build especially on our research based on the Daily Life and Care in Old Age (DACO) dataset (Aaltonen and Van Aerschot, 2021) and in-depth interviews of persons with dementia and their spousal carers (Aaltonen et al, 2021; Van Aerschot et al, 2021; 2022). Both datasets were collected in

Finland. We also present some updated, unpublished results from the latest DACO survey, collected in 2020.

We argue that the current service system in Finland is insufficiently prepared to meet the complex care needs of home-dwelling people with dementia, which may lead to their unmet needs, or, when those needs are met by an informal carer, to the carer's unmet needs. We show that unmet needs may be due to a lack of practical, daily assistance and help, but also to a lack of care and support that is vital for social and emotional well-being. Unmet needs may be physical, psychological, emotional or social and experienced by persons with dementia but also by informal carers.

In Finnish, the word 'memory illness' or 'memory disorder' is often used instead of dementia. Thus, the term memory disorder (in Finnish, *muistisairaus*) has been used in Finnish data collection. In this chapter, we use the term dementia to refer to people who have been diagnosed with a progressive disease that impairs memory or other cognitive capacity, because dementia is a commonly used concept in English. When we discuss the survey data we use for empirical analysis, we use the term 'memory problems' because that is the literal translation of the wording used in the Finnish questionnaire.

Health and social care for people with dementia in Finland

In Finland, as we saw in Chapter 7, tax-funded and needs-tested care services are organised by public authorities (MSAH, 2023). Public funding covers a large part of the services and user fees cover the rest. Many countries have reduced institutional and residential care, and the political priority is to provide long-term care services at home (Rostgaard et al, 2022). Finland is no exception. Public care services are needs-tested and increasingly targeted to older people with higher care needs (Kröger, 2019). Especially access to residential care has been restricted, and only very frail older persons are entitled to a place in care homes (Van Aerschot and Kröger, 2023).

According to the Finnish Institute for Health and Welfare (THL), the national goal in Finland is for older people to live in their own homes for as long as possible, even until the end of their lives (FIHW, 2023). As over 90 per cent of people over 75 years old live in their own homes, home care is the main service for older people with care needs. The vast majority of persons receiving long-term care have dementia (Linna et al, 2019; FIHW, 2022). The share of home care users with dementia is also significant: in 2022 about 40 per cent had a dementia diagnosis and about 54 per cent cognitive decline (measured by a cognition test) (THL, 2024).

Even though care services are publicly organised and subsidised in Finland, a major share of care is provided informally. Older persons rely to a significant extent on informal care provided by spouses, adult children and next-of-kin (Omaishoitajaliitto, 2021), and the number of informal carers receiving public support has increased since the 1990s (Noro et al, 2014; THL, 2021). In 2000, 3 per cent of persons over 75 years old received informal care based on an agreement between the public authorities and the carer. In 2021, the share was 4.6 per cent, which is about 26,000 older adults (THL, 2022: 56). It is estimated that in addition to the informal carers with such an official contract, about 350,000 Finns are so-called primary carers to someone, and about 60,000 of them provide binding and high-intensity informal care (Omaishoitajaliitto, 2021). The majority of informal carers are unpaid. When informal care is based on an official agreement, however, public authorities provide support, including a carer's allowance, services for the older or disabled person, carers' support services, and respite care.

Nevertheless, not all older people have persons in their family or other social networks that could provide informal care. Also, in the case of spousal care, the less frail person often provides care for the frailer one, which often becomes too demanding as needs increase (Bertogg and Strauss, 2020). This is almost inevitable when caring for a spouse with progressing dementia.

In addition to informal care and formal home care services, people with dementia may receive acute care and other health and social care. These are not always delivered as a comprehensive and coordinated package of services. As a consequence, fragmented and poorly coordinated care is associated with negative health outcomes and high costs, including excessive health care encounters and premature placements in residential care (Kolanowski et al, 2018). Such problems in meeting the needs of persons with dementia and their informal carers have been recognised already in the early 2000s. In 20 years, the supply of social and health care services has diversified, but the needs of care dyads living in the community remain at least partly unrecognised and unmet (Eskola and Jolanki, 2022).

Unmet needs in Activities of Daily Living: the DACO study

Unmet needs of older persons with memory problems have been examined using data from the DACO survey, collected in 2010 and 2015 in two cities in Finland, and most recently in 2020 for the whole country (for a general description of the data, see Kröger et al, 2019; Aaltonen and Van Aerschot, 2021). Our study (Aaltonen and Van Aerschot, 2021) used the combined data from 2010 and 2015 and included the respondents (n=1,928) who had one or more long-term illnesses or impairments that limited their daily activities and who had answered the question 'Do you have problems with memory?' (1=not at all, 2=somewhat, 3=a lot). Nine per cent of this group of respondents (n=185) were classified as having memory problems as they had chosen the response option 'a lot'. These respondents were compared with those who had answered 'not at all' or 'somewhat'. The 2020 data

(N=3,279) are representative of the whole population aged 75 and over in Finland. As with the 2010 and 2015 datasets, we restricted also the new dataset to those with one or more illnesses or impairments (n=1,910). 8 per cent (n=158) of this sample have reported having a lot of memory problems.

Unmet needs were examined first by asking in general: 'Do you receive enough help?'. The response options were (1) 'I do not need help', (2) 'Yes, I receive enough help' and (3) 'I do not receive enough help'. Those who chose option 3 were considered to have unmet needs. Second, specific needs were asked about with an eight-point question concerning Instrumental Activities of Daily Living (IADLs) and a five-point question regarding Activities of Daily Living (ADLs). The response options for each daily activity were: (1) 'I can cope without difficulty', (2) 'I do not cope by myself but I get enough help' and (3) 'I do not cope by myself and I need more help' (see also Chapter 7). Again, those who chose option 3 were considered to have unmet needs regarding the activity in question.

Results from the combined 2010 and 2015 dataset showed that people with a lot of memory problems needed and received more care than people with other types of impairment or illness. However, they also had unmet care needs more often, as about a quarter (26.3 per cent) of people with a lot of memory problems reported not receiving enough help, while less than a fifth (18.7 per cent) of others gave the same answer (Aaltonen and Van Aerschot, 2021). In 2020, 13 per cent of those with a lot of memory problems did not receive enough help compared to 7 per cent of those without memory problems.

Those with a lot of memory problems experienced more unmet needs in all IADLs (for example, grocery shopping, managing financial affairs, cleaning and cooking) as well as in ADLs like bathing and getting in or out of bed. Among older persons who received a combination of public home care and informal care, memory problems and a high number of ADL limitations predicted unmet needs. Among those who relied solely on informal care, low incomes and a high number of ADL limitations predicted unmet needs (Aaltonen and Van Aerschot, 2021).

Comparing unmet needs for specific I/ADLs among respondents in the 2020 dataset, people with memory problems were still more likely to not receive enough help than people without memory problems (Table 11.1). For example, only 2 per cent of respondents without memory problems do not receive enough help for grocery shopping or banking, whereas 16–17 per cent of those with memory problems have unmet needs with these IADLs.

These results from the latest wave of the DACO survey confirm the earlier findings and show that, during the previous decade, the difference between unmet needs of people living in the community with and without memory problems regarding daily activities has not disappeared. This means that care services for older people are still not accessible and sufficient enough for the

Table 11.1: Share of respondents not receiving enough help or care in selected activities in 2020: a comparison between people with (n=158) and without memory problems (n=1,607)

	People without memory problems % (n)	People with memory problems % (n)
Going to hobbies/activities/meetings	6 (99)	23 (33)
Grocery shopping	2 (36)	17 (26)
Acquiring home care/other services	6 (76)	17 (24)
Banking	2 (24)	16 (25)
Minor repairs or refurbishments at home or gardening	9 (139)	22 (32)
Taking medication	1 (10)	11 (18)
Bathing	1 (15)	11 (17)

Source: DACO wave 2020 dataset.

multiple and changing needs of persons with dementia. As the number of people with dementia increases due to increasing longevity (GBD, 2022), this, in the worst-case scenario, may mean that the number of people with unmet needs will increase in the future.

Unmet needs experienced by people with dementia and their spousal carers: a qualitative study

The qualitative data were collected as thematic, in-depth, semi-structured life-course interviews of 15 couples and five carers whose spouses with dementia did not want or were not able to participate. Altogether, 35 persons participated in the interviews conducted in Finland between October 2018 and March 2019. The interviews were audio-recorded and transcribed verbatim.

The participants were recruited with help from the Alzheimer Society of Finland and Carers Finland (Omaishoitajaliitto). The interested participants contacted the researchers themselves. The health conditions of the interviewees with dementia varied from mild to severe according to their knowledge and own perception. All participants were in sufficiently good health to give informed consent and participate in the discussion. The dyads were free to choose whether to be interviewed together or separately in a convenient place. In most cases, participants wished to be interviewed together in their own homes. Three dyads (six persons) felt they could express themselves more freely if they were interviewed separately.

The interviewees were asked about their everyday lives: their state of health and ability to function, social relationships, living arrangements and satisfaction with their current life situation. They were also asked to describe which health and social care services they had used and whether they had been satisfied with the help and care received. In addition, they were asked if there was some help or care they felt they needed but did not receive.

The qualitative research showed that older persons with dementia and their carers were not left without any help or services, but quite often they expressed a more diverse need for help than for which they received support or services. Unmet needs concerned poor organisation of care services, inadequate respite care, inaccessible medical services, a lack of continuous professional care relationships and emotional support. Some people with dementia and their carers wished they could talk to a social and health care professional about the disease and its consequences. A discussion about individual symptoms, the future and one's own feelings in the midst of the changes caused by progressing dementia was considered important. However, only a few had the opportunity for such a discussion.

The spousal carers supplemented or replaced the shortfalls in care provided by public services, and thus, the consequences of unmet care needs were directed at the spousal carer, not so much at the person with dementia. The carers provided a wide range of help and care, from psychosocial support and meeting basic needs of dressing, eating and hygiene to clinical procedures such as catheterisation. Informal carers also navigated the health and social care service system and advocated for people with dementia (Bressan et al, 2020; Aaltonen et al, 2021; see also Chapter 12). Sometimes informal caregiving employed all of the carers' personal resources, and the carers felt overly strained. In these cases, the help and support received from services was insufficient or completely missing. Even when services were received, they did not always cover all needs. In some cases, even if interviewees would have had the right to receive publicly provided care services, they could not access them because the service system was perceived as confusing and unclear (Aaltonen et al, 2021). Sometimes the informal carers did not know what services were available and where. Thus, navigating the system burdened the carers. When the person with dementia can no longer organise services themselves, this work falls to the spousal carer.

Care homes offer short-term care known as respite care for persons with high-level care needs who live at home supported by an informal carer. Respite care should enable the person with dementia to engage in social activities and provide rest and personal time for the informal carer. Some of the interviewees with dementia used respite care. Spousal carers and persons with dementia often considered the care provided in care homes as insufficient or of poor quality (Van Aerschot et al, 2021). They felt that there were shortcomings in taking care of basic needs, such as hygiene or safety. The interviewees often expected more or were promised extra support, such as rehabilitation or social interaction, but these expectations were not met.

If the quality of respite care was considered very poor, the service was not used even if this meant that the spousal carer missed the needed rest and the person with dementia missed the opportunity for rehabilitative care. The need for rest and time off from caring responsibilities was the most urgent need among spousal carers. Especially as dementia progresses, the multiple symptoms, like restlessness and staying awake at night, cause burden and sleep debt (Van Aerschot et al, 2021). The lack of rest and time off from caring responsibilities caused carers to worry about their ability to cope. This suggests that excessive responsibilities are put on informal carers as they top up and fill in insufficient care, which can further lead to their exhaustion.

Sometimes health care services should have been more easily accessible. A person with dementia may experience rapid changes in their condition or develop a comorbidity. However, some of the persons with dementia and their spousal carers reported difficulties in getting a doctor's appointment in the public sector, where the service users pay only a low fee (Van Aerschot et al, 2021). Private medical services are easily available, but the costs are too high for many older persons. Thus, they could not count on receiving health care services when they needed them. This could also cause repeated visits to emergency care, which in turn further burdens acute care services (Aaltonen et al, 2021).

Our qualitative research shows that the spousal carers of persons with dementia often experience unmet needs and care poverty due to inadequate support for caring and inaccessible or insufficient services. The spousal carers did their best to meet the needs of their partner with dementia, even if that meant experiencing burden or having to give up their own needs for rest or recovery.

Discussion

We have shown that persons with dementia have more care needs and receive more care but also have more unmet needs than other older persons. The survey data show that about one in five persons with dementia have unmet needs related to IADLs, such as moving outside the home or grocery shopping, and one in six have unmet needs with banking or accessing care services (Table 11.1). The qualitative analysis revealed that even if people with dementia were offered a service, their needs were left unmet if the social and emotional side of care was neglected. This was the case with respite care, which was not used if it was considered of poor quality and unreliable. The non-take-up of respite care leads to unmet needs as the carer misses the opportunity for rest and the care user misses the possibility for rehabilitative care. This shows how a failure to respond to care needs may have an impact not only on the well-being of the person with dementia but also on their informal carer.

The lack of reliable services and support for a person with dementia may thus turn to care poverty faced by the informal carer, usually a family member. In a system such as the Finnish one, where adequate care services are to be provided through a publicly funded system and people often assume that sufficient formal services are available, the extensive role of informal care is easily hidden or not entirely recognised. However, as family members provide care in addition to or instead of care services and cover up the possibly insufficient formal care, they may experience unmet needs due to an undue burden of care. According to our empirical research, the care of older persons living in the community with dementia is not socially sustainable when insufficient care services cause unmet needs and informal carers compensate for insufficient services even at the cost of their own well-being. In the worst case, the family member may no longer be able to take care of the person with dementia, and their own health and functioning may decline.

Socio-emotional care poverty, understood as the need for more quantity or quality of social, emotional, and psychosocial contacts and support, is one of the three domains of care poverty (Kröger, 2022: 39, 42–4). In our qualitative research, psychosocial needs that were not fully met included the need for social activities such as social contact, companionship and emotional support. Informal carers especially expressed the need to talk with someone who could relieve their stress and worries. People with dementia and their carers expressed the need for a personal relationship with the care staff. This is in line with results from other European countries. A study conducted with data from dementia and non-dementia care dyads from three countries – Finland, Austria and Slovenia – revealed that the unmet needs of the person receiving care and their relatives were often first and foremost psychosocial (Van Aerschot et al, 2022; see also Dunatchik et al, 2016). It seems that the task-oriented service system does not pay enough attention to people's needs for support and social interaction. Simply providing care and services that the care users do not feel meet their needs can be seen as a waste of resources.

Our studies show that unmet needs are often due to people not knowing what services are available and how to attain them. People living at home with dementia or their informal carers need to have enough information about the available services. Now it seems that navigating the service system and finding suitable and needed services is often too complex. Hence, in addition to the lack or insufficiency of services that cause unmet needs, the confusion related to available services and the lack of a sense of control put a considerable strain on both people with dementia and their informal carers.

Person-centred care, recommended specifically for people with dementia, can help identify insufficient care and unmet needs and help plan how to respond to them. Fazio et al (2018) provide recommendations for person-centred care, which includes knowing the person with dementia, recognising and accepting their reality, identifying and supporting ongoing opportunities for meaningful engagement, building and nurturing genuine, caring relationships, and creating and maintaining a community that supports individuals, families and staff. By implementing these recommendations, better opportunities for psychosocial support and recognition of the actual needs of people with dementia as well as their family members could be achieved. However, it is clear that due to frequent staff changes, and if the time spent with the person with dementia is only mainly for physical treatment procedures, these recommendations are difficult to implement.

Nevertheless, it is important to remember that not all persons with dementia have unmet needs. For many, especially in the condition's early stages, living at home and continuing an independent life is not a problem. The minor needs caused by dementia can usually be managed with little help from services or informal help. However, as dementia progresses, increasing needs and worsening of the condition are inevitable. Predicting the timing, increase and extent of care needs in advance can be difficult. For this reason, easily available information on help and services as well as the accessibility of services are crucial for persons with dementia.

At the societal level, the number of people needing help increases with longevity, and the number of people with unmet needs will likely increase unless the accessibility and availability of services and support for informal care are improved. As people tend to take care of their next-of-kin and family members, even at the cost of their own well-being, the risk of unmet needs has to be considered for both care users and informal carers.

Policy implications

Care needs due to dementia will increase rapidly in the coming decades in Finland and worldwide. Dementia has become more prevalent along with the increasing life expectancy and the fact that an increasing number of people live to a very advanced age. Worldwide, about 55 million persons have dementia and the number is predicted to increase to 140 million by 2050 (WHO, 2023). Insufficient help and care, therefore, affects an increasing number of people – both those with dementia and their family members.

People with dementia and their carers may lack information on the services they could receive and what would be available. When several different services are needed, navigating the system requires a multi-professional plan and monitoring how the services are integrated. The importance of dementia care planning has been recognised, but it still seems not to be consistently realised. Services must be better coordinated, and collaboration between professionals and health and long-term care sectors must be improved to enable integrated services that respond to the real needs of persons with dementia. In advanced dementia, continuity of care and the ability to revise the care plan according to the changing needs are essential. A better understanding of and response to psychosocial needs and adopting person-centred care principles would help solve some unmet needs. In discussing policy implications, it is essential to consider what kind of needs can be assumed to be covered by public services, what role private services or the third sector can play, and what role is appropriate for informal care.

Conclusion

The current service system in Finland is insufficiently prepared for the complex care needs of home-dwelling people with dementia, leading to unmet needs and care poverty. This, in turn, can be reflected in the informal carer's increased responsibilities and strain. Our studies lead to three important conclusions. First, persons with dementia have an increased risk of care poverty. Second, when informal carers either provide care or replace and top-up insufficient support and services at the cost of their well-being, the risk of care poverty is shifted from persons with dementia to their informal carers. Third, while persons with dementia have more unmet care needs related to ADLs and IADLs than older persons without dementia, they also experience socio-emotional care poverty.

The care poverty experienced by persons with dementia and their informal carers hampers the well-being and dignified old age of individuals, cost savings at the societal level, and the larger goal of social sustainability. The service system must be able to recognise and meet the changing needs, also psychosocial needs, of persons with dementia and their carers. Understanding the different dimensions of unmet needs, particularly for people with dementia, is crucial as the population ages, and the number of people with dementia and the need for care inevitably increase.

References

Aaltonen, M.S. and Van Aerschot, L.H. (2021) 'Unmet care needs are common among community-dwelling older people with memory problems in Finland', *Scandinavian Journal of Public Health*, 49(4): 423–32.

Aaltonen, M.S., Martin-Matthews, A., Pulkki, J.M., Eskola, P. and Jolanki, O.H. (2021) 'Experiences of people with memory disorders and their spouse carers on influencing formal care: they ask my wife questions that they should ask me', *Dementia*, 20(7): 2307–22.

Bertogg, A. and Strauss, S. (2020) 'Spousal caregiving arrangements in Europe: the role of gender, socioeconomic status and the welfare state', *Ageing & Society*, 40(4): 735–58.

Bressan, V., Visintini, C. and Palese, A. (2020) 'What do family caregivers of people with dementia need? A mixed-method systematic review', *Health and Social Care in the Community*, 28(6): 1942–60.

Brodaty, H. and Donkin, M. (2009) 'Family caregivers of people with dementia', *Dialogues in Clinical Neuroscience*, 11(2): 217–28.

Cao, Q., Tan, C.C., Xu, W., Hu, H., Cao, X.P., Dong, Q., et al (2020) 'The prevalence of dementia: a systematic review and meta-analysis', *Journal of Alzheimers Disease*, 73(3): 1157–66.

Connors, M.H., Seeher, K., Teixeira-Pinto, A., Woodward, M., Ames, D. and Brodaty, H. (2020) 'Dementia and caregiver burden: a three-year longitudinal study', *International Journal of Geriatric Psychiatry*, 35(2): 250–8.

Dunatchik, A., Icardi, R., Roberts, C. and Blake, M. (2016) *Predicting Unmet Social Care Needs and Links with Well-being*, London: Ipsos MORI Social Research Institute.

Erhola, K., Kehusmaa, S., Hammar, T., Noro, A. and Mäkelä, M. (2018) Avun antaminen [Giving help], in P. Koponen, K. Borodulin, A. Lundqvist, K. Sääksjärvi and S. Koskinen (eds) *Terveys, toimintakyky ja hyvinvointi Suomessa: FinTerveys 2017 –tutkimus* [Health, Functional Ability and Well-being in Finland: The FinTerveys 2017 Study], Helsinki: Terveyden ja hyvinvoinnin laitos.

Eskola, P. and Jolanki, O. (2022) 'Mikä muuttui 20 vuoden aikana? Pohdintaa ikääntyvän puoliso-omaishoitajan asemasta ja kotiin saatavasta tuesta' [What changed in 20 years? Discussion concerning the position of the ageing spousal carer and support available at home], *Gerontologia*, 36(4): 412–19.

Eurocarers (2023) 'About carers', *Eurocarers*. Available from: https://eurocar ers.org/about-carers/ [Accessed 6 February 2024].

Fazio, S., Pace, D., Flinner, J. and Kallmyer, B. (2018) 'The fundamentals of person-centered care for individuals with dementia', *The Gerontologist*, 58(suppl_1): S10–19.

FIHW (Finnish Institute for Health and Welfare) (2022) 'Memory disorders', *Finnish Institute for Health and Welfare*. Available from: https://thl.fi/en/ web/chronic-diseases/memory-disorders [Accessed 4 February 2024].

FIHW (2023) 'Home care', *Finnish Institute for Health and Welfare*. Available from: https://thl.fi/en/topics/ageing/older-people-services-undergoing-a-change/home-care [Accessed 4 February 2024].

GBD (GBD 2019 Dementia Forecasting Collaborators) (2022) 'Estimation of the global prevalence of dementia in 2019 and forecasted prevalence in 2050: an analysis for the Global Burden of Disease Study 2019', *Lancet Public Health*, 7(2): e105–25.

Isaacs, B. and Neville, Y. (1976) 'The needs of old people: the "interval" as a method of measurement', *British Journal of Preventive and Social Medicine*, 30(2): 79–85.

Kauppinen, T., Mattila-Holappa, P., Perkiö-Mäkelä, M., Saalo, A., Toikkanen, J., Tuomivaara, S., et al (2013) *Työ ja terveys Suomessa 2012* [Work and Health in Finland 2012], Helsinki: Työterveyslaitos.

Kerpershoek, L., de Vugt, M., Wolfs, C., Woods, B., Jelley, H., Orrell, M., et al (2018) 'Needs and quality of life of people with middle-stage dementia and their family carers from the European Actifcare study: when informal care alone may not suffice', *Aging and Mental Health*, 22(7): 897–902.

Khanassov, V., Rojas-Rozo, L., Sourial, R., Yand, X.Q. and Vedel, I. (2021) 'Needs of patients with dementia and their caregivers in primary care: lessons learned from the Alzheimer plan of Quebec', *BMC Family Practice*, 22(1): Article 186.

Kolanowski, A., Fortinsky, R.H., Calkins, M., Davangere, P.D., Gould, E., Heller, T., et al (2018) 'Advancing research on care needs and supportive approaches for persons with dementia: recommendations and rationale', *Journal of the American Medical Directors Association*, 19(12): 1047–53.

Kröger, T. (2019) 'Looking for the easy way out: demographic panic and the twists and turns of long-term care policy in Finland', in T.-K. Jing, S. Kuhnle, Y. Pan and S. Chen (eds) *Aging Welfare and Social Policy: China and the Nordic Countries in Comparative Perspective*, Cham: Springer, pp 91–104.

Kröger, T. (2022) *Care Poverty: When Older People's Needs Remain Unmet*, Cham: Palgrave Macmillan.

Kröger, T., Mathew Puthenparambil, J. and Van Aerschot, L. (2019) 'Care poverty: unmet care needs in a Nordic welfare state', *International Journal of Care and Caring*, 3(4): 485–500.

Kuzuya, M., Enoki, H., Hasegawa, J., Izawa, S., Hirakawa, Y., Shimokata, H., et al (2011) 'Impact of caregiver burden on adverse health outcomes in community-dwelling dependent older care recipients', *American Journal of Geriatric Psychiatry*, 19(4): 382–91.

Linna, M., Silander, K., Hörhammer, I., Koivuranta, P., Mikkola, T., Virta, L., et al (2019) *Iäkkäiden muistisairaiden sosiaali- ja terveyspalvelujen käyttö ja kustannukset* [Use and Expenditures of Social and Health Care by People with Dementia], Helsinki: Suomen Kuntaliitto.

Luppa, M., Luck, T., Brähler, E., König, H.H. and Riedel-Heller, S.G. (2008) 'Prediction of institutionalisation in dementia: a systematic review', *Dementia and Geriatric Cognitive Disorder*, 26(1): 65–78.

MSAH (Ministry of Social Affairs and Health) (2023) 'Services for older people', *Ministry of Social Affairs and Health*. Available from: https://stm.fi/en/older-people-services [Accessed 11 January 2023].

Ngandu, T. and Kivipelto, M. (2018) 'Monimuotoiset elintapainterventiot muistisairauksien ehkäisyssä' [Multidomain lifestyle interventions in the prevention of memory disorder epidemic], *Duodecim*, 134: 2547–53.

Noro, A., Mäkelä, M., Jussimäki, T. and Finne-Soveri, H. (2014) 'Ikäihmisten palveluiden kehityslinjoja 2000-luvulla' [Development of care services for older people in the 2000s], in A. Noro and H. Alastalo (eds) *Vanhuspalvelulain 980/2012 toimeenpanon seuranta* [Monitoring the Implementation of the Act on Services of Older People 980/2012], Helsinki: Terveyden ja hyvinvoinnin laitos, pp 19–30.

Nunez, F.E. (2021) 'Factors influencing decisions to admit family members with dementia to long-term care facilities', *Nursing Forum*, 56(2): 372–81.

Omaishoitajaliitto (2021) 'Tietoa omaishoidosta' [Information about family care], *Omaishoitajaliitto*. Available from: https://omaishoitajat.fi/mita-on-omaishoito/tietoa-omaishoidosta/ [Accessed 4 February 2024].

Rostgaard, T., Jacobsen, F., Kröger, T. and Peterson, E. (2022) 'Revisiting the Nordic long-term care model for older people – still equal?', *European Journal of Ageing*, 19(2): 201–10.

THL (Terveyden ja hyvinvoinnin laitos) (2021) *Sosiaali- ja terveysalan tilastollinen vuosikirja 2020* [Statistical Yearbook on Social Welfare and Health Care 2020], Helsinki: Terveyden ja hyvinvoinnin laitos.

THL (2022) *Sosiaali- ja terveysalan tilastollinen vuosikirja 2022* [Statistical Yearbook on Social Welfare and Health Care 2022], Helsinki: Terveyden ja hyvinvoinnin laitos.

THL (2024) *Iäkkäiden toimintakyky ja palvelutarpeet: RAI-vertailutiedot 2022* [Functioning and Service Needs of Older People: Comparative RAI Information 2022], Helsinki: Terveyden ja hyvinvoinnin laitos.

Van Aerschot, L. and Kröger, T. (2023) 'Suomalaisen vanhuspalvelujärjestelmän ongelmakohdat' [Problems of the Finnish long-term care system], in T. Sihto and P. Vasara (eds) *Hoivan pimeä puoli* [Dark Side of Care], Helsinki: Gaudeamus, pp 237–54.

Van Aerschot, L., Eskola, P. and Aaltonen, M. (2021) 'Muistisairaiden ja puoliso-omaishoitajien kokemuksia tuen riittämättömyydestä' [Experiences of inadequate support by people with dementia and spousal carers], *Gerontologia*, 35(3): 264–82.

Van Aerschot, L., Kadi, S., Rodrigues, R., Hrast, M.F., Hlebec, V. and Aaltonen, M. (2022) 'Community-dwelling older adults and their informal carers call for more attention to psychosocial needs: interview study on unmet care needs in three European countries', *Archives of Gerontology and Geriatrics*, 101: 104672.

Verbeek-Oudijk, D., Woittiez, I., Eggink, E. and Putman, L. (2014) *Who Cares in Europe? A Comparison of Long-Term Care for the Over-50s in Sixteen European Countries*, The Hague: National Institute for Social Research.

Wennberg, A., Dye, C., Streetman-Loy, B. and Pham, H. (2015) 'Alzheimer's patient familial caregivers: a review of burden and interventions', *Health & Social Work*, 40(4): e162–9.

WHO (World Health Organization) (2023) 'Dementia', *World Health Organization*. Available from: https://www.who.int/news-room/fact-sheets/detail/dementia [Accessed 24 January 2023].

Williams, J., Lyons, B. and Rowland, D. (1997) 'Unmet long-term care needs of elderly people in the community: a review of the literature', *Home Health Care Services Quarterly*, 16(1/2): 93–119.

Zhou, Y., Slachevasky, A. and Calvo, E. (2018) 'Health conditions and unmet needs for assistance to perform activities of daily living among older adults with dementia in Chile', *International Journal of Geriatric Psychiatry*, 33(7): 964–71.

12

Reproducing inequalities: unmet care needs and managerial care

Petra Ulmanen

Introduction

Managerial care is a family caregiving task involving handling contacts with health and social care services in order to make them meet the care needs at hand. While caregiving is often understood as providing direct, hands-on care, managerial caregiving implies an indirect provision of care, including identifying what services are needed and managing their provision by others (Archbold, 1983). Brody (2004) described managerial caregiving as an ongoing task involving 'knowing or finding out what entitlements the older person has ... identifying what services are needed and knowing whether they are available in the community ... gaining access to and mobilising those services ... and following through to see that services are actually received and are satisfactory' (Brody, 2004: 35).

Managerial care has received limited research interest, especially in a Nordic context. According to the few surveys that have been identified that include questions about managerial care, it is provided by the majority of caregivers. Unlike most other caregiving tasks, managerial care is equally common among men and women and more common among caregivers with higher socioeconomic status (Rosenthal et al, 2007; Ulmanen, 2015; AARP, 2020). It contributes to a specific form of caregiving burden, referred to as the structural burden of caregiving, arising from 'managing complex interactions with the fragmented structures of formal health and social care systems' (Taylor and Quesnel-Vallée, 2017: 20). Funk and colleagues point out that the 'structural features of formal care systems influence the amount, difficulty, and complexity of what carers do as they interface with those systems' (Funk et al, 2019: 426). Managerial caregiving has a negative impact on carers' well-being and work performance (Rosenthal et al, 2007; Ulmanen, 2015). Finding out about available care services and accessing them is perceived as time-consuming and difficult, and locating and coordinating care services increases stress for caregivers (Peel and Harding, 2014; Taylor and Quesnel-Vallée, 2017; Funk et al, 2019; Ulmanen et al, 2023).

By introducing the concept of care poverty for 'the deprivation of adequate coverage of care needs resulting from an interplay between individual and societal factors', Kröger (2022: 26) links unmet care needs at the individual level to social inequalities and welfare state policies. He describes care poverty as a lack of adequate care, including both formal and informal sources, resulting in a situation where care needs remain at least partially unmet. In this chapter, managerial caregiving is regarded as a response by family members to their perceptions of unmet care needs, and a practice aimed at avoiding care poverty by ensuring that care services meet these needs. Thus, managerial caregiving can potentially reduce informal care responsibilities without leading to care poverty. If care services do not meet the perceived needs, despite managerial caregiving efforts, family members, however, often try to avoid care poverty by providing hands-on care. They may either reduce or increase their caregiving responsibilities and burden by providing managerial care, depending on whether it is successful or not. Thus, successful managerial caregiving implies the possibility of meeting the needs of both care receivers and their informal carers.

Nevertheless, managerial caregiving will likely exacerbate socioeconomic inequalities among both family caregivers and care receivers. Caregivers with higher socioeconomic status are likely to be more successful in accessing adequate care services, thereby improving the situation of those they care for and their own situation by reducing their responsibilities. A middle-class advantage has been identified in accessing appropriate social services. It is created by the cultural and social capital possessed by service users in terms of education, networks, skills and resources, which are helpful in negotiating with service providers. In addition, professionals are more likely to empathise with service users who share a similar class background, resulting in preferential treatment (Hastings and Matthews, 2015; cf Shim, 2010).

Family members with more social and cultural capital are assumed to have greater chances to attain more appropriate publicly financed care services, similarly as economic capital increases their possibilities to purchase services on the market. Cultural capital is understood as 'the repertoire of cultural skills, verbal and nonverbal competencies, attitudes and behaviors, and interactional styles' that influence interactions with care professionals (Shim, 2010: 1). Social capital is regarded as resources, such as knowledge about how the care system works, accessed from social networks, including family and friends, networks established through paid employment and connections with care professionals (cf Barrett et al, 2014).

Besides class, gendered norms influence care professionals' expectations of individuals' behaviour and may imply a gender bias in needs assessment and treatment. For example, expectations of stoic men and emotional women may lead professionals to take women's needs less seriously (Samulowitz et al, 2018). Women might find it more difficult to make demands on care services to relieve them from what is perceived as their personal responsibility, and professionals might be less responsive to their demands. In a vignette experiment on needs assessment, an older woman received less home care services if she had a daughter than if she had a son (Jakobsson et al, 2016).

In exploring how gender and class influence managerial caregiving, this chapter will use an intersectional framing described by Anthias (2013). Intersectionality is primarily understood as 'a heuristic device for understanding boundaries and hierarchies of social life' (Anthias, 2013: 4). Gender and class are seen as social categories or divisions that are mutually constitutive and involved in boundary-making and hierarchy-making processes producing inequality and disadvantage. How these processes play out varies by time and place, and therefore, social divisions do not always matter in particular contexts or they may matter in unexpected ways. Therefore, Anthias stresses that an intersectional analysis must carefully attend to context, meaning and variability.

From an understanding of managerial caregiving as a practice aimed at ensuring that care services meet care needs, it is assumed that managerial caregiving reproduces inequalities by affecting the quantity and quality of care services received and, in turn, the extent to which care needs are met. This chapter aims to explore family members' managerial caregiving in terms of the tasks involved, the resources used and the challenges faced, and whether and how the interplay between gender and class matters for these issues.

Context: Swedish long-term care

For over three decades, long-term care has been rationed in Sweden. Although Sweden still fares fairly well in long-term care coverage compared to most European countries, it is among the countries with the most dramatic decline in nursing home beds (Spasova et al, 2018). Although the number of nursing home beds has declined by more than 30 per cent since the year 2000, home care coverage has remained unchanged (Socialstyrelsen, 2009; 2020; Ulmanen and Szebehely, 2015). As increasing numbers of older persons with extensive needs, who would previously have lived in nursing homes, now remain at home, home care users have more extensive and complex needs than before (Brändström et al, 2022). Home care did, however, not receive the resources necessary to meet the increased care needs in the community, and both family care and privately purchased services have increased (Ulmanen and Szebehely, 2015). Due to increased standardisation and fragmentation of home care, more users receive many short visits from different care workers. Those receiving at least two visits daily meet an average of 16 different care workers over a two-week period

(Socialstyrelsen, 2020). Further, more than half of home care visits last 15 minutes or less (Strandell, 2020).

Sweden has a highly decentralised care system, in which 290 municipalities in the country are responsible for financing and providing long-term care, and 21 regions are responsible for financing and providing most health care. The provision of long-term care is governed at the national level through the Social Services Act, a framework legislation not providing any detailed regulations or specific rights. The responsibility for the specific design and execution of the law is devolved to the municipalities. Local politicians instruct needs assessors or their managers to make decisions in accordance with the law, and they are often urged to follow the local assessment guidelines. Although the national law states that individual needs should determine access to care, the municipalities are free to decide what level of needs is required and many municipalities' assessment guidelines have become more restrictive due to budgetary constraints (Dunér and Nordström, 2006; Socialstyrelsen, 2011).

If an application for long-term care is approved, users in many municipalities can choose from both public and private care providers, the vast majority of which are for-profit. The number of providers from which users can choose, as well as the amount and type of support provided by needs assessors to help users make choices, varies considerably between local authorities and over time. However, the increasing standardisation and fragmentation of home care means that users generally have limited choice about which care workers will support them, when, with what and how (Strandell, 2020). Nevertheless, Swedish legislation strongly emphasises the right to self-determination and that providing long-term care services should be based on voluntary participation. Services cannot be provided against an individual's will. Even in cases of severe cognitive decline, individuals cannot be declared incompetent in making decisions concerning long-term care, and their right to self-determination cannot legally be taken away (Nedlund and Taghizadeh Larsson, 2016).

Methods

Family members, mostly adult children, of home-dwelling older persons with complex health and social care needs living in different municipalities in Stockholm County were interviewed twice in 2017–20. Thirty-two individuals were interviewed, 22 women and ten men. Around half a year or a year after the first interview, a follow-up interview was carried out with 24 of the interviewees. Most of the interviews lasted for more than an hour and, in total, the material consists of more than 67 hours of interviews.

Most of the interviewees were recruited by municipal needs assessors. Family members who participated in care planning meetings at hospital discharge or were the contact person in the social services file were asked to participate. As the needs assessors recruited fewer interviewees than planned,

Table 12.1: Socioeconomic characteristics of the sample

	Men (n=10)	Women (n=22)	Total (n=32)
Higher education	4	10	14
Lower education	6	12	18
White-collar job	9	15	24
Blue-collar job	1	7	8

Source: Family member interviews.

municipal family care advisors (social workers providing information and emotional support to family carers) were asked to do additional recruitment. They recruited seven interviewees, all women.

Table 12.1 shows the socioeconomic characteristics of the sample. Although almost half of both men and women had higher educational attainment (defined as a tertiary education of at least three years), men more often had white-collar jobs. Only one of the interviewed men had a blue-collar job.

A thematic analysis was performed (Braun and Clarke, 2006), using the NVivo software. During the initial coding of the material, a broad and mainly inductive approach was used. The material was read for any themes related to experiences of and contacts with care services. Later readings identified themes driven by specific research questions. The initial emerging patterns and potential coding schemes were adjusted repeatedly to ensure the accuracy of the content on the emerging themes.

In the second step of the analysis, drawing on Brody (2004), cases were compared to identify the managerial caregiving process over time. Summaries of this process were written on each case, focusing on the themes, and they were, in turn, reviewed and adjusted according to the processes. Five main themes emerged: *triggers and tasks*; *knowledge and skills*; *the right to self-determination*; *being difficult*; and *buying your way out*. The findings were anonymised, and they are presented in the next section grouped according to the themes.

Results

Triggers and tasks

When family members perceived that the older person had unmet care needs and difficulties in accessing care services or getting them to meet the needs at hand, they started to provide managerial care. Thus, it was triggered by perceptions of unmet care needs and aimed at making care services meet the needs at hand.

Figure 12.1: Conceptual model of the process of managerial caregiving

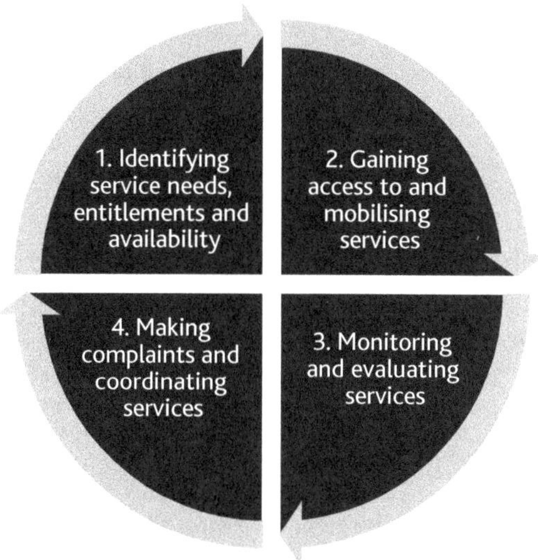

Four main managerial caregiving tasks were identified. They were generally performed in a specific chronological order, forming a process of managerial caregiving, illustrated in Figure 12.1. First, when unmet care needs were detected, family members tried to *identify service needs and find out if the older person was entitled to services and if they were available*. This entailed navigating the care system and gathering information. The second main task was trying to *gain access to and mobilise services*, which often included several more specific tasks: motivating the older person to accept services, advocating for services and mobilising different care providers.

The third main task involved *monitoring and evaluating services* to find out if needs were met, which included watching over the older person's health status and the provision of care services. The fourth main task was to *make complaints and coordinate services* when they did not meet the needs at hand, which included advocacy and coordination work. As family members often continued to monitor and evaluate services after they had made complaints or tried to coordinate services to see if there were any results, there was feedback from the fourth task to the third.

The tasks in the managerial caregiving process were often reiterated due to changes in either the older person's needs or service provision, such as an appreciated care worker being replaced or a home care company going out of business. As the older persons were very frail and many suffered from several serious medical conditions, their care needs often changed fast and unpredictably.

Depending on how well the care system worked and if the older person accepted care services or not, it varied among family members how many managerial caregiving tasks they performed and if the process was reiterated. Some family members went through the whole process repeatedly, performing all four tasks again and again, while others only did one sequence including the first two tasks. Family members who performed all four tasks repeatedly provided managerial care for longer periods of time and assumed more responsibility for service provision. They were almost exclusively women, and they were more burdened by their caregiving compared to those who only performed the first two tasks.

As the aim of managerial caregiving was to make care services meet the needs at hand, it paused or decreased when family members thought that the older person's care needs were met to a reasonable extent and in a reasonable way, or when they simply did not have the energy or possibility to continue.

Knowledge and skills

Many family members described a lack of knowledge regarding how the care system works, the older person's needs and the best way of satisfying them as key challenges in managerial caregiving. As the decision-making involved in managerial caregiving often implied assuming a heavy responsibility and could be a matter of life or death, lack of knowledge also contributed to stress.

Such a situation was described by Kjell, a son with higher educational attainment and a white-collar job. His father ended up in hospital for ten days when he got a high temperature, fainted and fell. According to Kjell, the hospital stay could easily have been avoided if home care or home nursing had taken his temperature when he asked them to. He described himself as 'a beginner in this' without the knowledge required to handle the situation:

Who is actually responsible for his health? … Is it me as next of kin who is going to check all the time or when home nursing is there [at his father's]? It beats me, but it doesn't feel like they are taking the lead, like they have the main responsibility. And maybe that is how it is supposed to be, I don't know … I'm a beginner in this and I don't know which authorities, who is leading what.

A hospital nurse had told Kjell that his father needed more assistance because of a high risk of falling, but she did not participate in the care planning meeting at hospital discharge. When Kjell's father denied needing any home care, the needs assessor asked Kjell how much home care his father needed. 'I have no idea! … I'm not a doctor!', he said and explained that he did not want to take on the responsibility for that decision:

Even if he gets [home care] five times [a day], he could fall between the visits. Suppose that he falls, then maybe I would feel responsible and say 'Damn it, I should have asked for one time more then maybe he wouldn't have fallen'. Emotionally that is really difficult to handle.

Later, however, Kjell said, 'Now I'm beginning to get the hang of who to call and where to press.' Many family members, irrespective of gender and socioeconomic status, described developing their cognitive knowledge by gathering information and their managerial caregiving skills by increasing their experience.

Nevertheless, the resources available for family members in their managerial caregiving differed by gender and professional background. Among the interviewees, only women had an education in care, and most of them worked in the care sector. They accounted for using their professional knowledge and skills on how the care system works and how to identify and satisfy care needs as resources in all four main managerial caregiving tasks. They also accessed relevant information through their professional networks and received better treatment from care providers they knew professionally.

Anna-Lena, a daughter with higher educational attainment who worked as a manager at a long-term care unit at the municipality, explained how her professional knowledge was helpful for her when dealing with needs assessors to gain access to services:

> I know how one should bring forward an application, how one should say it and what one should demand. … It's enough if you talk about what you work with, then you end up in a different situation. So, I can imagine that it could be pretty difficult if you are not at all familiar with … because it's not as if they would inform you about your rights.

Also, when monitoring, evaluating and making complaints about services, Anna-Lena thought that her knowledge made it easier for her to speak up and that this improved her father's situation:

> Sometimes I wonder if I would not have been so demanding and said no to things, how things would have been, if it would have been even worse. I sometimes think about that because you are not born with this knowledge, and many family members maybe don't dare to be difficult or question things.

However, having the relevant knowledge often implied an increased responsibility for managerial caregiving without any guarantee of success. Several women in care occupations described that their professional knowledge made them notice more deficiencies and realise how serious they were; and if their complaints were not successful, this made them feel even more upset and powerless.

This was the case for Ylva, a daughter and an assistant nurse. Despite her extensive professional skills, she found managerial caregiving very challenging: 'I have worked with health care and doctors my whole life actually, and I know how to fight for these things. ... You have to fight and persistently ask them for things and nothing really happens anyway. Time just goes by and it's actually quite frustrating.' It became much more manageable for Ylva when her mother moved to a nursing home, as she knew the manager and the nurses professionally:

I know all the registered nurses because we have a close collaboration with them at my health care centre, and in some way, it becomes a bit easier. ... Maybe it's not supposed to be that way, but ... I know who they are. They say 'Right, you work at the health clinic', and I know the manager too. We had cooperated a lot and he is very good.

Men also described using professional skills in their managerial caregiving. Several men with white-collar jobs explained how they used their professional skills in getting people to do what they wanted as a resource when making complaints and negotiating with needs assessors and care providers. One example is Björn, who did not have any higher educational attainment and ran his own business as a landlord. He had a lot of contacts with the needs assessor and her manager when trying to get a nursing home placement for his mother:

I have run businesses of my own my whole life. You cannot sit and wait for people to do things; you have to press them all the time. ... For the last 20 years, we have had blocks of flats, and we have renovated and reconstructed apartments. Then you have the bureaucracy with building permits and paperwork and you need to check on the workmen, see that the work is running smoothly and that there is building material. It has been my task to see that everybody can work. So, you have had to be difficult and persistently ask people, and see to it that it actually happens the day it is supposed to happen.

Björn pondered how to make the most effective argument and did a great deal of research. He explained that it is not only about convincing the needs assessor. Just as he saw to it that there were building materials for the workmen, he was also feeding the needs assessor with facts and good arguments for her discussion with her manager, who made the decision on the placement. The decision was in his favour.

Björn's account is an example of the more systematic and deliberate strategies for information gathering and negotiations described by family members with white-collar jobs. While they talked about 'doing research' and working on strategies, a reactive approach was more common among family members in blue-collar jobs. For example, Gunnel and Karin were two sisters with blue-collar jobs and no higher educational attainment who cared for their mother. Although they gave detailed accounts of extensive experiences of problems in service provision, they did not describe doing any systematic information gathering or working on strategies for their efforts. They supported each other but did not access any other resources for their managerial caregiving. They just kept on making complaints when something happened. Gunnel said: 'My husband says "You are just nagging all the time, do something instead." Well, what the hell should I do?'

The right to self-determination

A major challenge concerned how to handle the older person's right to self-determination when he or she did not accept care services. This challenge was especially pronounced for family members assisting an older person with dementia, which was more common for female family members. Many described needs assessors and home care workers refraining from motivational work and asking the older person in a way seemingly intended for the older person to decline assistance. For example, home care workers asked the service user if he or she had eaten or wanted to take a walk or a shower, and immediately accepted the answer. Care workers argued that the right to self-determination prevented them from doing anything the service user objected to. This implied that the older person's care needs remained unmet although they received care services, and that extra motivation and coordination work was required from family members to make services meet these needs.

This challenge often resulted in increased caregiving responsibilities primarily for women. If their managerial caregiving did not result in increased use of care services, they continued or increased their provision of hands-on care to meet the older person's care needs. In other words, their caring responsibilities were increased rather than reduced.

This was the case for Kerstin, a daughter with higher educational attainment who had retired from a white-collar job. Her mother had dementia and did not accept home care services. Their strategy was that home care workers would first pretend to visit as guests and later on start to provide care. Her mother accepted the new guests on a daily basis, but as she did not allow them to do any practical care work, Kerstin had to continue to provide hands-on care every day in order for her mother's needs to be met:

> Home care visited once a day and she paid the full fee. But when they were there, she said 'No, I don't need anything.' And they cannot do anything if she says no. ... They came, but I did the grocery shopping,

I saw to that she got up in the mornings. And then we made food, but my husband and I agreed to not more than three times a week in our place, so I went to her in the evenings and brought her dinner.

Being difficult

Although both men and women used their professional skills in making demands or complaints, men more often described themselves as confident in this role and women more often expressed unease. Only women said that they did not want to be a nuisance, 'a difficult daughter' or 'a difficult family member'. Although more women reported receiving crucial advice and support from care professionals, they were more likely to report receiving poor treatment. None of the men described being treated badly or talked about being a difficult son or anything similar. When asked if they thought that they were regarded as difficult, several men answered yes. On the question of how this made them feel, they gave almost identical answers. For example, Krister said, 'I'm not worried about people thinking that I'm difficult', Kjell said, 'I don't give a sh★★ about it', and Tomas said, 'I have no problem with that'.

Although both men and women expressed that they focused on the older person's needs in these situations, rather than how they themselves appeared or felt, it seemed to have different meanings for them. While several men explained that they did not seek conflict or did not want to prove themselves to be right, several women described a struggle against their feelings of unease. In addition, a few women but no man described feelings of self-doubt in suspecting that they exaggerated the problems in service delivery.

Hillevi, a daughter with higher educational attainment and a white-collar job, was helping her mother. She had made many complaints about home care services and nursing home care. She described being worried that if she complained too much, the care workers at the nursing home would treat her mother badly. She also struggled with the feeling that maybe she was in fact the problem, not how care services worked, and suspected that her standards were too high:

> Oh my God, now I'm doing it again! I'm starting to think that it's my own fault. Am I nuts, or maybe I have to do what my friend is talking about, to have more acceptance, like 'I'm accepting that it is like this; she may well sit in her pee'. And I cannot really tolerate it. I guess that it's about your personality and how much you have developed your Mindfulness. I wish I was more like that but I haven't succeeded yet.

Several family members who performed all four managerial caregiving tasks repeatedly described, as Hillevi, lowering their standards over time.

As their energy declined, they had to focus on the most serious threats to the older person's health and well-being to be able to continue their managerial caregiving.

Buying your way out

Among the family members who had extensive experience with serious problems in service delivery, which remained despite their numerous complaints, a few daughters chose another strategy: to try to buy their way out by hiring private helpers. This was the case for Ann-Charlotte, who had higher educational attainment and a high-level position. When she suffered burnout, she realised that she could not make home care services work, no matter how hard she tried. She hired three individuals privately to provide care for her mother, one of them assisting her on a daily basis and handling some of the contacts with the municipal home care. Ann-Charlotte instructed and supervised all care workers, both the regular ones and those she hired privately. For example, when the municipality sent in new home care workers, they could not use the machine her mother needed to breathe, so she had to teach them.

Although hiring private helpers was a strategy intended to reduce Ann-Charlotte's extensive care responsibilities, she reported increased responsibilities in managing these arrangements, including meeting the emotional needs of helpers:

> When I have to fix and call and arrange all these things, I get this feeling of sickness, like I'm on the minus side. … Even though you don't have the energy to talk with them, things happen in their lives and then you talk with them and support them. That's how it works. That's why I have to make sure that they get on well and give them a small Christmas gift and a small Easter egg. It's not a big thing, but you have to show them appreciation and make them feel that they get on well, but it adds to the things on my list.

Discussion

The assumption behind this chapter is that family members' use of economic, cultural and social capital in trying to make care services meet the older person's needs reduces their caregiving responsibilities and structural burden without increasing the risk of care poverty. The results, however, show the opposite for female carers. Although they seem to have used all resources available – economic, cultural and social – in their extensive managerial caregiving, they seldom succeeded in making care services meet the needs at hand. So, instead of reducing their care responsibilities, their managerial care work increased for long periods of time. To avoid care poverty, they assumed greater caregiving responsibilities, both regarding hands-on care and managerial care, and suffered more structural burden than men.

For women with a professional background in care, this was an essential resource for their managerial caregiving. But it also made them realise the severity of the problems in service delivery and the risks implied for the service user, which made them increase their efforts, and if they were not successful, they felt even more upset and powerless. Women with access to money to hire private help used it as a valuable resource in their managerial caregiving. However, the work involved in organising, instructing and supervising these private helpers and attending to their emotional needs seemed to add to, rather than reduce, their already extensive responsibilities. In addition, the challenge related to the older person's right to self-determination often resulted in increased caregiving responsibilities, primarily for women, as they more often cared for an older person with dementia.

Whereas both men and women with higher socioeconomic status generally described more systematic and deliberate strategies for information gathering and negotiation, the intersection of gender and class proved to matter in unexpected ways. Access to economic, cultural and social capital did not seem to give women any clear advantage, although it did benefit the care receivers. For men, the pattern is harder to detect, probably because only one man had a blue-collar job, and the main resource identified among men was their professional skills, which were primarily developed in white-collar jobs. Men used their professional skill of getting people to do what they wanted them to do and were more confident and unconcerned about making demands and complaints than most women. This may indicate a specific male middle-class advantage in accessing appropriate care services.

Women found it more difficult to make demands and complaints about care services, expressed unease and did not want to be 'a difficult daughter'. This could be an effect of gendered norms regarding care responsibilities. There may still be a taboo for women against demanding to be relieved of what is seen as their personal responsibility – meeting other people's needs. The fear of being perceived as 'a difficult daughter' could thus be related to a fear of being 'a bad daughter'. Women could also be regarded as responsible for meeting care professionals' needs, making it even harder to be demanding. Another possibility is that women actually make higher demands on care services to legitimise a relief from what is perceived as their personal responsibility, which would make them more difficult.

A key issue concerns the perception of unmet needs that triggers managerial caregiving, and the standards by which needs can be considered met or unmet. If gendered norms create expectations of emotional women that lead care professionals to take women's needs less seriously, the corresponding expectations of stoic men may lead professionals to be more sensitive to their demands (cf Samulowitz et al, 2018). The question is whether men are actually better negotiators, or whether they face less resistance from care professionals. If women place higher demands on care services, it would be difficult for them to be successful negotiators.

While access to various resources in managerial caregiving did not seem to reduce women's caregiving responsibilities and burden, it did benefit the care receivers and possibly male carers. Thus, while managerial caregiving alleviated care poverty, the needs of female carers, in particular, remained unmet.

References

AARP (2020) *Caregiving in the United States 2020*, Washington, DC: AARP and National Alliance for Caregiving.

Anthias, F. (2013) 'Intersectional what? Social divisions, intersectionality and levels of analysis', *Ethnicities*, 13(1): 3–19.

Archbold, P.G. (1983) 'Impact of parent-caring on women', *Family Relations*, 32(1): 39–45.

Barrett, P., Hale, B. and Butler, M. (2014) *Family Care and Social Capital: Transitions in Informal Care*, Dordrecht: Springer.

Brändström, A., Meyer, A., Modig, K. and Sandström, G. (2022) 'Determinants of home care utilization among the Swedish old: nationwide register-based study', *European Journal of Ageing*, 19(3): 652–62.

Braun, V. and Clarke, V. (2006) 'Using thematic analysis in psychology', *Qualitative Research in Psychology*, 3(2): 77–101.

Brody, E. (2004) *Women in the Middle: Their Parent-Care Years* (2nd edn), New York: Springer.

Dunér, A. and Nordström, M. (2006) 'The discretion and power of street level bureaucrats: an example from Swedish municipal eldercare', *European Journal of Social Work*, 9(4): 425–44.

Funk, L.M., Dansereau, L. and Novek, S. (2019) 'Carers as system navigators: exploring sources, processes and outcomes of structural burden', *The Gerontologist*, 59(3): 426–35.

Hastings, A. and Matthews, P. (2015) 'Bourdieu and the Big Society: empowering the powerful in public service provision?', *Policy & Politics*, 43(4): 545–60.

Jakobsson, N., Kotsadam, A., Syse, A. and Øien, H. (2016) 'Gender bias in public long-term care? A survey experiment among care managers', *Journal of Economic Behavior & Organization*, 131(Part B): 126–38.

Kröger, T. (2022) *Care Poverty: When Older People's Needs Remain Unmet*, Cham: Palgrave Macmillan.

Nedlund, A.C. and Taghizadeh Larsson, A. (2016). 'To protect and to support: how citizenship and self-determination are legally constructed and managed in practice for people living with dementia in Sweden', *Dementia*, 15(3): 343–57.

Peel, E. and Harding, R. (2014) ' "It's a huge maze, the system, it's a terrible maze": dementia carers' constructions of navigating health and social care services', *Dementia*, 13(5): 642–61.

Rosenthal, C.J., Martin-Matthews, A. and Keefe, J.M. (2007) 'Care management and care provision for older relatives amongst employed informal care-givers', *Ageing & Society*, 27(5): 755–78.

Samulowitz, A., Gremyr, I., Eriksson, E. and Hensing, G. (2018) ' "Brave men" and "emotional women": a theory-guided literature review on gender bias in health care and gendered norms towards patients with chronic pain', *Pain Research and Management*, 25: 6358624.

Shim, J.K. (2010) 'Cultural health capital: a theoretical approach to understanding health care interactions and the dynamics of unequal treatment', *Journal of Health and Social Behavior*, 51(1): 1–15.

Socialstyrelsen (2009) *Vård och omsorg om äldre: Lägesrapport 2008* [Health and Social Care for Older People: Progress Report 2008], Stockholm: Socialstyrelsen.

Socialstyrelsen (2011) *Hälso- och sjukvård och socialtjänst: Lägesrapport 2011* [Health and Social Care: Progress Report 2011], Stockholm: Socialstyrelsen.

Socialstyrelsen (2020) *Vård och omsorg om äldre: Lägesrapport 2020* [Health and Social Care for Older People: Progress Report 2020], Stockholm: Socialstyrelsen.

Spasova, S., Baeten, R., Coster, S., Ghailani, D., Peña-Casas, R. and Vanhercke, B. (2018) *Challenges in Long-term Care in Europe: A Study of National Policies 2018*, Brussels: European Commission.

Strandell, R. (2020) 'Care workers under pressure: a comparison of the work situation in Swedish home care 2005 and 2015', *Health and Social Care in the Community*, 28(1): 137–47.

Taylor, M.G. and Quesnel-Vallée, A. (2017) 'The structural burden of caregiving: shared challenges in the United States and Canada', *The Gerontologist*, 57(1): 19–25.

Ulmanen, P. (2015) 'Kvinnors och mäns hjälp till sina gamla föräldrar: innehåll, omfattning och konsekvenser' [Women's and men's help to their elderly parents: content, extent, and consequences], *Socialvetenskaplig tidskrift*, 22(2): 111–32.

Ulmanen, P. and Szebehely, M. (2015) 'From the state to the family or to the market? Consequences of reduced residential eldercare in Sweden', *International Journal of Social Welfare*, 24(1): 81–92.

Ulmanen, P., Lowndes, R. and Choiniere, J. (2023) 'Accessing nursing home care: family members' unpaid care work in Ontario and Sweden', in P. Armstrong (ed) *Unpaid Work in Nursing Homes: Flexible Boundaries*, Bristol: Policy Press, pp 18–32.

PART IV

Conclusions

13

Towards an understanding of care poverty

*Kirstein Rummery, Teppo Kröger,
Nicola Brimblecombe and Ricardo Rodrigues*

Introduction

In this chapter we will draw together some of the key lessons on care poverty from the theoretical and empirical contributors to this volume. As explained in Chapter 1, care poverty is the inadequate coverage of care needs resulting from a combination of individual and societal factors. However, our intention is not to produce a meta-theory of care poverty. We are aware of the dangers of grand theorising and attempting to create a theoretical framework capable of explaining the experience of giving and receiving care would fail to capture some of the vital nuances of those experiences. However, it is our view that previous theories concerning the giving and receiving of care have not yet adequately explained those phenomena, and it is our intention to push the debate forwards, rather than bring it to its conclusion.

We aim to develop a more theoretically sophisticated understanding of care poverty through examining the empirical evidence and methodological contributions that we have to date. This evidence is by its nature limited to those who contributed to this volume. Nevertheless, the empirical basis of this volume is fairly wide-reaching and covers many care scenarios and contexts. We have explored the experiences of paid and unpaid carers, of inter- and intra-generational family care, of people with dementia who pose particular challenges to theoretical models of care, of contexts where there is paid care widely available and where it is seen in policy terms as a 'last resort', and the intergenerational and intersectional impact of caring. This volume incorporates also different methodological contributions for the analysis and advancement of our understanding of care poverty.

We acknowledge that there are some very notable gaps in our review of the current state of the art in empirical terms. We do not include any chapters looking at care in underdeveloped welfare states or the Global South. Our evidence base for those receiving care is largely older people, and sometimes younger disabled adults – we have not yet explored the issue of disabled children and the interface between care poverty and parenting (however, see Kröger, 2010). And we are by the nature of this volume all academics: although some of us have lived experience of care and care poverty, we are all drawing on our theoretical and empirical research for these contributions. In chapters using qualitative methods, we have directly heard from people experiencing care poverty. However, the voices of those actually living with care poverty remain underdeveloped in our academic analysis. We have also not really explored the situation of formal paid care workers in addressing care poverty other than through policy analysis (for example, in Chapters 6 and 8, but see Mathew Puthenparambil, 2023) and in challenges to existing theory (Chapter 3). Throughout this chapter, unless otherwise stated, 'carers' refers to family/kinship carers rather than paid care workers.

Understanding care poverty from a theoretical perspective

There are several theoretical developments which underpin our ideas about care poverty. The first is the differences between and synthesis of ideas about unmet need, inequalities in care and care poverty. These are interlinked concepts, but our analysis showed that they are not necessarily interchangeable. Kelly, in Chapter 3, examines the idea of 'unmet need' and points out that this term has historically and in policy analysis always meant the lack of provision of a service to meet need – allowing that this could be a formal health or social care service, or unpaid care, or a mixture of both. However, as several writers in this volume point out, the provision of care does not necessarily in itself meet needs. The issue of care poverty is one of structural significance, not just private relationships.

Moreover, as Mathew Puthenparambil et al point out in Chapter 7, in conceptualising unmet need both academics and policy makers have tended to focus on intimate personal care needs – what are commonly referred to as the Activities of Daily Living (ADLs), based on Katz et al (1963). These are highly medicalised and impairment/body focused and are considered to be key life tasks that people wishing to live 'independently' need to be able to accomplish, such as eating, bathing and dressing. Being able to do these things – with or without care – offers a very limited life that is about existing rather than social participation. Taking on Sen's (1999) poverty framework, these would be equivalent to 'functionings', while a broader understanding of what is the aim of care would also include what Sen terms as 'capabilities' – activities that are about community engagement and self-determination – namely by including also Instrumental Activities of Daily Living (IADLs) (see Lawton and Brody, 1969). The inability to carry out ADLs *and* IADLs is therefore, under care poverty theory, a situation requiring a political response that is about addressing structural inequality and social citizenship, not simply providing a subsistence level of care.

The provision of care to address care poverty is uneven, with consequences for inequality of both carers and those who need care. The idea of a care poverty threshold, as explored by Medgyesi et al in Chapter 5, further engages with the inequality of care poverty. By treating care poverty in the same way as material poverty, there is an absolute threshold below which it is politically untenable for a citizen to fall. Medgyesi et al further develop this idea by exploring the concept of the intensity of care poverty: not only it is multidimensional (much as material poverty is no longer seen as being simply about income) but a complex interaction of the individual (medical/impairment) and the structural (social divisions, material poverty, networks, practical and emotional support). As Potočnik et al discuss in Chapter 9, there is a strong overlap between care poverty and material poverty, and how individuals can manage and address their care poverty is linked to social networks as well as income – inequality in access to care exists across several domains.

The second theoretical approach underlying our ideas about care poverty is the tension between feminist and disability theory in the area of care. Feminists have historically focused on the labour – both emotional and physical – demanded of women when providing care. Disability theory has focused on the exploitative nature of that care – particularly when delivered by unpaid family carers. Instead, they have conceptualised the right to receive care as one of social citizenship: like other welfare provisions, it should be seen as a resource to enable social participation. Rummery argues in Chapter 2 that the advantage of care poverty as a conceptual lens over both feminist and disability theory is that the provision of care becomes a political, rather than a private, issue. It is about the social citizenship of both carers – their right to not suffer material poverty or ill-health that would prevent social participation – and of those who need care – their right to self-determination, well-being and support that enables social participation. Moreover, as Vlachantoni et al discuss in Chapter 6, care poverty includes a socio-emotional dimension – what feminists would recognise as the relational aspects of caring (linked, for example, to emotional labour or the distinction between caring about and caring for), which has its counterpoint in the emotional poverty of being without sufficient care.

The empirical basis for care poverty

Rostgaard in Chapter 8 demonstrates that the reduction of formal care provision is not necessarily matched by family care filling the gaps, particularly for those with more complex care needs. Care poverty in this case can be said to be increasing even in one of the most developed and highly state-subsidised care economies (Denmark in this case). In another highly developed welfare state with high levels of public financing of care

(Finland), Mathew Puthenparambil et al demonstrate that care poverty is highest among those who are getting both formal services and family/kinship care – so even the combination of these resources is not enough to address the care poverty of those with the highest levels of need (Chapter 7).

Aaltonen et al in Chapter 11 confirm this finding with regards to people with dementia and their carers. They find that the formal home care system is insufficiently prepared for the complex care needs – particularly the socio-emotional needs – of those with dementia and their carers. This is an interesting finding, and challenging to Rummery's conclusion in Chapter 2 that the state provision of personalised formal care would address the theoretical and practical tensions that exist when reliance is placed on family care to address care poverty. Namely, that state-provided formal care is vital to address the gendered costs of family care and the self-determination needs of those who need care. Family care is largely, but not exclusively, unpaid care by women and thus has gendered implications for material poverty and social inequality. As families (as Rummery in Chapter 2 points out) are often the only place where the socio-emotional needs of people with dementia can be met to address care poverty, there is a corresponding concern that this places a huge socio-emotional burden on family carers that the state/formal care cannot easily address.

As noted before, none of our case studies includes the experiences of the parents of disabled children, tasked with providing both practical and socio-emotional care for their children through parenting and caring, but these too would likely find themselves in a similar situation: state or formal care cannot easily step in and relieve the burden or address the care poverty of disabled children.

In Chapter 9, Potočnik and her colleagues show that the weak availability of formal home care in a less developed formal care economy (Slovenia) has significant consequences for the care poverty of lower-income households. This is an interesting finding as it clearly demonstrates the links between material poverty, the lack of social capital and care poverty. Leiber and Brüker in Chapter 10 demonstrate further evidence of this: by drawing on a study comparing the situation in East Germany (with former high levels of state support) and West Germany (with a reliance on a mix of family and state support) they show that an intersectional approach is needed to understand the complexity of care poverty even within the same country, and this needs to take into account different political and cultural histories.

Finally, Ulmanen in Chapter 12 discusses the idea of 'managerial care' and reminds us that care itself is not limited to giving assistance with ADL or even IADL tasks: it can also involve the accessing of systems, management of the intersections between formal and family care, and navigating the wider welfare state to support those who might be living in both care poverty and material poverty. This emotional labour is highly gendered and has an impact on the social and emotional well-being of carers, as well as having time and resource costs for them.

Defining and measuring care poverty

'Need' remains a key and disputed concept in the context of care poverty. Hill et al in Chapter 4 provide a detailed account of the different disciplinary approaches to 'need' from different etiological perspectives (harms, rights, collective obligations, individual autonomy, empowerment, choice, distribution and poverty, to name a few). Besides these approaches, a dichotomy remains between self-assessed and third-party or externally assessed need, with a strong tradition from health and other disciplines to rely on self-assessed need. Yet, as Hill et al in Chapter 4 show in their review of needs–assessment instruments, unmet needs and their causes (particularly systemic ones) are seldom included in needs assessment instruments. Moreover, none uses the concept of care poverty or attempts to define thresholds for unmet needs. A necessary next step is therefore to bring care poverty into assessment – the real world of practitioners and street-level bureaucrats, not least of all because 'assessment tools shape care providers' and care receivers' perceptions of needs to be met through services, priorities and "policy problems"' (Chapter 4, based on Dickson et al, 2022).

Medgyesi et al in Chapter 5 show that the definition of needs is also key for the advancement of methods to assess care poverty. The concept of care poverty highlights the systemic factors that underline the mismatch between needs and care, and as access to (affordable) care is often based on an assessment of needs (which presupposes a definition of it), this is indeed a key concept for care poverty.

The concept of care poverty is underpinned by a structuralist approach (Kröger, 2022). Comparing care poverty across different long-term care systems or countries, or even within countries before and after major policy reforms, could shed light onto the determinants of care poverty and successful measures to address it. This area, however, remains relatively unexplored in the literature. While there is some discussion about the use of self-perceived unmet needs for international comparison (for example, due to differences in the anchoring of expectations), Medgyesi et al in Chapter 5 point to the potential for relative measures of care poverty to enable cross-country comparisons.

Building on the vast literature on (income) poverty, Medgyesi et al point in Chapter 5 to some dimensions that can add to the relevance of the concept of care poverty. Two of them stand out. The first of these is 'intensity of care poverty', defined as 'how distant a particular individual may be from having their needs met by care'. The second is the distinction between different types or reasons for care poverty, mirroring what is already done for unmet needs for health care (for example, the distinction between unmet needs due to financial reasons, unavailability, lack of quality). Both are of particular relevance to guide policy. Medgyesi et al in Chapter 5 did not review existing data sources, but while care poverty may require new methods or metrics that enable this concept to be impactful in policy and ultimately people's lives, it is nonetheless clear that it may also require new data and indicators. For example, when assessing care use, many of the most commonly used international survey datasets today do not or only imperfectly account for quality of care, intensity and frequency of care used. This is a parallel development that needs to take place as well.

Among the causes of care poverty, affordability ranks as one of the most relevant across different long-term care systems. For example, Potočnik et al in their analysis of care trajectories among care dyads in Slovenia (Chapter 9) and Mathew Puthenparambil et al in their study on care receivers in Finland (Chapter 7) concur in the relevance of affordability. In the former study, affordability is a crucial reason for unmet needs, not only among care recipients but also among carers. In both cases, care recipients were using a mix of formal and informal care, which highlights that informal care cannot always fully fill the care gap left by unaffordable care services. In both studies, affordability issues and unmet needs appear to be more prevalent among less affluent individuals despite targeting policies in place (for example, income-related out-of-pocket payments or exemptions from payments based on income).

Mathew Puthenparambil et al in Chapter 7 present higher needs as a determinant of care poverty, but it is possible that the causality runs the other way around, with care poverty as a determinant of poorer health outcomes (that is, as an enhancer of needs) (cf Komisar et al, 2005 and other studies cited in Chapter 6). This calls for longitudinal studies, which would enable us to see the effect of care poverty over time, while at the same time analysing another relevant metric: persistent care poverty (Chapter 6).

The focus on affordability may, however, also reflect a 'streetlamp effect' in existing data, especially quantitative datasets, which for the most part fail to distinguish between different reasons for care poverty. Qualitative studies, on the other hand, have the ability to provide us with insights into different reasons for care poverty based on people's own experiences. Potočnik et al in Chapter 9 show that besides affordability, lack of available care on particular days or time periods (for example, holidays and vacations) is also a key reason for unmet needs. Other reasons for unmet needs uncovered by this qualitative study include tasks that professional carers are unable to carry out (for example, certain personal hygiene tasks or nursing care). Filling those gaps or unmet needs remains a key motivation for the provision of informal care. Kelly shows in Chapter 3 how much of these gaps are routed in the care economy (Peng, 2018) and how it is organised, and very importantly, financed. Going back to the study of Potočnik et al on care dyads (Chapter 9), it is also clear that unmet needs among care recipients have clear consequences for caregivers, exacerbating care burden and creating their own unmet needs.

Kröger's (2022) initial definition of care poverty considered different dimensions of care poverty such as personal and practical care poverty. The relevance of this distinction between different dimensions of care poverty, but also its variety, is well expressed in a number of findings that highlight different trends, prevalence of unmet needs and even possible underlying causes for the different dimensions of care poverty (Chapters 6, 7 and 9). For example, Potočnik et al show in Chapter 9 that needs for social interaction and socialisation are consistently left unmet by care services, a finding that is echoed by other studies (for example, Van Aerschot et al, 2022).

Policy and practice implications of our findings on care poverty

First, it is clear that the theoretical idea of care poverty – distinct from unmet need – has provided an extremely useful development in trying to make sense of the work of care, from both a structural and socioeconomic perspective, and from an individual relational and socio-emotional perspective. We can clearly see how care poverty is both a political and theoretical lens that can add nuance and a deeper understanding of the complexities of care in modern developed welfare states.

This has clear implications both for policy and practice in our case study welfare states. Those who are living in care poverty – whose needs are not met and who are socially excluded due to the lack of adequate care – need to be able to access and navigate existing care and support systems more easily. The complexity of formal support, with responsibilities divided between national, regional and local governments, public and private providers, and health, long-term care and welfare systems, is disastrous and adds bureaucratic barriers to addressing care poverty, particularly for those with complex support needs. Existing support also needs to be better matched to existing needs, particularly where those needs are variable and change over time.

There is a political as well as a theoretical discussion to be had about who is responsible for providing care that would address care poverty. Feminist and disability theory and evidence to date would suggest that the provision of formal paid personalised care services is the optimal route to address care poverty of those who need care and support without increasing the material and socio-emotional poverty of carers – resulting in high levels of women's poverty. However, we already mentioned how the socio-emotional element of care poverty of those with dementia and those with little material capital may be best addressed by family/kinship care – and in fact, it may not be possible for formal provision of services and support to provide adequate care to address care poverty in these situations, although improvements in formal care such as the ability and time for care workers to build and develop relationships and have time to spend on socio-emotional support may help. If the responsibility is to lie with family carers, the effects of this need to be recognised and addressed through adequate support and financial protection.

Better policies to address care poverty would recognise the need for, and the benefits of, investment in long-term formal social care provision. Part of this needs to be in recognition of both the costs and the political inacceptability of high levels of care poverty, particularly in wealthy developed welfare states. However, even highly developed formalised care economies are increasingly relying on family/kinship care – and liberal and familial based welfare systems always have relied on family/kinship care at the expense of gendered inequality. The empirical findings presented here show the limits of such policy in addressing care poverty, as those using a mix of care services and informal care were often more likely to experience care poverty, while at the same time highlighting the issue of care poverty among informal carers. For these reasons, policies to address care poverty in all developed welfare states need to include the voices of, and meet the needs of, family/kinship carers and not just those who need care and support.

Finally, it is worth noting the important lessons for policies indicated by the work of Hill et al in Chapter 4. They note that policy is often driven not just by ideological and empirical aims, but also by what is measurable and achievable, due to a push towards evidence-based policy making (Oliver and Cairney, 2019). There is a significant need for interdisciplinary approaches to theorising, researching and measuring care poverty. Measures that are somewhat limited, and questionable from a disability theory perspective as being overly individualised and medicalised, such as ADLs and IADLs, are universally used because they are simple and easily measurable without any significant challenges to the normative frameworks that underpin policy with regards to care poverty. If we are to develop new policies that are universal and recognise the tensions inherent in addressing care poverty, then we need to address the normative frameworks underpinning policy, and correspondingly develop new ways of measuring when we have got there. When the concept of care poverty was introduced, Kröger (2022) linked it to a 'policy failure' and it is therefore in and to public policies that we must impact and return to if we are to correct these failures and enable older citizens and their carers to have their needs met adequately.

A blueprint for future work

We have demonstrated in this volume that the development of care poverty has a theoretical sophistication that can get us beyond understandings of unmet need and inequalities, as well as providing a conceptual synthesis between feminist and disability theory. We have also demonstrated that this conceptual clarity can be applied to a range of academic challenges, from researching to measuring to theorising care poverty and its policy implications. Our empirical findings indicate that intersectionality is an important element of identifying and addressing care poverty. It is not possible to divorce people from their social, cultural and political context, so we cannot ignore that different social divisions such as gender, class, age and ethnicity have differential impacts on both the incidence of, and the qualitative experience of, care poverty.

However, this volume is very much the beginning rather than the end of a conversation. There are several areas left unexplored in this collection which require urgent attention. First, our developing theoretical understanding of care poverty needs to continue evolving. While we have tested the theory out in various empirical scenarios, there are several important perspectives missing from our theoretical development. We need to test these theories out in situations where the challenges of identifying and measuring care poverty, as well as designing solutions for it, are complex, just as the lives of people who are experiencing and trying to tackle care poverty are complex. It is clear that material poverty and care poverty are inextricably linked, and the ability to address one affects the ability to address the other. We need to think further about ideas that underpin our understanding of care poverty, in particular conceptions of need, absolute and relative care poverty, and social citizenship, while at the same time developing and testing further indicators to measure care poverty (for example, intensity and persistence of care poverty).

Several voices and perspectives are missing from the theoretical developments begun here. We have not drawn on evidence and stakeholders living in underdeveloped welfare states, or in countries where material poverty is endemic and systematic. We have relied primarily on academic voices to critically engage with the theories and evidence but, in the future, more co-production with carers and those who need care is needed.

Second, the theoretical gaps in our knowledge are also matched by the empirical gaps. In this volume we have managed to raise more empirical questions than we have answered. What are the implications of care poverty for groups of people who need care but who cannot easily advocate for themselves in navigating both formal and family/kinship care? For example, there are challenges in applying theoretical ideas around care poverty and self-determination to people with dementia, some groups of learning disabled adults, those in extreme mental distress and disabled children. Do our theoretical framings stand up to empirical enquiry with these groups?

We also do not know much about the application of care poverty theories to the lived experience of formal care workers. Does it help us understand their lives? What role do they play in addressing care poverty? While there is a substantial evidence base for practitioner challenges, little of it to date draws on care poverty theory as an explanatory factor, nor as a framework to develop better policies and practices for this group (see, however, Mathew Puthenparambil, 2023). Most empirical research presented in this volume relied on secondary data that was not purposely developed to capture important dimensions of care poverty, such as its causes. Some of the qualitative studies unearthed possible important dimensions or causes for care poverty that must be further explored in the future with purposely collected data. Knowing the causes of care poverty and inequalities in care poverty is crucial in knowing how to address it.

There are many interesting single country case studies presented here, but there is a dearth of comparative care policy research that is informed by care poverty theories. What kinds of systems and practices address care poverty? What kinds of systems and practices increase the risk, and the detrimental effects of, care poverty? What measures of care poverty are better suited for cross-country comparisons? How can the theoretical and empirical contribution of care poverty be used in an ageing world to address the widening gap between those at risk of and living in care poverty and those who are not?

References

Dickson, D., Marier, R. and Dube, A.-S. (2022) 'Do assessment tools shape policy preferences? Analysing policy framing effects on older adults' conceptualisation of autonomy', *Journal of Social Policy*, 51(1): 114–31.

Katz, S., Ford, A.B., Moskowitz, R.W., Jackson, B.A. and Jaffe, M.W. (1963) 'Studies of illness in the aged: the index of ADL: a standardized measure of biological and psychosocial function', *JAMA*, 185(12): 914–9.

Komisar, H.L., Feder, J. and Kasper, J.D. (2005) 'Unmet long-term care needs: an analysis of Medicare-Medicaid dual eligibles', *Inquiry*, 42(2): 171–82.

Kröger, T. (2010) 'Lone mothers and the puzzles of daily life: do care regimes really matter?', *International Journal of Social Welfare*, 19(4): 390–401.

Kröger, T. (2022) *Care Poverty: When Older People's Needs Remain Unmet*, Cham: Palgrave Macmillan.

Lawton, M.P. and Brody, E.M. (1969) 'Assessment of older people: self-maintaining and Instrumental Activities of Daily Living', *The Gerontologist*, 9(3 Part 1): 179–86.

Mathew Puthenparambil, J. (2023) 'Being able to provide sufficiently good care for older people: care workers and their working conditions in Finland', *International Journal of Care and Caring*, 7(4): 691–707.

Oliver, K. and Cairney, P. (2019) 'The dos and don'ts of influencing policy: a systematic review of advice to academics', *Palgrave Communications*, 5: Article 21.

Peng, I. (2018) 'Why Canadians should care about the global care economy', *Canadian International Council* [Open Canada], 16 March. Available from: https://opencanada.org/why-canadians-should-care-about-global-care-economy/ [Accessed 1 February 2024].

Sen, A. (1999) *Development as Freedom*, Oxford: Oxford University Press.

Van Aerschot, L., Kadi, S., Rodrigues, R., Hrast, M.F., Hlebec, V. and Aaltonen, M. (2022) 'Community-dwelling older adults and their informal carers call for more attention to psychosocial needs: interview study on unmet care needs in three European countries', *Archives of Gerontology and Geriatrics*, 101: 104672.

Index

References to figures appear in *italic* type; those in **bold** type refer to tables.

Q

R

S